Doctrine of Baptism

THE
DOCTRINE
OF
BAPTISM

Edmund Schlink

Translated by
Herbert J. A. Bouman

Concordia Publishing House
Saint Louis / London

Edmund Schlink
"Die Lehre von der Taufe"

Original publication by Johannes Stauda Verlag Kassel
Germany

© Johannes Stauda Verlag Kassel, Germany 1969

Translated by permission of Johannes Stauda Verlag
Kassel

Library of Congress Catalog Card No. 78-159794
ISBN 0-570-03726-3

Copyright © 1972 by Concordia Publishing House
for English edition

Manufactured in the United States of America

Table of Contents

Introduction   7

Chapter One

The Basis for Baptism   9

1. The Baptismal Command   9
2. The Historical Antecedents of Christian Baptism   12
   a. Ablutions in the Old Covenant and the promise of eschatological cleansing
   b. The Baptism of John
   c. The Baptism, death, and resurrection of Jesus
   d. The outpouring of the Holy Spirit
3. The Historical Problem of the Origin of Christian Baptism   26
4. Variety and Structure of the New Testament Statements About Baptism   31
5. The Starting Point for the Doctrine of Baptism   37

Chapter Two

The Saving Activity of God Through Baptism   42

1. Baptism into Christ   42
   a. Baptism as assignment to the crucified and risen Christ
   b. Given into Jesus' death and resurrection
   c. The gift of the new life and the admonition to walk in newness of life
   d. The danger of detaching the understanding of Baptism from the history of Jesus Christ
2. Baptism by the Holy Spirit   58
   a. The activity of the Spirit through Baptism
   b. Effects of the Spirit in connection with Baptism
   c. The gift of the Holy Spirit and the admonition to walk in the Spirit
   d. The danger of restricting the activity of the Spirit in the understanding of Baptism
3. Reception into the Church   72
   a. Baptism as incorporation into the people of God, the body of Christ, and the spiritual temple
   b. Incorporation into the church and commissioning for service to the world
   c. The danger of reducing the understanding of Baptism to external church membership
4. The New-Creating Deed of the Triune God   82
   a. Baptism as the deed of God in Christ through the Holy Spirit
   b. The name of the Father and of the Son and of the Holy Spirit
   c. The interaction of Word, washing with water, and God's saving deed
   d. The danger of letting the statements about the Word, the washing with water, and God's saving deed fall apart
5. The Necessity of Baptism   105

Chapter Three

The Administration and Reception of Baptism   109

1. The Single Reception of Baptism   109
2. The Administration of Baptism   114
   a. The baptizing church
   b. The church as instrument of the baptizing God
   c. The administration of Baptism separated from the church
3. The Reception of Baptism   120
   a. Faith in Jesus Christ
   b. The threefold connection between faith and Baptism
   c. The reception of Baptism separated from faith
4. Infant Baptism   130
   a. The origin of infant Baptism and its rejection
   b. Individual theological arguments for and against infant Baptism
   c. Inferences from the understanding of Baptism for the attitude toward infant Baptism
   d. Inferences from the understanding of the church for the attitude toward infant Baptism
   e. The dogmatic justification of infant Baptism
   f. The practical problems of infant Baptism
5. The Most Profound Difference in the Understanding of Baptism   166

Chapter Four

The Form of the Baptismal Act   172

1. The Administration of Baptism in the New Testament   172
2. The Problem of the Form of the Baptismal Act   176
3. The Constitutive Center of Baptism   183
4. Developing the Baptismal Act Through the Word   186
5. Developing the Baptismal Act Through Further Acts   194
6. The Danger of Obscuring the Understanding of Baptism   199

Conclusion: The Ecumenical Significance of Baptism   206
Notes   211

Introduction

Baptism is one of the *foci* of Christian thought in our time. It is again playing a leading role similar to that in the ancient church, though in a quite different orientation. Two points of departure are especially characteristic of the current discussion concerning Baptism.

On the one hand, there is a new awareness of Baptism as a bond of fellowship. Aroused to a sense of shame because of its disunity, Christendom has taken note of the fact that nearly all churches acknowledge each other's Baptism as valid. The question is being raised concerning the implications of this fact for the unity of the churches. If the words of Paul, "we were all baptized into *one* body" (1 Cor. 12:13), are taken seriously, does it then not follow from the reciprocal recognition of Baptism that all the baptized who believe in Christ are members of the one body of Christ in spite of the separation of the churches? But if they are members of *one* body, they cannot remain separated from each other. This separation manifests itself most noticeably in the lack of Communion fellowship. Must not the unity of Baptism exert an influence also on this area? It is one and the same body of Christ into which they are baptized and which is nurtured in the Lord's Supper by the gift of the body and blood of Christ. If all the baptized have become Christ's, then this oneness in Christ cannot remain hidden under the separateness of the churches. It should rather assume visible form in their unification. Thus reflection on Baptism has released strong ecumenical impulses both in the history of the World Council of Churches and in the deliberations and resolutions of Vatican II.

At the same time voices have been raised which emphatically question the traditional baptismal practices of their church. Especially in Reformed churches Karl Barth's objections to infant Baptism have influenced some groups to reject its further practice. Also within churches committed to the Lutheran Confessions, qualms about the historic practice have arisen here and there, and even among many members of the Roman Catholic Church a sense of uncertainty in this area is evident. Such criticism of infant Baptism, or even its rejection, does indeed place into question what the separated churches in their mutual recognition of Baptism have hitherto regarded as self-evident and what in our time had become a common point of departure for ecumenical efforts at unification. Such opposing positions with respect to infant Baptism profoundly affect the consciousness of the churches. These positions must be taken all the more seriously because they concern not only questions about baptismal practice but the understanding of Baptism itself. Such incisive antitheses in the understanding of Baptism have here become manifest that the question must be raised whether the mutual recognition of Baptism may serve as a reliable and adequate point of departure for the uniting efforts of the separated churches.

Thus the new reflections on Baptism in our day lead to contradictory effects: gathering together and splitting apart, promoting unity and calling the existing unity into question. It is true, such challenges may also produce unitive effects. For the criticism of infant Baptism leads to new possibilities for the Baptist bodies to participate in the endeavor for unity. Thus the status of the debate is highly contradictory and complex. The task of treating the doctrine of Baptism has not become easier but more difficult. Today it cannot confine itself in any church to an interpretation of accepted dogmatic decisions, but it must take up the new questions that have been raised.

The current reflection on the central significance of Baptism has found expression in a deluge of publications, especially in German and in English. These do not deal only with one-sided points of view and practical suggestions, as is customary in casual conversation. On the contrary, an impressive number of thorough and scholarly studies have been published, studies that concern themselves with the baptismal statements of the New Testament and the baptismal theology of the reformers and of the Baptist movement. It cannot be the purpose of this introduction to provide a complete listing of the recent literature on Baptism. We shall confine ourselves to those studies which introduce the reader to the problems in an especially comprehensive or distinctive way or which make further relevant literature accessible. Reference to additional publications will be made at appropriate places in this book.

CHAPTER ONE

The Basis for Baptism

1. The Baptismal Command

The church baptizes on the basis of her Lord's commission, "Go therefore and make disciples of all nations, baptizing them in the name of the Father and of the Son and of the Holy Spirit." (Matt. 28:19 RSV)

This command has been handed down as a word of the Risen One who has been exalted as Lord of all. "All authority in heaven and on earth has been given to Me" (v. 18). While during His earthly ministry Jesus had referred to the coming Son of Man as to another person, He now speaks as the Exalted One who claims for Himself the word from Daniel's apocalypse, "And to Him [the Son of Man] was given dominion and glory and kingdom, that all peoples, nations, and languages should serve Him; His dominion is an everlasting dominion, which shall not pass away, and His kingdom one that shall not be destroyed" (Dan. 7:14).[1] Jesus is here speaking as the Exalted One who has all things under His feet, as the Lord whom God has installed at His right hand. But having been given all authority does not mean that it is already acknowledged by all. Putting all things under Him does not yet mean that all things are obedient to Him. The world's resistance is already futile and will one day be shattered in the Judgment. But those who acknowledge His rule and become His disciples will be saved. It is this saving pervasion of all that has been made subject to the exalted Lord that is the concern of the baptismal command. The concern is in every respect with the whole: "*All* authority" has been given Jesus, "*all* nations" are to be made His disciples, "*all*" that Jesus has commanded is to be taught and observed, and Jesus will be with His people "*all* the days until the close of the age."

This commission sets those who have been sent by the Lord into a movement that pervades space and time—a movement which cannot rest with any part of humanity but must spread like a fire over the whole earth "until the close of the age." The disciples are disciples of

9

their Lord only as they hasten and make disciples of others. In this commission the sequence of baptizing and teaching is noteworthy (no matter how the Greek participles are construed in relation to each other). Must not teaching precede Baptism? Or is the emphasis here merely on the connection between teaching and baptizing without reference to a chronological sequence? At any rate this sequence suggests that Baptism is the antecedent for the observance of what Jesus has commanded. The sequence baptizing-teaching corresponds to the distinctive character of the admonitions in the New Testament letters which also proceed from Baptism as the basis for the new life and call it to remembrance. A legalistic understanding must be excluded from the teaching of what Jesus has commanded. We are dealing with the transmission of His imperious summons by means of which He has at once expounded, broken through, transcended, and fulfilled the Law. For it is the Christ who is here issuing orders. As for the rest, it is self-evident that the proclamation of this name of Christ, and thus the saving deeds of God in Jesus Christ through the Holy Spirit, is preceded by a Baptism "in the name of the Father and of the Son and of the Holy Spirit." It is to be noted at once that it is not a Baptism in the *names* of the Father and of the Son and of the Holy Spirit, but in the one *name*.

This baptizing and teaching is to be carried out "to the close of the age." The time and the space for the activity of the disciples between Jesus' resurrection and His return does not remain an empty time and an empty space. The promise is made to those who baptize and teach: "Lo, I am with you always, to the close of the age" (Matt. 28: 20). This promise involves not a mere spectator presence of the Exalted but His present activity. Just as Jesus had promised His disciples that those who heard their message heard Him and those who received them received Him, so this promise of His active presence applies to succeeding generations to the close of the age, also as far as the practice of Baptism is concerned.

It is on the basis of this command of the Lord that the church baptizes — whether by appealing to this command in her baptismal instruction or by explicitly reciting this command in her baptismal liturgy. It is true, the explanation of this close of Matthew's Gospel does not yet answer the historical question regarding the origin of Christian Baptism. In this respect the text raises considerable problems which will be considered later. Yet long before these problems of historical research became evident, the church did not confine herself to this baptismal command in answering the question concerning the institution of Baptism. From ancient times also the Baptism of Jesus by John has been designated the institution of Baptism. In this sense Thomas Aquinas understood Jesus' Baptism as the sacramental consecration of water as the baptismal element.[2]

By means of scholastic distinctions Bonaventure gave a fourfold answer to the question, "When was Baptism instituted?": Materially, when Christ was baptized; formally, when He arose and gave the baptismal formula in His baptismal command, Matt. 28:19; effectively, when He suffered on the cross whence Baptism gets its power; and finally, when He proclaimed the necessity and benefit of Baptism, John 3:5.[3] In his baptismal hymn Luther too proclaimed Jesus' Baptism as the institution of Baptism:

> To Jordan came our Lord, the Christ,
> To do God's pleasure willing,
> And there was by Saint John baptized,
> All righteousness fulfilling;
> There did He consecrate a bath
> To wash away transgression,
> And quench the bitterness of death
> By His own blood and passion;
> He would a new life give us.[4]

In fact Christian Baptism can no more be separated from the history of Jesus Christ than the Gospel can. The Gospel proclaims the history of Jesus Christ, and Baptism assigns the baptized into that account. Jesus Christ is not only the One who sends people to proclaim the message, but with His history He is the ground of the Gospel and Baptism, and at the same time the One who gives Himself and is active through Gospel and Baptism. Jesus Christ, His death and His resurrection, belong necessarily to the institution of Baptism.

In addition, the institution of Christian Baptism cannot be separated from the Old Testament antecedents, that is, the promise and demand of the Old Covenant. For Jesus is confessed as Christ and Lord only when He is confessed as the fulfillment of the Old Testament promise and the end of the Law. This is equally true of the preaching of the Gospel of Jesus Christ and of Christian Baptism. The specifics of Christian Baptism can be recognized only as one takes note of the connection and the difference between Christian Baptism and John's Baptism and, beyond that, between Christian Baptism and Old Testament and Jewish ablutions. In the same way, the Lord's Supper must be understood not only on the basis of Jesus' last meal with His disciples but also His previous table fellowship with sinners and His promise of the coming meal in the kingdom of God—as well as the Old Testament statements about covenant meal and sacrifice.

In view of this state of affairs the concept of institution in the doctrine of Baptism cannot be restricted to the transmission of the baptismal command. The concept of institution must either be broadened so as to include the Old Testament antecedents and the history of Jesus Christ, or it must be replaced by the concept of logical defense.

2. The Historical Antecedents of Christian Baptism

a. Ablutions in the Old Covenant and the promise of eschatological cleansing

The Old Testament law contains numerous prescriptions for cleansing through washing and sprinkling. The occasions when this is to be done are precisely depicted in Lev. 11—15 (cf. also 6:20 f., 16:24 ff., 17:15 f., and otherwise) and Numbers 19. These are cases of touching unclean animals or corpses; defilement through natural or diseased emissions; various aspects of the sex life; certain conditions regarding lepers, contact with lepers, and others. At the same time the duration of the state of uncleanness and the time for cleansing are indicated. In these cases either the whole person, or only the affected parts of the body, or also the clothes are to be washed. Also objects defiled by touch must be cleansed; earthen vessels must be broken and bronze ones rinsed in water (Lev. 6:28). Beyond this, there is also a purification by fire. Of the spoils of war all metal objects "you shall pass through the fire," but "whatever cannot stand the fire, you shall pass through the water" (Num. 31:22 f.). The defiled person who was excluded from the worshiping congregation was readmitted to it and the cultic sacrifice through cleansing. In addition to the cleansing by water an atonement through sin offering and burnt offering was prescribed in certain cases (e. g., in the cleansing of a leper, Lev. 14:8 and

19 ff.). The washings were performed with any kind of water (only occasionally is "living water," that is, spring water, expressly prescribed. Lev. 15:13, cf. 14:5 f. and 50; Num. 19:17). Two cases, however, call for the use of specially prepared water: In the case of defilement through contact with corpses and graves the person shall be sprinkled with water mixed with ashes of the burnt sin offering (Num. 19.17). In the case of leprosy the person is to be sprinkled with water mixed with the blood of a sacrificial bird (Lev. 14:5 f.). Here sacrifice and washing were combined in one act of purification. In a few cases the washings were prescribed also after touching holy objects and after performing sacred acts.[5] . . . Important statements of prophetic preaching would be unintelligible if ablutions for cleansing had not been a widespread custom. "Your hands are full of blood. Wash yourselves; make yourselves clean" (Is. 1:15-16). "O Jerusalem, wash your heart from wickedness, that you may be saved" (Jer. 4:14), et al.

These prophetic imperatives obviously presuppose ritual ablutions. Yet they do not demand physical washings with water but the cleansing of the heart from evil, namely, repentance. "Wash yourselves; make yourselves clean" means "remove the evil of your doings from before My eyes; cease to do evil, learn to do good; seek justice, correct oppression; defend the fatherless, plead for the widow" (Is. 1:16-17). In their relationship to the ritual washings these demands resemble the relationship to the sacrificial worship.

The prophetic preaching did not, however, stop with the imperatives of the call to repentance. In view of the impenitence of the nation a future sovereign act of divine washing and cleansing was proclaimed: "When the Lord shall have washed away the filth of the daughters of Zion and cleansed the bloodstains of Jerusalem from its midst by a spirit of judgment and by a spirit of burning. . . ." (Is. 4:4). One might be inclined to regard this proclamation as being a part of the threat of judgment. But Ezekiel promised this eschatological washing as a new-creating saving deed of God: "I will sprinkle clean water upon you, and you shall be clean from all your uncleanness, and from all your idols I will cleanse you. A new heart I will give you, and a new spirit I will put within you; and I will take out of your flesh the heart of stone and give you a heart of flesh. And I will put My spirit within you, and cause you to walk in My statutes and be careful to observe My ordinances" (Ezek. 36:25-27). Into this context belong perhaps also the statements about the spring of water issuing from below the threshold of the eschatological temple and about the sanative effects of the water flowing from the sanctuary (Ezek. 47:1-12), and certainly the expectation of Zechariah concerning the fountain that will one day be opened up in Jerusalem "to cleanse them from sin and uncleanness" (Zech. 13:1). When, therefore, the pious man prayed, "Wash me thoroughly from my iniquity, and cleanse me from my sin" (Ps. 51:2; cf. v. 7), he was not thinking of the ritual ablution, but he was praying for the creation of a clean heart and the gift of the Holy Spirit—just as God is not pleased with sacrifices and burnt offerings, but rather with the sacrifice of a broken and contrite heart (vv. 16-17). Even though the prophetic preaching does not proceed against the ritual ablutions in the same way as against sacrifices and temple, these washings are in reality equally put into question.

In the course of the history of post-exilic Judaism until the appearance of Jesus, these ritual washings became increasingly significant. This dogmatic treatise cannot enter upon an analysis of the highly controverted particulars that accompany the exegesis of the transmitted texts and the attempts at reconstructing historical dependences between various baptismal rituals and groups. We must confine ourselves to featuring such aspects as are essential to an understanding of the distinctive character of Christian Baptism.

When the attempts at keeping the Law and being cleansed as a condition for the expected saving deed of God became more radical, the washings were not restricted to the cases explicitly prescribed by the Law, but they were demanded of all Jews and were to be frequently repeated. Also the ritual act as such was given greater attention. Whereas even the Priestly Code left open the question whether the washings were to be performed by bathing and immersion or by pouring and rinsing,[6] the immersion of the whole body became more and more obligatory, and bathing facilities were provided for the synagogs. In the process the Jewish washings and other existing rites of purification "did not develop along the lines of sacral magic, but exclusively along legalistic lines. Their one goal was ritual purity. . . . Rabbinic Judaism thinks of washing only in terms of purification from cultic uncleanness. . . . Forgiveness can be compared to this, but neither it, nor especially ethical purity, can be mediated by it."[7] The purifications were understood primarily as acts of fulfilling the precepts of the divine law, hence as deeds of human obedience, rather than as a pardoning act of God done to man. Within official Judaism the Pharisees made particularly rigorous demands of purification. They even had to purify themselves by a bath of immersion when a non-Pharisee touched them.[8]

But even apart from official Judaism, washings and baths had spread to Jewish sects which had separated themselves for the purpose of a more rigorous keeping of the Law. Among the baptismal movements in Palestine[9] the Essene community is especially significant. Since 1947 we are no longer entirely dependent on the references in Philo and Josephus. In that year important parts of the library of one such religious colony, perhaps the motherhouse of a larger part of this movement, were discovered in caves near the Dead Sea. The Essenes had separated themselves from the Jerusalem temple cult and priesthood, which for many Jews had become suspect since the time of the Hasmoneans and especially since Hadrian. The Essenes appealed to Is. 40:3, "in the wilderness prepare the way of the Lord," for their move into the desert for the purpose of preparing themselves as "the house of Israel," as the "holy planting," after the eschatological wars between the "children of light" and the "children of darkness," to offer the priestly service in the cleansed temple of God. This preparation was to be achieved through the repentance, the asceticism, and the strictest discipline of the communal life, and baths of purification played a large role, larger even than among the Pharisees. From the moment of acceptance into the order these purifications accompanied the daily course of life. Even when an Essene was touched by another Essene of a lower rank such defilement had to be removed by a bath. It is not certain from the texts whether beyond a ritual purification, atonement for sin was expected from these baths. The absence of the cultic sacrifices would seem to suggest that an expiatory significance was now ascribed to the immersion. Yet, however clearly the texts speak of a cleansing from sins through the Holy Spirit and of an expiation for transgression,[10] the relationship to the immersion is not unequivocal — it is clear only with reference to repentance: "Only by a spirit of uprightness and humility can his sin be atoned."[11] Further statements indicate that forgiveness is granted to him who repents and denied him who refuses to repent. However, repentance and the bath which follows are distinguished. Hence the assumption seems most reasonable that "the Qumran washings do not provide . . . forgiveness and expiation." They are derived "from an intensification of the Old Testament demands of Levitical purification" (Herbert Braun).[12] Only the significance of a ritual purification can be established beyond doubt. For the rest the conclusion must be drawn, from the multiplication of baths and the fact that the first bath did not have the significance of a decisive ritual of initiation, that the Qumran community did not ascribe to Baptism a once-for-all pervasive spiritual renewal of man.

In the context of an increased estimate and spread of ritual baths within the Judaism of the time *proselyte Baptism* also derives its origin. Its more precise age is controverted. There is some evidence in favor of the claim that it arose already before the ministry of John the Baptist.[13] Since the Jews considered the Gentile unclean because he did not fulfill the laws of Levitical purification, it seemed natural to demand that the Gentile submit to a bath of Levitical purification on his entrance into the Jewish cultic community. But at what time proselyte Baptism became an established custom cannot be determined. Reliable references can only be found in later sources. The Talmud lists three requisites for the reception of the proselyte into the Jewish community: 1. circumcision; 2. an immersion for Levitical purification; and 3. a sacrifice in which blood is poured out for his atonement. The manner of Baptism was this, that the proselyte, in the presence of Jewish witnesses, immersed himself — if possible in running water. Faith in the one God and a knowledge of the principal commandments of the Law were presupposed. As a result of this Baptism the proselyte was considered ceremonially clean and thus achieved access to the cultic community and the sacrifice. It is important to observe that, according to the extant Jewish texts, "confessions of sin were very rarely connected with proselyte Baptism." [14] It is therefore unlikely that this Baptism was understood as an act of the forgiveness of sins over and above the establishment of Levitical purity. This seems to be contradicted by the statement that "at his conversion [to Judaism] the proselyte is like a newborn child." [15] But the explanation of this and similar passages is debated. They can hardly be interpreted in the sense of a regeneration and new creation brought about by the forgiveness of sins,[16] but they acknowledge the new legal status of membership in Judaism.[17] "When the proselyte is described as a 'newborn child,' this relates only to his theocratic and casuistic position. . . . There is no thought of any natural, let alone ethical, death and regeneration." [18] This legal understanding is supported by the fact that a sacrifice had to be offered after the prose-lyte Baptism. The Gentile remained "without atonement until blood was sprinkled for him." [19]

b. The Baptism of John

In the midst of the manifold baths and washings of his time John the Baptist proclaimed his message. He confronted the Jewish nation as an individual, not as a member of the priestly caste (although according to tradition the son of a priest) or one of the lawyers or one identified with any of the Jewish Puritan movements, whether Pharisee or Essene. In the radical situation of imminent expectation he revived the prophetic message of the day of Jahweh's wrath and the judgment by fire: "Do not presume to say to yourselves, 'We have Abraham as our father'; for I tell you, God is able from these stones to raise up children to Abraham. Even now the axe is laid to the root of the trees" (Matt. 3:9-10). John was particularly critical of the Pharisees and Sadducees. "The dark storm cloud, which the faithful Jewish observer of the Law saw, with a mixed feeling of horror and pride, looming on the horizon of the godless Gentile world, now suddenly hung menacingly over his own head and threatened dire destruction." (Martin Dibelius) [20]

Conscious of being the herald and way preparer for the Coming One, the "mightier one" (Mark 1:7), John proclaimed Him as the executor of the divine judgment. At the same time John looked to Him for the fulfilment of the prophetic promise concerning the outpouring of the Spirit: "I have baptized you with water; but He will baptize you with the Holy Spirit" (Mark 1:8). This announcement of salvation may not be deleted as an accretion from the Christian tradition. Yet John's annunciation of the Coming One as the judge was so dominant a feature of his message that later in prison he perhaps doubted whether Jesus, the friend of sinners, was the One whose coming he had proclaimed.

Since God's judgment is imminent, immediate repentance is called for. John demanded not only confession of sin but also a turning away from sin. "Bear fruit that befits repentance" (Matt. 3:8). Whoever does not bear fruits of repentance "is cut down and thrown into the fire" (v. 10). Also these demands correspond to the summons with which the prophets had confronted the people. In connection with this preaching of repentance John called for Baptism. In spite of the many baths and washings current in John's environment his Baptism was regarded as a unique event to such a degree that he was called "the Baptizer."

What is the significance of this "Baptism of repentance"? In any case it was not a matter merely of an external cleansing of the body, nor only a cultic-ceremonial purification. It was rather a matter of preparing the whole man for his encounter with the coming judge. This Baptism did not concern itself with the removal of stains that had resulted from isolated offences such as contacts with the unclean, but rather with total conversion, the last chance to escape the impending judgment. In view of the conscientious and even desperate efforts of pious Jews to keep the divine law, more will have to be ascribed to this Baptism than merely a public confession of sins or a sign that the repentance of those who had been struck by the message of judgment was accepted. On the contrary, through this Baptism the penitent sinner was placed into repentance, and because of it appropriate fruits of repentance and safety in the coming judgment were to be expected. For Matthew, at any rate, John's Baptism was not only a "baptism *of* repentance" but also a Baptism "*for* repentance" (εἰς μετάνοιαν Matt. 3:11).

Since in all accounts John's Baptism is clearly distinguished from the future cleansing and renewal by the Holy Spirit, some questions have been raised about designating it "a baptism of repentance for the forgiveness of sins" (Mark 1:4; Luke 3:3). On the one hand, the thought arises that expression is here given to the reference to the future forgiveness and deliverance in the announced judgment.[21] Accordingly this Baptism would have been performed in view of the eschatological forgiveness. That is to say, John's Baptism did not effect forgiveness but prepared the repentance in which the future forgiveness might be expected. Matthew probably avoided the expression "baptism for the forgiveness of sins" because he wanted to exclude the misconception that John's Baptism was already supplying what only Jesus Christ provided. On the other hand, Mark and Luke use the same prepositions in connection with this Baptism to designate it as a "baptism of repentance for the forgiveness of sins," as Matthew does when he speaks of a "baptism for repentance." It must be noted, furthermore, that a performance of righteousness without forgiveness of prior sins appears unthinkable. Consequently there are exegetes who regard John's Baptism "as an eschatological sacrament producing repentance and forgiveness."[22] On the contrary, it must be observed that in the Gospels

18

Jesus is indeed accused of forgiving sins, but never John. If John's Baptism is to be understood not only as preparation for the future forgiveness but already as the consummation of forgiveness, then it should in every case be clearly distinguished from what the Coming One would accomplish through the Holy Spirit. There can be no weakening of the antithesis in the proclamation, "I have baptized you with water; but He will baptize you with the Holy Spirit" (Mark 1:8; cf. Matt. 3:11; Luke 3:16; Acts 1:5). Not John but the One coming after him will carry out the eschatological cleansing and renewal through the Holy Spirit, as promised by the prophets. "Baptism of repentance" or "baptism for repentance" is less ambiguous than "baptism for the forgiveness of sins." "Baptism for repentance" surely means not only that repentance is demanded as a condition for receiving this Baptism over and above a consciousness of ritual uncleanness. The sinner is in fact given over into that repentance in which the people of God are to meet the Coming One. John's Baptism demands repentance, gives over into repentance, and acknowledges repentance as eschatologically valid. In this respect John's Baptism may be characterized as being an efficacious seal of repentance.

John's Baptism contains elements that are also known from other Jewish baths and ablutions. For some time the attempt was made to trace its origin to proselyte Baptism, and recently some have tried to derive it from the Baptism of the Essenes. John's Baptism shares with other Jewish baths and ablutions the motif of preparation for the encounter with God. Nils Astrup Dahl has pointed to the relationships between the priestly washings in preparation for the temple worship and John's Baptism in preparation for the eschatological feast of the assembly of the saved.[23] Yet the differences are greater than the correspondences. Over against all Jewish immersions and ablutions John's Baptism was in a decisive respect an innovation. In spite of various similarities it cannot be derived from existing rites. If John's contemporaries had not regarded his Baptism as something new they would not have called John "the Baptizer" and would not have singled out his Baptism from the totality of his preaching and baptizing ministry as the decisive element.

Disregarding proselyte Baptism for the moment, John's Baptism was distinguished from other Jewish immersions and ablutions by the fact that it was not repeated. It possessed an eschatological finality.

Furthermore, it was not a self-administered Baptism, but was applied by John to the candidate. Above all, this Baptism was distinguished from the rites of ritual purification in that it was combined with the announcement of the immediately imminent judgment and was administered "for repentance." It has indeed been assumed that John had been close to the Essenes, as he also labored in their geographical neighborhood.[24] However, their immersions were constantly repeated and seem above all to have had a ritual character. A further important difference was that John summoned the whole Jewish people to Baptism, while the baths of the Essenes were open only to the small circle of those who had already made their vows and had demonstrated their efforts at holiness. "We must be cautious about a derivation [of John's Baptism] from the baptismal practices of Qumran. There is no demonstrable connection between the Baptizer and the sect—his eventual membership in the sect is a hypothetical construction!—and the analogies in the baptismal practices are insufficient for a genealogical relationship." (Erich Dinkler) [25]

John's Baptism is like proselyte Baptism in that it was applied only once, but it differs already in that it was not self-administered. "The expressions [that refer to John's Baptism in the New Testament] mean more than that he simply induced people to take the bath or be immersed and that he supervised the act, as was done by the witnesses at the Jewish proselyte Baptism" (W. Brandt).[26] Above all, proselyte Baptism had only the ritual significance of establishing the Levitical purity which must then be followed by atonement through sacrifice. Yes, John's Baptism stood in direct contrast to proselyte Baptism in that John baptized Jews, not converts from the Gentiles. If at the time of John proselyte Baptism had already been established, his Baptism would have been an insult in that he was expecting the Jews to submit to a onetime Baptism similar to the proselyte Baptism that was demanded of converting Gentiles.

What is new about John's Baptism over against the other washings and immersions of his day rests on his commission to proclaim the immediately imminent judgment. By means of this message he is the last in the series of Old Testament prophets and the forerunner of the Coming One. This imminent expectation would seem to explain the single application of his Baptism as well as the fact that precisely his Baptism was not self-administered. In the expectation of the imminent final judgment man cannot save himself by his own deed. He can be prepared for salvation only by God and those sent by God. In this sense we must understand the question of Jesus, "Was the Baptism of John from heaven or from men?" (Mark 11:30)

c. The Baptism, death, and resurrection of Jesus

Before His public appearance Jesus too came to John to receive his Baptism of repentance. Thus He aligned Himself with the members of His people who repented and accepted Baptism in expectation of the divine judgment proclaimed by John. There are other references to the fact that Jesus acknowledged John's special divine mission and sided with him.

All the Gospels report a unique incident in connection with Jesus' Baptism, whereby this Baptism was profoundly distinguished from all the rest of John's baptizing. John indeed baptized Jesus in the same way as the others, but here the Holy Spirit descended upon the One baptized. What the Baptist had proclaimed as the deed of the Coming One, namely the Baptism by the Holy Spirit, is here reported as having happened to Jesus. The Spirit who, according to the Biblical witness, moved upon the waters at the beginning of the creation, the Spirit who had been active in the prophets and whom they had proclaimed as the divine gift of the End-Time, here descended upon Jesus. The comparison, "like a dove," is perhaps a reference to the beginning of creation, perhaps also to the dove that showed Noah the end of the Deluge — perhaps also to the symbolism of the royal bird, known from the history of religions, representing the divine power which the king receives. The prayer of the pious in the Old Testament, "O that Thou wouldst rend the heavens and come down" (Is. 64:1), here finds its answer (cf. Mark 1:10 and parallels). According to the reports, what John had not expected of his Baptism came to pass in the Baptism of Jesus, namely, the Baptism by the Spirit. Hence John's Baptism was transformed as Jesus submitted to it. This was not merely the eschatological seal of repentance. Through the descent of the Spirit upon the Christ, John's Baptism became Christian Baptism in its most proper sense. For this reason it has been said again and again in the course of church history that Christian Baptism rests on the Baptism of Jesus.

The Synoptic tradition further reports the sound of a "voice from heaven" which said, "Thou art My beloved Son; with Thee I am well pleased" (Mark 1:11). God declares Jesus to be His chosen Son. These words echo the royal psalm, "You are My Son; today I have begotten You" (Ps. 2:7). With this divine word of the coronation liturgy the kings were enthroned, and at the same time the words pointed beyond their historic reality to the eschatological saving deed by which God subjected all kings and nations in order that they might serve God in fear and joy. It is noteworthy that (with the exception of a few manuscripts of Luke's Gospel) the transmitted texts concerning Jesus' Baptism omit the words of the psalm, "Today I have begotten You." In their stead there is an echo of words from the Servant of God poems of the second part of Isaiah: "Behold My Servant, whom I uphold, My chosen, in whom My soul delights; I have put My Spirit upon Him. . . ." (Is. 42:1). While in the Old Testament the statements about the Messianic king and the Servant of God are made independently of each other, they are combined into one statement by the divine voice that spoke at Jesus' Baptism. In Psalm 2 the words, "You are My Son; today I have begotten You," constituted the formula by means of which God adopted a man as His son and installed him as king. This word makes him son and king. But in the Gospels it is presupposed that Jesus was the Son of God even before His Baptism. Hence it is no accident that the reports concerning Jesus' Baptism omit the words, "today I have begotten You." He who is the Son is proclaimed as Son by the baptismal epiphany. Also in other places, where Psalm 110 is used in the New Testament witnesses concerning the exaltation of Jesus, it is presupposed that Jesus had already previously been the Christ but was raised from the dead and established in His rule "at the right hand of God." The adoptionistic ideas known from the later history of theology are present neither in the Baptism reports nor in the New Testament testimonies to the exaltation. To be already Son and to be installed as Son are no either-or at this point (cf., for example, Rom. 1:3 f.). In general there is much to be said in favor of the opinion that "the concept of adoption, as applied to Christ, was completely foreign to primitive Christianity" (Ernst Lohmeyer).[27] Furthermore, the Gospels of Matthew and Luke presuppose that the Spirit of God did not begin to be active in Jesus at His Baptism but was in Him before that, indeed, that Jesus was "of the Holy Spirit." (Matt. 1:20)

But if Jesus was the Son already before His Baptism, why then did He desire John's Baptism of repentance? According to Matthew,

Jesus replied to John's unwillingness to baptize Him with the words, "Let it be so now; for thus it is fitting for Us to fulfil all righteousness" (3:15). "It is in accordance with God's plan that the Messiah, the divine king, associate with His people, that the Servant of God represent the 'many' (Is. 53:12). Jesus aligns Himself with those who are sinners" (J. Schniewind).[28] Also the word of the Baptist in John's Gospel: "Behold the Lamb of God, who takes away the sin of the world" (John 1:29), points in this direction.

There are some rather significant differences in the Gospel accounts concerning the Baptism of Jesus. According to Mark and Luke the voice from heaven is addressed only to Jesus, while according to Matthew the voice proclaimed to the assembled multitude Jesus as the Son, and John does not have these words at all. According to the Synoptics it was Jesus — according to John it was the Baptist — who saw the descent of the Spirit. These and other differences indicate that the Baptism of Jesus was transmitted by the community which was now itself baptizing and in this context took an increasingly greater interest in the significance of Jesus' Baptism, both for Jesus and for the community. Nevertheless, the tradition of Jesus' Baptism cannot simply be dismissed as an etiological cultic legend. Jesus' Baptism by John is a historical fact. The reported epiphany, and similarly the call visions and auditions of the Old Testament prophets, as well as the appearances of the Risen One. cannot be historically verified. It may be possible to isolate a Hellenistic interpretation from an older Jewish one in the texts,[29] but the historical sequence of events cannot be reconstructed in detail. Beyond the fact of this Baptism it is certain, however, that soon thereafter Jesus came forward with a claim that distinguished Him from all prophets, including John, and especially from the lawyers. He did not preach only by expounding the Scriptures like the rabbis, and He did not transmit a Word of God heard earlier, like the prophets ("thus says the Lord"), but He confronted the people in the unmediated authority of "but I say to you." It may therefore be assumed that the historical significance of Jesus' Baptism was not restricted to a reception of repentance, but that here a unique event of revelation took place which determined and released Jesus' subsequent activity.

What was begun in Jesus' Baptism was brought to completion in His death and resurrection. If Jesus through the Baptism of repentance entered the solidarity of sinners, He confirmed this solidarity by dying the death of a sinner on the cross—condemned not only by men but also by God who delivered Him up to the cross and forsook Him on the cross. In this context we must understand the Logion from the material peculiar to Luke, "I came to cast fire upon the earth; and would that it were already kindled! I have a Baptism to be baptized with; and how I am constrained until it is accomplished!" (Luke 12:49-50). This metaphorical language testifies to the connection between Jesus' Baptism and His death, yes, to the meaning of Baptism as a dying. The eschatological fire which Jesus brought to this earth is kindled through His death. If through the voice of God Jesus was at His Baptism singled out from among all sinners, this fact has been brought to completion by His resurrection from the dead. In this act God acknowledged the Crucified One as the Christ, as the Son. Now God has established Him as the One to whom has been given "all authority in heaven and on earth." Now He is manifest to the church as "His Son, who was descended from David according to the flesh and designated Son of God in power according to the Spirit of holiness by His resurrection from the dead." (Rom. 1:3-4)

It is especially Paul who taught that Jesus' death is the basis of Baptism (Romans 6). Yet in another way John's Gospel and the First Epistle also show this relationship. The emphatic reference of the Johannine Passion account to the outflowing of blood and water from Jesus' pierced side (John 19:34) bears witness not only to the reality of His death but also to the origin of Baptism and the Holy Supper in His death. It may be that the First Epistle of John also points to the relationship between Christian Baptism and Jesus' death when it says, "This is He who came by water and blood. . . ." (1 John 5:6; cf. vv. 5-8). There is some debate about the interpretation of this passage, but there is much to be said for the opinion that Jesus Christ, who in His Baptism and in His death entered into the death-bound reality of our flesh, is here proclaimed as the One who is present in the church through the Spirit, through Baptism, and the Lord's Supper. "What do these words say? Precisely what the author is saying: Jesus has passed through His Baptism in Jordan *and* through His death on the cross, Jesus has come into the flesh *realiter* and not just in appearance. 'Water' and 'blood' in the life of the Incarnate One continue to live, in a sense, in the church in the 'water' of Baptism and in the 'blood' of the Lord's Supper." (Edward Schweizer) [30]

24

d. The outpouring of the Holy Spirit

It is the common presupposition of all New Testament writings that after the death and resurrection of Jesus the Spirit of God was imparted to His people and since then is active in all believers. Indeed the Spirit of God had been active already in the Old Covenant in prophets, kings, and other members of the people of God. But now He has been poured out in His fullness: *every* member of the church of Christ receives the Spirit, every member of the church is enlisted by the Spirit as an instrument of the exalted Christ, and the Lord deals with the world in a judging and saving way through every member of the church. The newness of this outpouring of the Spirit is so strongly accented in John's Gospel that it is said of the time preceding, "as yet the Spirit had not been given, because Jesus was not yet glorified" (John 7:39). In a no less radical way Paul distinguishes the newness of this saving event from all that has gone before by opposing to the ministry of the Old Covenant as that of the written code the ministry of the New Covenant as that of the Spirit (2 Cor. 3:6). The outpouring of the Holy Spirit is — with manifold differences in understanding of the Spirit — attested not only in Acts but also in the writings of John and Paul.

The New Testament reports concerning the fundamental operation of the Spirit vary considerably. According to Acts 2:1-13 God imparted the Holy Spirit after the ascension of Jesus, while according to John 20 it was the Risen One who gave the Spirit. These reports cannot be harmonized by saying that the effective impartation of the Spirit in John 20:22 was merely the promise of a future outpouring of the Spirit, or that it meant nothing more than a special charisma for the office of the apostles. These reports do bear witness that the Holy Spirit was in special measure imparted after Jesus' death and resurrection and without water Baptism.

A sovereign act of God and of the Risen One, apart from the instrumentality of baptizing men, by the gift of the Holy Spirit created the community of those who were then authorized to proclaim the Christ message and administer Baptism in the name of Christ. Due respect must be given the sovereignty of this act of God which preceded the Christian Baptism with the Spirit. Its force must not be weakened by deliberating on the question how the pentecostal gift of the Spirit was possible without water Baptism. Moreover, it would be completely misleading to claim that the assembled crowd no longer needed Christian Baptism to receive the Spirit since they had already been baptized by John. This claim is contradicted by the account of the Baptism of the Johannine disciples (Acts 19:1-6). Nor does it seem proper to answer the question by pointing to the account in John's Gospel of Jesus washing His disciples' feet, as though this was their Baptism. Nor is there any indication in the Acts that the group of disciples at Pentecost were subsequently baptized. There is no support here for *a posteriori* conclusions from the much later concept of the necessity of Baptism for salvation. Rather, the outpouring of the Spirit which laid the ground for all subsequent effects of the Spirit and the growth of the church was just as sovereign and immediate an act as the appearances of the Risen One which silenced doubts. In a sovereign way God fashioned the instruments through whose preaching and baptizing He built His church. In this respect the initial outpouring of the Spirit also belongs to the antecedents of Christian Baptism.

3. The Historical Problem of the Origin of Christian Baptism

According to the New Testament the Christian community baptized from the start. This is not only the tradition of the Acts (2:38 ff.); also Paul's baptismal statements which presuppose his own Baptism lead us back to the earliest period of the primitive church.[31] There are no indications in the New Testament that the community began to baptize only at a later date. For linguistic and substantive reasons the conclusion is inescapable that a Baptism with water is meant wherever a Baptism in the name of Christ is mentioned. The Greek terms used (βαπτίζειν and βάπτισμα) include the use of water. Correspondingly, the Pentecost account in the Book of Acts, of the outpouring of the Spirit upon the disciples, does not label it a "baptism by the Spirit." A metaphoric use of the word, as in Luke 12:50, is demonstrable neither in the Acts nor in the New Testament letters nor in John's Gospel.

Like proselyte Baptism and the Baptism of John, Christian Baptism differs from other Jewish immersions and washings in that it is applied only once. It differs from proselyte Baptism also in that like John's Baptism it is not self-administered but administered by another. Furthermore, Christian Baptism is distinguished from John's Baptism in several respects: In the accounts of Acts it is called a Baptism "in the name of

Jesus Christ" (e. g., Acts 2:38 and 10:48) or "in the name of the Lord Jesus" (Acts 8:16 and 19:5). Along the same line are the Pauline statements about Baptism "into Christ Jesus" (Rom. 6:3) or "into Christ" (Gal. 3:27), as well as the warding off of the erroneous idea that the Corinthians had been baptized "in the name of Paul" (1 Cor. 1:13 ff.). An essential feature of Christian Baptism, furthermore, is that it was administered in the certainty of the Spirit's operation, as the New Testament texts agree in affirming. Hence, with her Baptism the church confessed that the prophetic promise of the Spirit's outpouring had now been fulfilled and that in Jesus the one proclaimed by John as the One who would baptize with the Holy Spirit had come. There are further differences between John's Baptism and Christian Baptism: Whereas John had not gathered a community, this happened through Christian Baptism. Whereas John had baptized only members of the Jewish people, Christian Baptism was soon administered also to Gentiles. The difference between the two Baptisms is frequently noted in the baptismal texts. The account in Acts 19:1-6 is particularly significant. Christian Baptism is a new Baptism which differs from and supersedes John's Baptism above all by the name of Christ and the operation of the Spirit. What is reported to have happened in connection with John's Baptism only once, namely at the Baptism of Jesus, is now said to be expected of Christian Baptism. The epiphany of the Spirit upon Him who is the Son now finds its continuation through Baptism in the name of Jesus Christ. Through it God by means of the Holy Spirit makes sinners His sons.

How did Christian Baptism originate? This historical question cannot be answered simply by referring to Matt. 28:19, since this text presents inescapable difficulties for historical thinking.

First of all, there is the problem of the "Trinitarian formula." Nowhere else does the New Testament speak of a Baptism "in the name of the Father and of the Son and of the Holy Spirit." It speaks only of a Baptism upon (in) the name of Jesus Christ (with slight variations). Not until the Didache (7:1 and 3) is the threefold name mentioned again. As a result, theology from Ambrose until late in the scholastic period suggested that the Christological and the Trinitarian baptismal formulae were originally used side by side. Since Bellarmine, Roman Catholic theologians have attempted to demonstrate that the New Testament statements about Baptism in the name of Christ merely *identified* Baptism, whereas the *baptismal formula* was the Trinitarian one from the beginning. The attempt has also been made to account for the absence of the threefold name in other New Testament writings by pointing to the Arcane Discipline [Arcana Disciplina]. Most probably Baptism was originally performed upon (in) the name of Christ [32] and this was later expanded, as in the expansion of the Christological confession into the tripartite creeds. In that case the baptismal command in its Matt. 28:19 form cannot be the historical origin of Christian Baptism. At the very least it must be assumed that the text has been transmitted in a form expanded by the church.[33]

The missionary commission as such presents a further difficulty. Does not its universality contradict the behavior of the primitive church as pictured in the Acts and the letters of Paul? If this missionary command of the Exalted One had been known, would the missionary advance toward the Gentiles have had to fight against so much opposition in the primitive church? It must be noted, however, that this opposition was directed less against the winning of the Gentiles than against their liberation from the demands of the Law (circumcision, etc.). The mission to the Gentiles was nothing new; it had been carried on by Jews before. What was new was the proclamation of the Gospel apart from the Law.

The chief difficulty which the transmitted baptismal command poses for the historian is that as a word of the Risen One it is as impossible to document historically as the resurrection itself. Historical scholarship can indeed document the certainty of the primitive church that Jesus rose from the dead. It can also assume visions and auditions which created this certainty. But historical research cannot prove that God raised Jesus from the dead. There is no experience of similar events that might serve to measure this message and to confirm its claim. The Gospel in fact proclaims the resurrection of Jesus as an utterly unique event through which the universally valid law of death in this world has been breached. By applying the principle of analogy, historical scholarship, on the basis of the universal experience of death, can only deny the truth of this message. If, however, it is radically open for the contingency of history, it can do no more than speak of an unprovable possibility. If, then, the resurrection eludes historical verification, the transmitted words of the Risen One are also open to question. This is true all the more because these words say something that is not supported by the transmitted words of the earthly Jesus.

The attempt has therefore been made to explain the origin of Christian Baptism without a prior command by Jesus. A start is usually made with John's Baptism and then steps of development within the history of primitive Christian Baptism are assumed—steps in which Christian Baptism received the characteristics that distinguished it from John's Baptism. Thus Alfred Seeberg[34] holds that the primitive church in its earliest period took over only the Baptism of John for forgiveness, performing it, of course, with the alteration to take place in the name of Jesus, and then subsequently associating with it the concept of the gift of the Spirit. This theory has been widely accepted— with individual differences. Rudolf Bultmann supports it, too, and assumes that in continuation of John's Baptism primitive Christian Baptism was administered solely for cleansing from sin and that the use of the Lord's name was added as a second motif. Finally, the bestowal of the Spirit was added as a third motif. "Since when that was the case we admittedly do not know. At any rate it was scarcely true in the earliest church, because there, where Jewish tradition was dominant, the baptismal water-bath can scarcely have been conceived otherwise than negatively—i. e., as a purification."[35]

But even this attempted explanation fails to remove certain important difficulties. In contrast to John the Baptist Jesus did not baptize during His ministry nor did He send out His disciples to baptize. Neither in the numerous Gospel reports concerning Jesus' encounter with individuals, nor in the passages that summarize His activity, nor in the instructions for the disciples compiled in Jesus' addresses when He sent them out, is there any mention of Baptism. It is true that John's Gospel mentions that Jesus baptized (3:22), and this statement is then qualified to the effect that not Jesus Himself but His disciples baptized (4:2). However, in view of the silence of the Synoptics it is not likely that this represents a reliable tradition. Perhaps in the overall conception of John's Gospel, which already witnesses to the earthly Jesus as the Exalted One, this passage is to be interpreted as indicating that the post-Easter baptizing by the disciples and their pre-Easter activity are interwoven. But if it must be assumed as historical fact that Jesus did not baptize during His public ministry and did not send His disciples to baptize, then we cannot understand why the primitive church administered Baptism from the very beginning.

Nor do the New Testament writings provide any support for the assumption that the primitive church did not at first baptize in the name of Christ. But if she did, then her Baptism was from the start not a continuation of John's Baptism but an innovation. No name was mentioned in connection with John's Baptism. Again, it cannot be overlooked that the New Testament assumes the connection between Christian Baptism and the reception of the Spirit as having existed from the beginning. This is clearly the case in the oldest accounts, the Pauline statements about Baptism; but this is also true in a different way about the baptismal reports in the Acts. Even where Baptism and reception of the Spirit are separated in time, the necessary connection of both is clearly expressed. Also Bultmann acknowledges this: "The passages, Acts 8:14-17, 10:44-48, in which the receipt of the Spirit and baptism are not contemporaneous, are only an apparent exception. In reality, the intent of both passages is to teach precisely the inseparability of baptism and the receipt of the Spirit. A baptism which does not bestow the Spirit is no proper baptism and hence must be supplemented by the receiving of the Spirit (8:14-17). The bestowal of the Spirit by God means that baptism must be given to the one so favored." [36] There is no warrant in the New Testament statements about Baptism for the assumption of an evolution of the Christian understanding of Baptism up to the time when its interpretation as forgiveness of sins was combined with the concept of the impartation of the Spirit.[37] The pneumatological statements can be eliminated from the New Testament texts all the less because they are concerned not only with a pneumatological *interpretation* of Baptism but with the *experience* of effects of the Spirit which Christians had in connection with Baptism.

In view of this state of affairs it remains unintelligible how the primitive Christian community came to perform this Baptism from the beginning, which was so different from John's Baptism, if the community had no baptismal command. It is all the less likely that the church invented this act when one considers how much the Jesus tradition meant to her and how long it took for the church, for example, to make a sacrament of the anointing of the sick (cf. James 5:14) for which no command of Jesus could be adduced. Thus we have the paradoxical situation that the command of the Risen One, which eludes historical grasp, is the most reliable historical explanation for the origin of Christian Baptism. In addition to Matt. 28:19 also the "appendix" to Mark's Gospel (16:16) points in this direction.

Like the origin of the message concerning the resurrection of Jesus, so also the origin of Christian Baptism is beyond strict historical verification. The resurrection message and the baptismal practice of the primitive church can be historically established, but not the resurrection itself nor the words of the Risen One. The institution of Baptism by Jesus Christ can only be believed. If, in spite of the historical problems, the church continues to baptize by appealing to the baptismal command of the Risen One, she is confessing thereby that she is here not acting on the basis of her own initiative but in obedience to the exalted Lord. The church cannot be satisfied with a belated reference of her Baptism to Christ by bringing her traditional practice into an interpretive relationship with Jesus Christ and the Holy Spirit. The church is rather confessing that the command of the Risen One has sent and authorized her to baptize. A Baptism content to rest upon the fact that the primitive Christian community has always baptized would rest on a poor foundation. No matter how the concept of the institution is defined, the baptismal command ought to have a special basic meaning within the whole foundational context — which is predetermined through prophetic promise; through Jesus' Baptism, death, and resurrection; and through the outpouring of the Holy Spirit.

4. Variety and Structure of the New Testament Statements About Baptism

The baptismal statements in the New Testament are numerous, far more numerous than those about the Lord's Supper. Similarly, the literature of the ancient church contains incomparably more statements about Baptism than about the Lord's Supper. Baptism provides decisive access to all the gifts which God has made available and now gives to the New Testament people of God.

Also the variety of the New Testament statements about Baptism corresponds to the basic significance of Baptism. This variety, too, is far greater than that of the passages about the Lord's Supper. This is true already of the passages which explicitly mention Baptism.

In the first place, the gift of Baptism is repeatedly designated as the forgiveness of sins, either in so many words (Acts 2:38), or as a washing away of sins (Acts 22:16), as cleansing (Eph. 5:26), as sprinkling the hearts clean from an evil conscience (Heb. 10:22), or something similar. Related in thought are the Pauline statements about being washed, sanctified, and justified (1 Cor. 6:11) and especially about the destruction of the sinful body through Baptism (Rom. 6:6). But already these references to the forgiveness of sins are quite different in their anthropological presuppositions and in their understanding of sin, and they cannot simply be equated with each other. Closely related to the forgiveness of sins is the witness to the "salvation" from the divine judgment resulting from Baptism. (E. g., Acts 2:40 and 47; Titus 3:5)

In the second place, the activity of the Spirit in connection with Baptism is referred to again and again. This too is done in a quite different manner. On the one hand, the gift of the Spirit is spoken of in the sense of special manifestations of power (notably in Acts); on the other hand, mention is made of the creation of a new existence through the "birth from above" (John 3:3), through "regeneration and renewal" (Titus 3:5). Renewal and the gift of the Spirit are also mentioned side by side (especially by Paul). Also sanctification and justification can be seen as the work of the Spirit (1 Cor. 6:11). These pneumatological statements, too, are to be taken seriously, each in its peculiarity, and must not be reduced to one of them or derived from one of them.

It is not possible, however, to assign all the New Testament passages concerning the significance of Baptism to the two themes of the forgiveness of sins and the imparting of the Spirit. If according to Rom. 6:3 ff. man has died to sin in Baptism in order to walk in newness of life and become a partaker of Christ's resurrection, and if according to Col. 2:12 (3:1) man has not only died in Baptism but has already risen from the dead, then forgiveness and the effectual operation of the Spirit are jointly effective in this matter of being taken into Christ's way. The same might be said of the statement that those who "were baptized into Christ have put on Christ" (Gal. 3:27). But here too the differences cannot be overlooked. To say that through Baptism into Jesus' death the future resurrection is guaranteed and to say that in Baptism the resurrection has already taken place are not the same. Forgiveness of sins and the activity of the Spirit are also implicitly together in the statements about being "added" to the people of God as a result of Baptism (Acts 2:41) and being baptized "into one body" (1 Cor. 12:13). Even these two assertions differ not only in their Christological and pneumatological significance but also in their eschatological reference.

If the people of God are going to meet the coming Christ, then the body is the presence of Christ.

The diversity in the understanding of Baptism that has here been merely indicated proves to be even greater when we do not confine ourselves to those passages which explicitly deal with Baptism. Surely we must include a large number of passages that do not mention Baptism specifically but speak of the foundation of the Christian life, even though we may not always be able to draw the line precisely. It is especially plausible that Baptism is intended in passages which elsewhere are expressly referred to Baptism (e. g., the statement about being "born anew," 1 Peter 1:3). Beyond this lies the understanding that a large number of additional statements deal with Baptism, for example, the statements about the seal (2 Cor. 1:22; Eph. 1:13; 4:30), about reception of the "guarantee of our inheritance until we acquire possession of it" (Eph. 1:14), about the gift of "His Spirit in our hearts as a guarantee" (2 Cor. 1:22; 5:5), the adoption of sons (Rom. 8:29-30), and the realization of the "new creation" (2 Cor. 5:17). Reference to Baptism may well be included also in the references to the call, the beginning of being in Christ or of being in the Holy Spirit.

It is better to arrange the variety of all these baptismal statements genetically rather than systematically. This variety reflects the breakthrough of the Christ proclamation from the Palestinian-Jewish Christian milieu into the Hellenistic world, whereby also concepts from the mystery religions and Gnosis were taken over. But even if we take note of the manifold genetic layers of the baptismal material, we are left in each case with a juxtaposition of several statements that cannot be reduced to a common denominator or derived from each other. Thus there are concepts mentioned side by side which derive from totally different areas, such as the forensic-legal and the creative-ontological. There is an exuberance about the New Testament baptismal material, a character of restlessness, since the event spoken of signifies so profound and revolutionary an inroad into the life of a person that *one* word cannot grasp it. It is not simply a matter of interpreting a rite but of bearing witness to the action of God which takes place through Baptism. Strictly speaking, therefore, it is inadequate to speak only of the *significance* of Baptism. We are dealing with the *gift* and the *effect* that are imparted through Baptism.

As a result the variety of the New Testament statements poses a

33

methodological problem for the church's doctrine of Baptism. In every case both confession and dogmatics deal with the multiplicity of Biblical statements by concentrating on a few concepts. The doctrine of Baptism presents the same methodological problem as exists for the dogmatic endeavor also in other areas of doctrine, such as Christology, ecclesiology, or soteriology. This problem arises from the fact that one and the same divine deed is given expression through a multiplicity of Biblical terms which are not simply interchangeable, even though each concept bears witness to the whole. Think, for example, of the large number of exalted titles applied to Christ, the many ways in which the saving significance of Christ's death is expressed, the many terms used to describe the church, or the juxtaposition of statements about justification, sanctification, vivification, etc. Dogma always selects individual concepts from among a large number in order to use them as basic concepts and by means of them to embrace the multiplicity of relevant Biblical statements. This selection can in principle be made along different lines. In the course of the history of theology different Biblical concepts have in fact been used as fundamental dogmatic concepts, and in the process these concepts were expanded considerably beyond their original content. In the formulation of dogmatic concepts there is ever the danger that the richness of the Biblical statements is no longer recognized, and consequently the unity of the church's confession is put into question. This danger is increased even more when dogmatics is shaped from without through comprehensive ontological conceptions or such as deal with the philosophy of history. Thus in view of the variety of New Testament baptismal statements the question arises concerning the systematic starting point from which this variety should be taken up dogmatically and given expression.

However, not only the content of the New Testament baptismal statements must be considered, but also the structure in which they are made. The dogmatic enterprise must give an account of the degree to which its formulations coincide with those of the New Testament or have undergone structural changes.[38] This is far from being merely a formal question. Many later problems in the doctrine of Baptism arose only because men departed from the structure of the New Testament baptismal statements and took a different position from which they attempted to think through the doctrine of Baptism and formulate it. Some of the contrasts in the baptismal teaching of different church bodies are linked with such structural changes in dogmatic formulations. There are other far-reaching differences in the history of dogma; for example, in the discussion of the problem of synergism, which presuppose such shifts in structure. Dealing with the relationship between divine and human activity leads to contradictory assertions when these are made either from the standpoint of being existentially struck by God's address or from the standpoint of being a spectator. The content of the New Testament baptismal statements may not be separated from their structure. Only if this structure is taken into account will the statements be correctly interpreted and incorporated in the church's baptismal theology in conformity with their content.

Let us start with the location of the New Testament baptismal statements.

The oldest statements are found in the letters of Paul. Since these letters, like others in the New Testament, are addressed to congregations, it is not a question of summoning them to Baptism but of reminding them of the Baptism they have received. The act of Baptism is not described, nor is a cohesive doctrine of Baptism set forth, but rather expression is given to what was done to the members of the congregation in Baptism, and this becomes the basis for the admonitions to walk in a new life, to persevere in trials, to keep from relapsing into sin, etc. This reminder may be given in different ways, either by pointing to the reality of God's deed in Baptism or by praising God for this deed. Furthermore, there are passages in the epistles which suggest that phrases are cited from the baptismal liturgy, or at least they are alluded to. This applies especially to 1 Peter 1:3-5, Titus 3:5-7, and Ephesians 5:14. In addition, other passages from 1 Peter, Ephesians,[39] and Colossians[40] have been interpreted in relation to the baptismal liturgy. An implicit recollection of Baptism may also be contained in Romans 13:11-14.

The other important source of baptismal statements is the Book of Acts. These statements are quite different from those in the epistles. Here the congregation is not directly addressed and reminded of the Baptism already received, but a report is made about Baptisms that were administered at the beginning of the church's history. These reports were in part taken over by Luke — in part shaped by him. All of them are in the perspective of the historical growth of the church. They are less interested in a detailed description of the process involved in Baptism

35

than in the addition of individuals and groups to the Christian community.

In spite of all differences the baptismal statements of the epistles and Acts have this in common that they are concerned above all to bear witness to what the Christian received in his Baptism, that is to say, what God did to him in Baptism, and that means what God did to the church. There is in the New Testament, however, no tradition of a specific order of Baptism, nor even of a more precise instruction on the manner of administering Baptism.

With regard to the structure of the New Testament baptismal statements there is therefore much less variety than in the concept itself.

Only rarely is there the form of the imperative: to bestow Baptism or to receive it (Matt. 28:19; Acts 2:38; cf. also Eph. 5:14). Reports of Baptisms are more numerous. They are cast in the form of historical instruction. While they were certainly assembled by Luke for the sake of the community, the community is not directly addressed, neither directly sent to baptize, nor directly reminded of the Baptism received. Most of the baptismal statements are in the form of New Testament admonition — more precisely in the recall and application of what happened to the recipients of the letters in their Baptism. Hence they emphasize the event through which the new life was opened to the addressees, and thus become the ground of the exhortation to walk in a new life and to praise God. Finally Baptism is indirectly expressed in the form of doxology, as for example in 1 Peter 1:3-4: "Blessed be the God and Father of our Lord Jesus Christ! By His great mercy we have been born anew to a living hope. . . ."

Thus the New Testament baptismal statements are not concerned with describing the baptismal ritual as such — nor with presenting the results of a theoretical study. For example, their theme is not the definition of the relationship between water and Word, washing and forgiveness of sins, immersion and death, emersion and renewal, etc. These familiar questions, that arose later in the history of theology, are not dealt with in the New Testament. Nor is the concern with an abstract doctrine of Baptism as such, a doctrine which demands acceptance apart from the bestowal or reception of Baptism in faith or in unbelief, and apart from the question whether God grants grace through it or not. For this question too, which later became so important, the New Testament offers no immediate answer. The New Testament does

36

not assume a position of reflection and thought to a certain extent independent of divine and human activity, a position from which both might be surveyed and defined in their mutual relationship and on the basis of which conclusions could then be drawn for the effect and value of Baptism for faith and unbelief. Rather, the form of the New Testament baptismal statements is determined by the fact that by faith in God's saving deed which takes place in Baptism they summon to Baptism, report on Baptisms, and recall the received Baptism to mind. From this we may not conclude that the New Testament has nothing instructive to say about Baptism; [41] but this instruction is for the most part embedded in the address to the congregation, where it is used as an argument in support of exhortation. The form of these statements is determined above all by the fact that they express the summons of faith to faith in the saving deed which God has done for the baptized.

The dogmatic teaching as such is neither historical report nor application and admonition, nor prayer and worship, but it must serve all these expressions of faith. This results in a much broader concept of doctrine than that contained, for example, in Paul's distinction between prophecy and teaching. Whereas Paul's concern with doctrine was primarily with the tradition and its interpretation, dogmatic teaching deals not only with the transmitted saving deeds of God but also with their concrete application and claim, as well as with prayer and doxology. This results in noteworthy shifts over against the original form of these statements — shifts which can be highly significant also for the content. It is therefore important for the church's doctrine to be made aware of these structural differences. Although the doctrine is not proclamation or prayer or doxology, it must avoid a position that is taken in isolation from an existential involvement and challenge, a position from which one thinks it possible to reflect and speak on God's activity for man and man's responses to God in the role of spectators. In view of the specific forms of the New Testament baptismal statements it is necessary to engage in a systematic search for those dogmatic formulations which come closest to doing justice to the New Testament witness.

5. The Starting Point for the Doctrine of Baptism

The doctrine of Baptism cannot confine itself to adopting and summarizing the results of New Testament exegesis. Starting with the New

Testament baptismal statements, the doctrine must take up the questions that are currently raised in connection with Baptism and attempt to answer them. So, for example, in the midst of the external and internal dissolution in many churches infant Baptism has become questionable for many. It is not only a question of whether it is proper to baptize children of unchurched parents, but whether infants should be baptized at all. It is not merely a problem about baptismal practice, but it concerns distinctions and contrasts in the understanding of Baptism. Such differences have in part been dogmatically and legally fixed even in church schisms, and in part they are present side by side in the same church. In every case we are dealing here with particularly ecumenical problems that did not exist in early Christendom and can therefore not be answered directly on the basis of the New Testament. For their solution we must draw on the history of the understanding and practice of Baptism. Without a knowledge of these today's problem-situation remains unintelligible. It is self-evident that in the course of church history problems in the doctrine of Baptism, for which the New Testament texts have no immediate answer, had to be discussed. It was only in the discussions of the ancient church, for example, that the problem of heretical Baptism became acute. Also the later problems of the state church and people's church [in Germany] were as foreign to the primitive church as the problems of a free church separated from the people's church. To that extent also the specific problems surrounding infant Baptism in our time were foreign to the primitive church. Only indirectly, by means of deductions from New Testament statements and new decisions on the basis of these statements, can such and similar questions be answered. The decisive factor is that both the current problems as well as the history of the doctrine and practice of Baptism are placed into question by the New Testament baptismal statements and that these be maintained as the norm for the discussion of all problems.

How then shall we begin in our study of the New Testament baptismal statements? The variety of their content and the particularity of their forms gives the dogmatic teaching a choice. Which approach and which form shall we choose?

a. It is true that in Baptism a human being is active. Yet all the interest of the New Testament statements is focused on what God is doing through this person to the one being baptized. It is true that the person being baptized also is active in coming to Baptism and submitting to it. Yet all the weight of the statements rests on what God is doing to the one baptized. At the decisive point the behavior of the baptizand [one being baptized] during his Baptism is passive, both over against the baptizer and over against God. The desire for Baptism on the part of the baptizand and the action of the baptizer are necessary components of the doctrine of Baptism. But since the real concern of the New Testament statements is with God's activity, we shall first treat God's deed (Chapter 2) and only then the administration and the reception of Baptism (Chapter 3).

b. In view of the multiplicity of the New Testament statements it is extremely significant that in every case a Baptism upon (in) the name of Jesus Christ is assumed. This name is of over-arching significance not only for the designation and administration of Baptism but also for its dogmatic understanding. In what follows we shall therefore begin with this name and proceed to develop systematically the variety of statements concerning God's activity in Baptism. In so doing, we shall not start with the universal religio-historical function of cultic names, nor with the universal phenomenon of the use of a name in the sense of an efficacious magical exorcism,[42] but we shall start with the historical Person who bears this name and to which baptizer and baptizand appeal: Jesus Christ, the crucified and risen, exalted to be Lord. What is decisive here is not the universal religio-historical function of cultic names but the history and authority of Jesus Christ. His suffering and His exaltation determine the specific power of His name upon which and in which people are baptized. On the basis of this approach God's activity through Baptism will be developed 1. Christologically, 2. pneumatologically, 3. ecclesiologically, and 4. in a Trinitarian manner.

c. We must not only consider the approach to the doctrine of Baptism as far as content is concerned, but we must also reach a decision about the position from which and the form in which the doctrine of Baptism is to be systematically developed. In each of the following sections our point of departure shall be what *faith* proclaims as happening in Baptism on the basis of the New Testament material. We decline to take a position isolated from the *believing* remembrance of the Baptism that was received and isolated from the invitation to receive Baptism *in faith*. In this way we shall remain in the structure of formulation that corresponds to the New Testament baptismal texts. We may not a priori dilute the formulations in the doctrine of Baptism by asking questions about the significance of Baptism for the nonbeliever. The doctrine of Baptism will, of course, have to ask and answer this question and all others connected with it. But the church's doctrine of Baptism should have the courage to begin with the saving deed experienced by faith in Baptism, rather than with the abuse of Baptism and the sickness of the church. Only in this way can the abnormalities in the understanding and practice of Baptism be appropriately discussed. Hence the dangers of an abuse of Baptism, as well as questions pertaining to a fixing of relationships between the act of Baptism and grace, "sign" and "substance," water and Word, etc., will always be discussed as the last item in the subdivisions of the following two chapters (Chapter 2, 1d, 2d, 3c, 4d and Chapter 3, 2c, 3c, 4).

d. The fact that the New Testament baptismal statements confront us as a call to faith in God's saving deed — above all as a consoling reminder of the saving deed which God has done to the baptized — and as an exhortation to live accordingly, makes it impossible to separate the baptismal statements from the imperative [the command]. For that reason the imperative to walk in the new life on the basis of God's saving deed shall in the following be given expression in the doctrine of Baptism itself. If Baptism itself is not to be misunderstood, the imperative dare not be left exclusively to theological ethics. Consequently Chapter 2 will present the doctrine of God's activity through Baptism by including the exhortation which has its basis in God's deed (1c, 2c, 3b).

e. The New Testament is not interested in an isolated doctrine of Baptism. Beyond the relationship between Baptism and exhortation, the New Testament baptismal statements are embedded in the totality of the responses which the believer offers to God in prayer and doxology, in confession and witness, and thus in the total life of the church. Hence the doctrine of baptism can be isolated neither from the message concerning Christ, nor from the Lord's Supper, nor from the church. Since the New Testament does not treat Baptism in isolation, the church's doctrine, even when Baptism is treated monographically, must constantly keep in view the relationship between Baptism and proclamation, Lord's Supper and church. It is precisely in the combination of all these events that God deals with man. In other words, the doctrine of Baptism must take note of the mystery of the riches of grace and the means of grace through which in different ways God bestows the same forgiveness, the

40

same new life, the fellowship of the same Christ and the same Holy Spirit. (Cf. especially Chapter 3, 1.)

f. Since the Biblical material about Baptism is not primarily interested in the form of the baptismal act, the question of the form in which Baptism is to be administered will be treated in Chapter 4. Finally, a brief concluding section will point to the special significance of Baptism in the relationship of separated churches to each other. In distinction from the Lord's Supper and holy orders most churches today acknowledge each other's Baptism. What does this mean for the unification of the churches?

CHAPTER TWO

The Saving Activity of God
Through Baptism

1. Baptism into Christ

a. Baptism as assignment to the crucified
and risen Christ

The New Testament speaks of Baptism upon (in) "the name of Jesus Christ" (Acts 2:38; 10:48), "of the Lord Jesus" (Acts 8:16; 19:5), or "of the Lord Jesus Christ" (1 Cor. 6:11), as well as of Baptism "into Christ" (Gal. 3:27) or "into Christ Jesus" (Rom. 6:3). The change in prepositions can be unambiguously clarified neither from the Hebrew nor secular Greek usage, nor from the Septuagint. It is particularly difficult to fix the meaning of the individual prepositions in the colloquial Greek used in the New Testament.[1] The meanings often coalesce. In any case the customary translation of the two basic Greek prepositions (ἐν and ἐπὶ τῷ ὀνόματι) with "in the name" need not mean "by command of" or "by authority of" Jesus Christ. It may also be rendered "through the name" and "on the basis of the name."[2] What is decisive for the meaning of the various prepositional combinations is the reference to the name and thus to the reality of Christ.

The predominant New Testament formulation is "upon the name," or more accurately, "into the name" (εἰς τὸ ὄνομα), or also "into Christ."[3] Baptism into the name of Christ, which must be assumed also in 1 Cor. 1:13-16, is identical with Baptism "into Christ" (Rom. 6:3). This prepositional combination is understood mostly in the sense of an assignment. Through Baptism "into the name of the Lord Jesus" the person is assigned to the Lord Jesus. "Through the name the baptized is signed, stamped, and sealed as the property of Christ" (W. Heitmüller).[4] Similarly R. Bultmann: "The meaning of this naming of the Name is first of all this: that by it the candidate is stamped as property of the Kyrios and placed under his protection. This is proved by the use of the term 'seal' (σφραγίς), which Paul clearly presupposes, for baptism."[5] In opposition to this interpretation G. Delling has pointed out that "quite generally εἰς can express relationship (including personal relationship)."[6] Accordingly, Baptism into Christ in Paul's writings should be understood not as assignment to Christ but as a Baptism with regard to Christ, especially with regard to the saving event in His death. Since the Baptism "into Moses" (1 Cor. 10:2) cannot mean an assignment to Moses, what the statements about Baptism into Moses and into Christ have in common is the common reference to the fact that God acted through both.[7] In a similar way the statements in the Acts are not understood in the sense of assignment but of the assurance of the salvation that is bound to the name of Jesus. The "into" "indicates the direction, the 'point of reference,' toward which Baptism is performed."[8]

However, these two interpretations need not exclude each other. The crucified Jesus is the present Lord. In Paul's understanding the insertion of the baptized person into the event of the cross is inseparable from assignment to the living Lord. It is furthermore striking that, according to the reports in Acts, Baptism was explicitly performed "into the name of the Lord Jesus."[9] Delling himself observes that the reference to the name of Jesus in Acts is less concerned with the event of the cross and the resurrection than with the crucified and risen One, and thus with the person of Jesus.[10] But since in contrast to Moses Jesus rose from the dead and was installed as Lord, Baptism into His name can never be referred back exclusively to God's historical saving deed, just as the present Lord can never be separated from the event of the cross. Since Baptism upon (in) the name of Jesus Christ takes place with reference to Jesus' death and resurrection, it effects at the same time the assignment to the crucified and risen Lord who is present in His community. The attempt has been made to explain the formula "upon (in) the name" as a technical term taken over from Hellenistic commerce in the sense of an assignment, "since the account bears the name of the one who owns it, and in baptism the name of Christ is pronounced, invoked and confessed by the one who baptises or the one baptised" (A. Oepke).[11] In that case Baptism to a certain extent would signify the transfer of the baptized into Christ's possession. It is unlikely that there is here a historical dependence, and yet this suggestion may be adduced to clarify the baptismal event in an allegorical way.

In opposition to the interpretation offered by the history-of-religions school, which by analogy understood the name of Christ into which one is baptized as a magical use of the divine name, identical with the divine reality,[12] it must be pointed out that Jesus Christ commissions and acts in personal freedom.[13] This aspect of freedom is evident above all in the New Testament statements concerning the relationship between Baptism, faith, and Holy Spirit. The extreme opposite of this magical understanding of Baptism is the thesis of Markus Barth: "Baptism is not an act of assignment by which the baptized becomes the property of Jesus Christ, a child of God or an heir of glory," [14] but rather "a seemly act of humiliation before God, of human fellowship and mutual love," [15] "a work which God commanded men to perform, a work by which they respond to God's saving work and to the proclamation of this saving work." [16] However, this thesis has rightly found no support in New Testament scholarship.

Being assigned to Jesus Christ, the Lord, as His property, this being placed under the present rule of the Crucified comes to the baptized as something done to him. Just as Christian Baptism is not a self-Baptism but a being baptized, so the baptized does not become Christ's property by placing *himself* under Christ, but rather he *becomes* Christ's property through Baptism. This is God's deed; this is acceptance by the Lord.

Because Jesus died for the world on the cross, the forgiveness of sins is imparted together with the assignment to Him. "Standing in a definite and absolutely indispensable historical context, baptism derives its force from the reconciling action of God in Christ, or more exactly from the atoning death of Christ (1 Cor. 6:11; Eph. 5:25-27; Titus 3:4-8; 1 John 5:6; cf. John 19:34; 1 Peter 1:2; Heb. 10:22)." [17] It is true that this relationship between Baptism, forgiveness of sins, and the death on the cross is not expressed in all the New Testament baptismal statements. It is lacking especially in the Acts. In its Christological formulas the resurrection of Jesus as God's saving deed stands in the foreground. Yet in reality the death of Jesus is the precondition for all baptizing upon the name of Jesus, for the person and the history of Jesus cannot be separated from each other. The forgiveness which is imparted through Baptism is determined by the fact that the baptized is assigned to the Crucified as to the living, present, and active Lord. Therefore in this forgiveness it is not simply a matter of removing a purely cultic impurity, nor of pardoning isolated transgressions of divine precepts, nor of the cancellation of a specific individual guilt Beyond all of this the forgiveness which is imparted through Baptism is a change of dominion. Through Baptism a man is removed from the dominion of sin and placed under the rule of Christ. Through Baptism God lays hold of the whole man, together with his past and his future. Through forgiveness the past has been rendered powerless, and the future will consist in so indissoluble a union with Christ that the baptized may live free from the claim of guilt. Thus Baptism effects not only the forgiveness of sinful deeds but the liberation of the person from the compulsion to keep on sinning—the liberation to a life in purity, righteousness, and holiness. In this way the New Testament statements concerning this forgiveness correspond to the Old Testament prophetic promise of the eschatological purification. "This cannot refer only to a removal of guilt. It must include removal of sin, that is, an actual deliverance from sin. This deliverance will be brought about by the purification and transformation of those who survive [the eschatological judgment]" (Hans Windisch).[18] In contrast to the problems associated with John's Baptism, Christian Baptism is concerned not only with an eschatological promise but with God's eschatological deed.

Because God has installed as Lord and Christ the same Jesus who died on the cross for the world and has given Him the judgment of the world, the assignment to Him through Baptism is salvation from the coming day of wrath and of judgment which the prophets and John the Baptist had announced and whose coming is also presupposed in Jesus' preaching of the imminent rule of God. Through Christian Baptism the deliverance in the final Judgment is not only promised, or only guaranteed, but actually accomplished, so that the baptized are going toward the coming day, the return of their Lord, as the rescued. Because they belong to Jesus it can be said of them, "Who is to condemn? Is it Christ Jesus, who died, yes, who was raised from the dead, who is at the right hand of God, who indeed intercedes for us?" (Rom. 8:34). Because the forgiveness of sins and deliverance from the judgment of wrath are imparted through Baptism, the Law loses its accusing and condemning force over the baptized, and death loses its terrors. Though the baptized are still moving toward death in this world, they have been snatched out of the judgment of death. Now the words apply, "None of us lives to himself, and none of us dies to himself. If we live, we live to the Lord,

45

and if we die, we die to the Lord; so then, whether we live or whether we die, we are the Lord's." (Rom. 14:7 f.)

Thus Baptism also effects man's deliverance from the dominion of the powers that through sin had gained control of him. It is true that in the foreground of the New Testament baptismal statements there is forgiveness of sins and rescue from God's judgment and not deliverance from the spell of the devil and the demonic powers. In the foreground are also the positive statements about the new existence which is opened up through belonging to Jesus as Lord. Also in the confession of Christ the renunciation of the world, which is in essence accomplished by the confession, is not necessarily given explicit expression. However, even though the New Testament baptismal statements only rarely say it in so many words, the assignment to Christ is *in fact* deliverance from the dominion of the powers of darkness. Even though Col. 1:12 f. does not explicitly speak of Baptism, this passage may in this sense be applied to Baptism: Give "thanks to the Father, who . . . has delivered us from the dominion of darkness and transferred us to the kingdom of His beloved Son, in whom we have redemption . . . ." This deliverance is also presupposed by the admonitions to watchfulness (1 Thess. 5:4 ff.) and to resistance to "your adversary the devil" (1 Peter 5:8). Because the baptized are not property of darkness but "sons of the day" (1 Thess. 5:5), they must be on their guard against darkness; because they are not under the dominion of the devil but are stalked by him (1 Peter 5:8), they must withstand him. The onesidedness with which W. Heitmüller understood Christian Baptism as exorcism [19] has no support in the New Testament but rests on transferring the exorcistic magic of the name in the history-of-religions environment to the use of the name of Christ in Baptism.

Thus through Baptism God enters deeply into human life; a separation between the life before and the life after takes place. Man's autonomy, which was in reality his enslavement through guilt and ruin, has come to an end. The new life as Christ's property, the life in freedom and hope, has opened up. This turning point, this new beginning is emphasized in the New Testament in the strongest possible way. It cannot be overestimated. Here we have not only the restoration of the earthly life without the obstacles set by sin and the powers but also the opening of the new life in fellowship with the Lord who, as the Risen One, has been removed from the conditions of existence in this world and transferred into a new mode of being. As the Exalted One He draws His own to Himself. The pathos of the New Testament baptismal statements applies to this new existence that has been brought about through being assigned to Christ as His property. The baptized may now live as those who have been washed, justified, sanctified, saved, liberated. Through the name of Christ they have been surrendered to Christ Himself. They now bear Christ's name and are Christ's possession.

b. Given into Jesus' death and resurrection

Paul understood Baptism not only as assignment to the person of Jesus Christ but also as assignment to His history. Baptism into Christ is Baptism into His death. "Do you not know that all of us who have been baptized into Christ Jesus were baptized into His death?" (Rom. 6:3). To be assigned to Christ is to be given into His death on the cross and into His grave. The Baptism event indeed takes place temporally removed from Jesus' death, but through Baptism the person is given into that death which Jesus Christ died once for all.

What happened to the baptized when he was given into Jesus' death? "We were buried therefore with Him by Baptism into death" (Rom. 3:4). "Our old self was crucified with Him" (v. 6). "We have died with Christ" (v. 8). Paul had received and passed on the creedal formula "that Christ *died* for our sins in accordance with the Scriptures, that He was *buried* . . ." (1 Cor. 15:3). Now he uses the same verbs to speak about what happened to the baptized. Paul may here even be referring to a confession in which "crucified, dead, and buried" were united in a formula that already went beyond 1 Cor. 15:3. The baptized was "crucified, dead, and buried" with Christ. Hence the judgment of death which the sinner deserved has been both executed and suspended in the case of the baptized. "The sinful body" is "destroyed" (Rom. 6:6). A new life has been opened.

Baptism is expressly mentioned only in Rom. 6:4. It is the means through which the sinners were *buried* with Christ. But this hardly justifies the conclusion that in Paul's opinion only the burial with Christ has taken place in Baptism, while being crucified with Him and dying with Him happened before Baptism, namely in Christ's death on the cross.[20] The question also arises whether 2 Cor. 5:14 can be adduced here and interpreted in this sense. The entire context of Rom. 6:3-11 is controlled by the reference to Baptism at the beginning, so that the three sentences mentioned (v. 4, 6, and 8) must

47

be understood as statements of one and the same Baptism (in the opinion of most exegetes).

V. 5a also speaks in favor of the assertion that the dying with Christ took place through Baptism: "We have been united with Him in a death like His." It is true, the interpretation of this half of the sentence is disputed.[21] What is the meaning of "a death like His"? It has often been understood as a reference to Baptism itself and words like "with Him," "with Christ," or "with Christ's death" were added. This part of the sentence would then be translated, "when through a death like His (namely through Baptism) we have been united with Him (Christ, His death). . . ." But opposed to this interpretation are the difficulties which then arise for an understanding of the second half of the sentence. If the likeness of death means Baptism and the two parts of the sentence correspond, what shall we make of the likeness of the resurrection which is distinguished from the likeness of death? This question remains unanswered even when the first half of the sentence, without changing the text, is interpreted to mean that we have been united *with* Baptism as the likeness of Christ's death. It is therefore not very likely that Paul designated the baptismal ritual as such the likeness of the death of Christ.[22] He does, however, say something in this verse about what has happened to the baptized in Baptism: His dying with Christ is the likeness of the dying of Jesus Christ. Through Baptism the baptized has been united with this likeness of the death of Jesus Christ. Through Baptism the person experiences the same thing by way of likeness that Jesus Christ experienced in His crucifixion, death, and burial.

In this connection it must be borne in mind that likeness means more than mere similarity. On the contrary, the likeness and the reality with which it is compared correspond so completely that the pictured reality is present in the likeness. Thus the special character of this likeness may be highlighted by the term "replica" [Gleichgestalt] (P. Brunner).[23] The replica of the death of Jesus is the dying with Christ which took place in Baptism through the giving into Jesus' death. The death which Jesus Christ died on the cross and the death which we die in Baptism are one and the same death. Hence the idea suggests itself to speak directly of the "identity" of[24] the death of Jesus Christ and the death of the baptized.

The statements about being crucified, dying, and being buried with Christ do not mean that the difference between Jesus Christ and those who were baptized into Him has been removed. Rather, within the *likeness* of the crucifixion, death, and burial this *difference* is most emphatically maintained. Christ's crucifixion, death, and burial are the *precon-*

dition for the crucifixion, death, and burial of the baptized and *make them possible.* Baptism takes place into Christ's death. "The death He died He died to sin, once for all" (Rom. 6:10). If in Baptism we "die to sin" with Him (Rom. 6:10 f.), this is based on the fact that He died to sin in a different manner than we. It is true, the accent of all statements in Rom. 6:4-11 rests on "with Christ," on "as Christ . . . we too." Furthermore, Paul furnishes a general basis for the freedom from the slavery of sin which was obtained through death, "he who has died is freed from sin" (v. 7),[25] which probably rests on the same thought as in Rom. 7:3, that is, that death frees from legal obligations and ties. Not for one moment, however, dare we overlook the basic difference between the dying of Christ and the believers' dying with Christ. "Christ died for our sins" (1 Cor. 15:3), He "was put to death for our trespasses" (Rom. 4:25). Antecedent to all statements about our having died *with* Christ in Baptism is the incomparable uniqueness of Christ's death *for* us. Hence antecedent to the understanding of Romans 6 are the statements of Romans 5 (especially vv. 17-19) concerning Christ as the Second Adam, the New Man, in whom humanity is now comprehended in a saving manner as it was formerly comprehended in the father of the race in a disastrous manner.

> The concept of likeness means more than mere similarity; it means replica, even identity, and yet this concept inescapably maintains the difference between the reality and the exact reproduction, namely, between Christ's death and that of the baptized. In his Christological assertion (Rom. 8:3) about the sending of the Son "in the likeness of sinful flesh" Paul preserved both the identity of His and our flesh and at the same time the difference between His not sinning in the flesh and our sinning. In the same way his statements about the Baptism event give expression both to the identity and the difference between Christ's death and our dying with Christ. In Baptism we are united with the same death which Christ died on the cross, and yet our dying differs from His death. He did not die for the sake of His sins, but we had become subject to death because of our sins. Because He died for us our sinful body died in Baptism unto life. In a nonreversible manner our dying is coordinated to Christ's death. His once-for-all death is the definitive and decisive historical event, and in Baptism we are united with Him in a death like His. Indeed through Baptism we have become the likeness of His death.

Since Jesus' "dying to sin" happened once for all as a death of obedience for our sins, it is true that "our old self was crucified with Him so that the sinful body might be destroyed, and we might no longer be enslaved to sin" (Rom. 6:6). Paul is here not speaking of the destruction of the sinful body as of a goal to be reached by the baptized at some future time, but as of a present reality from which the baptized is to move into the future: "Consider yourselves dead to sin" (v. 11). Through Baptism the dominion of sin has been broken so that now the Law has forfeited its accusing claim and death has lost its power. The baptized is no longer under the judgment of God's wrath but under God's grace. Along the same line Paul says, Gal. 2:19 f., "I through the Law died to the Law, that I might live to God. I have been crucified with Christ" (cf. 2:16). Even though Baptism is not explicitly mentioned here, it seems nevertheless to be presupposed as the event of dying. Beyond this, other Pauline statements about suffering and dying with Christ would seem to belong into this context even though Baptism is not mentioned. The death that took place in Baptism is the basis for the daily dying with Christ. Thus also in Col. 2:11-12 the admonition to "put off the body of flesh" rests on the fact that "you were buried with Him in baptism." Like Christ's death, so our death that took place in Baptism is a onetime historical event. As Paul proclaims Christ's death "for our sins" as the definitive saving deed in ever new ways, so he constantly reminds us of our dying with Christ as the saving deed which determines our entire future.

In the course of history the event of Christ's death and the event of Baptism are separated in time. We must not lose sight of this interval. Yet the Pauline statements are not interested in the interval but in the combination and even interpenetration of both events. Through Baptism the persons baptized have been inserted into the once-for-all death of Jesus Christ. Thus Paul is not speaking of subsequently experiencing in Baptism what befell Jesus Christ in His death, nor of an imitation of Christ brought about in Baptism, nor of Baptism as an acknowledgment of what happened in Jesus' death. Furthermore, he is not concerned about interpreting the act of Baptism as a symbolic copy of the death of Christ.[26] Neither through a symbolical interpretation of the baptismal ritual nor through assertions about what the baptized person experiences and does during this act does Paul establish a relationship between Baptism and the death of Jesus Christ on the cross.[27] He is rather concerned about the fact: "Through Baptism" we have been crucified, we have died, and have been buried with Christ. In spite of the interval between Christ's death and Baptism, both events are in their decisive point *one* event. In Baptism something happens that had not yet happened before Baptism. Formerly the person was under the dominion of sin; in Baptism this dominion is broken. Yet in its decisive point Baptism is not a saving deed different from the one accomplished on the cross, for through Baptism the sinner is given into Christ's death. In this way the temporal distance from Jesus' death loses its significance in the act of Baptism. As the Exalted One the Crucified is Lord without qualification, not only over the world but also over the structure of this world in space and time. Just as Christ, in overcoming the temporal interval between today and His Second Coming already assures faith of the justifying acquittal in the coming Judgment and grants him the future life of the resurrected, so also, in overcoming the temporal interval between the events surrounding His death and our Baptism, He grants participation in His once-for-all death. Through Baptism Christ gives the sinner into the death [He] once suffered as into his present death. We would not be doing justice to Paul's statements if we were to speak only of the benefit, effect, and fruit of Christ's death which are imparted through Baptism. All this is indeed included in the statements about dying with Christ, but beyond this we must acknowledge the presence of the death of Jesus Christ and the fact that the baptized person becomes contemporary with Jesus' death. In this way, it is true, we are going beyond the wording of Paul's statements. He is not interested in a theological clarification of the problem of time involved with Baptism but his concern is concentrated on the assurance: You are baptized into Christ's death, through Baptism you are crucified, dead, and buried with Christ — you have died to sin.

The problem of time posed by Romans 6 has in recent decades been discussed particularly in connection with a study of the mystery theology presented by Odo Casel.[28] Certainly the Pauline statements do not permit O. Casel's teaching of an exhibitory representation of Jesus' death in Baptism that could be distinguished from the appropriation of this saving deed through Baptism. Paul is not so much concerned with the presence of the death of Jesus in its historical factuality as such but with the presence of this onetime death for the baptized person. Furthermore, in contrast to the mystery religions to which Casel adverts, Paul does not feature the exhibitory function of the baptismal event as if in its symbol-

51

ism the death of Jesus on the cross were really present, and he certainly makes no reference to the church which by her exhibitory activity makes Christ's death present in Baptism. Yet, even though such limitations must be imposed on the mystery theology, [29] they cannot cancel the legitimacy of the assertion that Christ's death is present in Baptism. Luther has it too,[30] and in current evangelical theology it is supported especially by Peter Brunner.[31]

Though Paul is little interested in a theoretical clarification of these problems,[32] he is very much concerned about the consequences arising from dying with Christ. Since we have died with Christ we shall also rise with Him. Through Baptism our history has become so definitively interwoven with Christ's history that it is no longer only our own history with Him and in Him. Being given into His death we have been received into His way through death to life. "We were buried therefore with Him by Baptism into death, so that as Christ was raised from the dead, . . . we too might walk in newness of life" (Rom. 6:4). "But if we have died with Christ, we believe that we shall also live with Him" (v. 8). Paul draws the same conclusion from the fact that we have been united with Christ in the likeness of His death (v. 5). The language of the text permits the conclusion in the second half of the sentence to read, "so we shall also participate in His resurrection." But it is probably more appropriate to translate, "If we have grown together with the likeness of His death, we shall also have grown together with the likeness of His resurrection." Paul speaks of the likeness of death and the likeness of resurrection in the same way as of the replica [Gleichbild], even the identity, while maintaining the distinction, namely the foundational significance of Jesus' death and resurrection. By means of all these inferences Paul emphasizes that participation in Christ's death guarantees participation in His resurrection life. The affirmations about the life of the baptized are made in the future tense (Rom. 6:5 and 8). At the same time those who have died with Christ participate in this life already now. The baptized are to "walk in newness of life" (v. 4) and yield themselves to God "as men who have been brought from death to life" (v. 13). Because being given into Christ's death guarantees the resurrection, the baptized, as one who has died with Christ, participates already in the life that is to come.[33]

It is, therefore, not surprising that Colossians speaks not only of the burial of the baptized but also of their resurrection as of an event that has taken place in Baptism. You were "raised with Him through faith in the working of God, who raised Him from the dead." "You, who were dead in trespasses and the uncircumcision of your flesh, God made alive together with Him" (Christ) (Col. 2:12-14). "You have been raised with Christ" (3:1). Not only the fact of dying and being buried with Christ, but also the fact of being raised with Christ here forms the basis for the admonition to the congregation. Being raised together with Him also took place in Baptism. The sentence, "you were buried with Him in baptism, in which you were also raised with Him through faith" (2:12), does not refer to two different events. Faith and Baptism belong together. Yet we must not overlook that also the admonition in Colossians directs the baptized to the future. Their life is still "hid with Christ in God. When Christ who is our life appears, then you also will appear with Him in glory" (3:3). The resurrection that has taken place is the pledge for the future appearance of the baptized in glory. Whether Romans speaks of the rising with Christ as a future event, or whether Colossians speaks of it as an event that has already happened, both texts contain the tension between the "already" and the "not-yet" of the new life.

From the fact of our being given into the historical way of Jesus Christ the letter to the Ephesians draws a conclusion that goes even farther. Since God has raised Christ "from the dead and made Him sit at His right hand in the heavenly places" (Eph. 1:20), then it is now also true that "even when we were dead through our trespasses, [God] made us alive together with Christ (by grace you have been saved), and raised us up with Him, and made us sit with Him in the heavenly places in Christ Jesus" (2:5-7). When did this take place? It would seem that Baptism is implied.[34] It is true that this passage is not speaking of death and burial but only of being made alive, which embraces resurrection and exaltation, since it is a being made alive with Christ. Here too the decisive factor is the Christians' history interwoven with Christ's history, so that the affirmation of Christ's session "at the right hand of God" in the creed applies to them also.

Thus through Baptism God encompasses the entire course of human life. Even though in this world the baptized is still moving toward his death, he may be certain on the basis of his Baptism that he has already experienced his death, for he has been given into Christ's death. Even though the resurrection is man's future, he may be certain on the basis

53

of his Baptism that he already shares in the new life, and even that he has been set to take part in Christ's dominion. Thus through Baptism the temporal succession of the earthly life has in a peculiar way been abrogated even though it continues to exist. In the event of Baptism both origin and consummation of the Christian life coincide in a peculiar manner without permitting the Christian to stop looking forward to the future consummation.

c. The gift of the new life and the admonition to walk in newness of life

The assignment to Jesus Christ and the giving into His death for a life with Him are God's deed. As He accomplishes this deed through Baptism in the name of Christ He justifies the sinner, rescues him from judgment, delivers him from the dominion of the powers of destruction, and opens a new life for him. The New Testament baptismal statements, in spite of all their variety, testify most emphatically that God has done this to the believer through Baptism. They speak both of the Baptism received and of Jesus' death and resurrection as of a fact. This assignment to Christ is at the same time a sovereign act of the exalted Christ Himself who receives man through Baptism and makes him a partaker of His saving deed.

These statements become misleading when they are isolated from the imperatives that are connected with them.[35] The doctrine of Baptism must not forget that the statements in the New Testament concerning the saving deed done in Baptism are made mostly as arguments in admonitions, and that the indicatives which witness to the new life of the baptized are correctly understood only when the imperatives which call for the activity of the baptized are added. If the connection between indicative and imperative is not observed, the understanding of Baptism is in danger either of misinterpreting God's saving deed in the direction of a magical operation or of going in the opposite direction and reducing Baptism to a mere sign that has no effect.

Since the baptized have died to sin, they are commanded: "Let not sin therefore reign in your mortal bodies, to make you obey their passions" (Rom. 6:12). Since the baptized have been justified, they are commanded: "Yield . . . your members to God as instruments of righteousness" (v. 13). "Aim at righteousness" (1 Tim. 6:11). Since the baptized have been sanctified, the imperative applies to them: Strive

54

"for the holiness without which no one will see the Lord" (Heb. 12:14). Since they have been saved, they are commanded: "Work out your own salvation with fear and trembling" (Phil. 2:12). Since they have been delivered from the dominion of the powers of destruction, they are now summoned to the battle against the powers of destruction. All of these imperatives are the strongest kind of appeal to human decision—demands for a full involvement of watchfulness, of wrestling, and of perseverance. It is here a matter of a constantly new renunciation of sin on the part of the baptized and an obedient turning to God. In the process everything that the baptismal statements attest as fact returns as imperative. As those who have died with Christ the baptized are to die with Christ. As those who have been renewed they are to "put on the new nature" (Eph. 4:24). In the judgment toward which also the baptized are moving, salvation is promised to him who does not let up in this battle.

Do not these imperatives negate everything that the baptismal statements had affirmed as the saving deed of God? Do they not refute the statements about the saving deed accomplished through Baptism? At the very least, is not man placed into such a dialectic of indicative and imperative that it becomes impossible for him to be certain of this saving deed? Has he not, after all, been placed back under the Law, which promises him life as a reward for the works of obedience, and precisely in this way results in death—as a matter of fact?

The command to walk in newness of life does not abrogate the new life which God has created through Baptism, but it asks for the Yea of the baptized to this divine deed. In none of these imperatives does God demand anything different from what He has already bestowed in Baptism. He demands no works by which the baptized might have to acquire salvation. Rather, because God has saved the baptized, He calls for the activity of salvation. Because He has justified and sanctified, He demands the striving for righteousness and holiness. Because He has given the sinner into Christ's death through Baptism, He demands that the baptized die with Christ. Yes, since in Baptism God has already completely embraced the life of the baptized with his eschatological verdict of acquittal and his eschatological deed of resurrection, He asks the baptized to face the coming judgment and the coming resurrection in a manner consistent with this acquittal and this resurrection. "God is at work in you, both to will and to work for His good pleasure" (Phil. 2:13).

Hence the imperatives are not demands of the Law but admonitions of the Gospel, calling on the baptized to live as the people God has made us in Baptism—to make room in our conduct for what through Baptism has become our new reality. Since the imperatives are the unfolding of the indicative, they are not considered burdensome.

But precisely because these imperatives demand nothing that God has not already given in Baptism, they are so urgent, so full of warning, even adjuring. Since the walk in newness of life follows so self-evidently from the reality of the new life, the admonitions become menacing, warning, scolding, and even judging where the baptized do not live in conformity with God's saving deed. Since in Baptism God has savingly embraced the whole life of man, the latter must now yield this entire life of his to the Savior. The disobedience of the baptized is no refutation of the saving deed which God performed on him. The saving deed, however, refutes the disobedience. The saving deed turns into judgment for the baptized if he denies it by his conduct. Thus not only is Baptism the basis for ethics, but the refusal of the prescribed obedience places the baptismal grace in question. "Thus Baptism and ethics are bound to each other and interwoven with each other." Paul links "not only ethics to Baptism but also Baptism to ethics" (N. Gäumann).[36] It is therefore impossible to continue in sin "that grace may abound." (Rom. 6:1)

d. The danger of detaching the understanding of Baptism from the history of Jesus Christ

It is of decisive importance for the doctrine of Christian Baptism that the name of Christ be not understood unhistorically and that it be referred not only to the glorified *Kyrios* who has been removed from earthly history. It is rather the Crucified and Risen One to whom the sinner is through Baptism assigned as to his Lord. Without this reference to the Crucified One as the present Lord the name of the triune God is also open to misunderstanding, since the basis for Baptism is not the eternal Son as such, but the Son of God who became man, and therefore the God who revealed Himself in history through the sacrifice of His Son and the sending of His Spirit.

This primarily Pauline reference of Baptism to Jesus' death and resurrection, interpreting Baptism as a dying with Christ, was surprisingly pushed into the background in the history of baptismal theology during the first two centuries. This is all the more surprising since the influence of the Hellenistic mysteries on the understanding of Baptism increased, and before long the Baptism of blood was recognized as a substitute for water Baptism. "In general it is noteworthy — and this is the mark of a new age — that quite soon after Paul or behind 'primitive Christianity' the concept of a personal 'union' with Christ (immersion in Christ Himself) is almost totally lost sight of." The "into His name" "did not long retain its energy but fell to the level of a 'formula.'" "'Christ' appeared only in His benefits" (Ferdinand Kattenbusch).[37] Consequently Baptism is no longer understood as a being given into the history of Jesus Christ but as the bestowal of the gifts disclosed with the name of Christ: forgiveness, cleansing, deliverance, sanctification, etc. In this way the effect of Baptism is described onesidedly in the dimension between above and below, while the historical dimension, the "contemporaneity" of the baptismal event and Christ's death or the baptismal event and Christ's death and resurrection, is neglected. But in this way also the once for all — the eschatological finality — of Baptism is diluted and the accent falls on such gifts as are not imparted only in Baptism, although they are initially imparted here too.

However, an insufficient concern with the once for all of the death and resurrection of Christ is bound to have its effect on the understanding of the imperative with which the New Testament admonition confronts the baptized. The less Baptism is understood as death with Christ, and thus as the fact which embraces the entire subsequent life of the baptized in an eschatological way, the more the consoling character of the New Testament admonition is weakened. It is no accident that in the ancient church before long the New Testament imperative was called a new law.

Not until the third century do the Eastern theologians again feature the Pauline understanding of Baptism. Origen, Cyril of Jerusalem, and Basil again saw Baptism as a dying and rising with Christ. In the West this Pauline accent was taken up again especially by Ambrose and Augustine. As the candidate steps down into the water and comes up again, he experiences dying to sin with Christ and rising again. Later Thomas Aquinas attached central importance to these Pauline statements. With systematic cogency he derived all sacraments from Christ's death on the cross, but in his doctrine concerning the effects of Baptism [38] he did not further pursue the special exegetical problems of the relationship between Christ's death and the sinner's death in Baptism. Yet on this Christological basis his teaching about the law of love *(lex caritatis)* again featured aspects of the New Testament admonition.[39]

In his Small Catechism Luther cites Romans 6 in answer to the question concerning the significance of Baptism. The water Baptism "signifies that the old Adam in us, together with all sins and evil lusts, should be drowned by daily sorrow and repentance and be put to death, and that the new man should come forth daily and rise up, cleansed and righteous, to live forever in God's presence." By appealing to Romans 6 Luther at this place does not teach the onetime fact of dying with Christ in Baptism but teaches the admonition to die with Christ constantly. A look at Luther's total baptismal theology will show that he also taught most emphatically the onetime definitive factuality of our dying with Christ in Baptism. Through Baptism into Christ's death the old man has been killed and buried. "Both things are said: Christ's death and Baptism accomplish this. It is Baptism that brings men death and the new life, but it is Christ's death that does this through Baptism. . . . The saving event not only provides the historical background for the baptismal event and the suprahistorical origin of its effect, but the saving event is itself efficaciously present in the baptismal event" (Otto Hof).[40] Thus the death of the old man in Baptism is not only a result and fruit of Christ's death, but Christ's death is present in Baptism, and into this present death of His the sinner is given.

By the way, the separation of the understanding of Baptism from the history of Jesus Christ is more widespread than the history of the dogma of Baptism would lead us to expect. In many churches the preaching about Baptism not infrequently confines itself to very general statements about the promise of grace which God imparts through Baptism.

2. Baptism by the Holy Spirit

a. The activity of the Spirit through Baptism

Baptism in the name of Jesus Christ is at the same time Baptism by the Holy Spirit. It is the common conviction of the primitive Christian church that Baptism takes place by the Holy Spirit and that the Holy Spirit is imparted with Baptism:

"You were washed, you were sanctified, you were justified in the name of the Lord Jesus Christ and in the Spirit of our God" (1 Cor. 6:11). All of this happened to the baptized in a *single* act. "By one Spirit we were all baptized into one body" (1 Cor. 12:13a). It is debatable whether the rest of the sentence refers to Baptism or to the Lord's Supper, "and all were made to drink of one Spirit" (v 13b). Yet Paul is also here speaking of a definite event of the past, while the Lord's Supper is always received again. Probably the activity of the Spirit in Baptism is clarified by the thought that "we have been deluged, drenched, permeated" with the Spirit, "'and all have been drenched over and over (through the overflowing) of the one Spirit'" (R. Schnackenburg).[41] It is quite possible that also the statements about the sealing and anointing by the Holy Spirit refer to the onetime and foundational act of Baptism. "It is God who establishes us with you in Christ, and has commissioned [anointed] us; He has put His seal upon us and given us His Spirit in our hearts as a guarantee" (2 Cor. 1:21-22; cf. Eph. 1:12 f.; 4:30; 1 John 2:20-27). Another reference to the Spirit's activity in Baptism is Titus 3:5: By His mercy God saved us "by the washing of regeneration and renewal of the Holy Spirit, which He poured out upon us richly through Jesus Christ our Savior." "Renewal in the Holy Spirit" means renewal through the Holy Spirit.[42] In this act of salvation all human activity is expressly excluded (Titus 3:5a). It is done entirely by God's deed, by the one act of the washing and the activity of the Spirit through which regeneration and renewal take place. The unity of the baptismal event and the activity of the Spirit is also presupposed in John 3:5: "Unless one is born of water and the Spirit, he cannot enter the kingdom of God." Man cannot give himself a new origin. This can only be given him "from above" (v. 3). This birth from above takes place "of the Spirit" (v. 6), and that means, "of water and the Spirit" (v. 5). As man comes from his mother's womb, so the reborn man comes forth from water and the Spirit. Water and Spirit belong together in the act of regeneration. There is no textual tradition in which mention of the water is missing,[43] and there is no indication that "water" is here to be construed as a metaphor which is then clarified by "Spirit." [44]

The cited New Testament passages on Baptism have this in common that they speak of Baptism and the Spirit's activity as *one* act. Christian Baptism takes place through the Spirit; the Spirit works

59

through Christian Baptism. At no place is a distinction made between "water Baptism" and "Spirit Baptism," or also between forgiveness of sins and the Spirit's activity, as two different acts. The statements about Baptism through the Holy Spirit are the basis for the common Christian conviction that through Christ's death and resurrection the turning point which the prophets of the Old Covenant had foretold had been reached. The time of the Messianic salvation has now come, the Holy Spirit has now been poured out, and He washes sins away and creates new hearts. He whom John the Baptist had proclaimed as the Coming One has now appeared, and His Baptism with fire and Spirit has become a reality.

The Book of Acts also witnesses to the relationship between the activity of the Spirit and Baptism. What happened at Pentecost in a foundational way to the small circle of apostles and women without Baptism happens subsequently to all others who come to faith and submit to Baptism. Without anticipating [45] the special problem of the temporal relationship between Baptism and reception of the Spirit as posed by the Lukan baptismal texts, it cannot be denied that here too water Baptism in the name of Christ and the activity of the Holy Spirit belong together in principle and in fact.

It is self-evident that Baptism in the name of the Lord Jesus Christ is at the same time Baptism by the Holy Spirit, if it is presupposed that through Baptism in the name of Christ the baptized is assigned to Jesus Christ Himself. The exalted Christ is active through the Holy Spirit, His rule over His own takes place as the activity of the Spirit. If we have been assigned to Christ through Baptism we have therewith been given into the Holy Spirit's sphere of activity. In the New Testament writings the connection between the lordship of Christ and the activity of the Spirit is developed in a variety of ways, but it is always a very close connection. To be "in Christ" and to be "in the Spirit" is the same thing for Paul. Both statements are interchangeable (Rom. 8:4; cf. 14:17 f. and elsewhere). Since God's Spirit is at the same time the Spirit of Christ (Rom. 8:4), the Spirit of the Son (Gal. 4:6), the Spirit of the Lord (2 Cor. 3:17), it is impossible to belong to Christ without being moved by the Spirit. "Any one who does not have the Spirit of Christ does not belong to Him" (Rom. 8:9b). The rule of the exalted Christ and the activity of the Spirit are so much one and the same ruling and acting that the sentence, "the Lord is the Spirit," can mean both "the Spirit is Lord" and "Christ is the Lord who is active as Spirit." Christ, "the last Adam," is "a life-giving spirit" (1 Cor. 15:45). "This means that the Spirit is the earthly presence of the exalted Lord. In the Spirit the Risen One reveals Himself more accurately with the power of His resurrection" (E. Käsemann).[46] John's Gospel distinguishes Christ and Spirit more sharply than Paul does. The Holy Spirit is the "other Paraclete" who will come after the departure of the Paraclete Jesus Christ. Yet He is sent by God the Father through the Son. He will not speak on His own authority but will bring the Son to remembrance. He will bear witness to the Son and glorify Him and guide into the truth which is Jesus Christ. Thus the Holy Spirit is the presence of the Word that was made manifest in the Incarnation. Here too the presence of the Exalted One and the activity of the Spirit cannot be isolated from each other. In the Acts the exaltation of Jesus Christ and the outpouring of the Spirit are conjoined in yet another way. But even though the outpouring of the Holy Spirit is here distinguished from God's saving deed in Jesus Christ, through the accented temporal interval between Ascension and Pentecost as a separate act of God, both are nevertheless bracketed together by the fact that the Risen One promised the coming of the Spirit and commanded His disciples to wait for the Spirit, and that the Pentecostal Spirit, wherever He is poured out, arouses people to praise the name of Christ. With all the variety of the New Testament statements the connection between Christ and the Spirit is so intimate that Baptism, through which the assignment to Christ occurs, is also a giving into the activity of the Spirit.

What, then, is the meaning of Baptism "by the Holy Spirit"? Wherein does the Spirit's activity in Baptism consist? What the New Testament has to say about Baptism by the Spirit must be understood in the context of all that the New Testament says about the activity of the Spirit in general. From this perspective the answer must be developed in a systematic way:

Through Baptism the Holy Spirit assigns the believer to Christ the Lord. He gives him a share in Christ's righteousness, holiness, life, and glory. He nullifies the temporal interval which separates us from Jesus' death and resurrection but also from the return of the Exalted One. He assigns the believer to the Lord who is present as the One who has come and will come.

By assigning man to Christ, the Spirit makes him a child of God.

61

"All who are led by the Spirit of God are sons of God" (Rom. 8:14). Indeed, Christ is the eternal Son of God made man, and the Holy Spirit makes us His brothers who die and live with Him and in Him. He makes the believers adopted sons in Him, the incarnate Son. Not only are we "called" children of God, but we "are" so; not only shall we become God's children in the future, but we are that already (1 John 3:1). In the hearts of the believers the Spirit stirs up the prayer of the children to God the Father. "Because you are sons, God has sent the Spirit of His Son into our hearts, crying, 'Abba! Father!'" (Gal. 4:6)

By assigning the sinner to Christ through faith and making him God's child, the Holy Spirit makes the sinner alive (cf. 1 Cor. 15:45; 2 Cor. 3:6; John 6:63). By giving the sinner into Jesus' death, the Spirit lets him share in the life of the Risen One. But inasmuch as Christ lives in him he shares in the life of God which was made manifest in Jesus Christ and into which man was received in the incarnation of the Son of God. Thus the Holy Spirit snatches man out of the transitory, out of death and corruption, and transfers him, the creature, who in contrast to God the Creator has a beginning and in rebellion against the Creator has forfeited life, into the eternal life with Christ in God. The Holy Spirit transports man into the life that had been promised him from the beginning but which he had forfeited. This life has made its appearance in the resurrection of Jesus from the dead.

By giving man a part in the divine life, the Holy Spirit at the same time places him into the service of divine love which does not desire the death of sinners but their life. The same love by which God created all things and by which He delivered up His Son breaks into the world through the Holy Spirit so that it might be exhibited in the midst of the world by those who have been seized by the Spirit. In this way "the fruit of the Spirit is love, joy, peace, patience, kindness, goodness, faithfulness, gentleness, self-control" (Gal. 5:22). In this way the Holy Spirit creates a new fellowship of mutual service. Gift of the Spirit and stimulation to service are one and the same thing. This service is performed in the reciprocal love of those who have received the Spirit, and at the same time it moves out of this community and turns to the world. Since God's love in Christ has reached out to the world, no one has the right to keep the Spirit's gifts for himself. On the contrary, by His very gift the Holy Spirit places men into service to the world. This service consists above all in the witness to Christ.

Thus the Holy Spirit not only influences man but He enters into him, dwells in him, is active in him and impels him, gives Himself to him and enlists him in service. But everything said about the activity of the Spirit would be misleading if we did not at the same time take into consideration that, unlike the birth, death, and resurrection of Christ, the outpouring of the Spirit at Pentecost was not a onetime event. Rather, it was an initial event followed by further outpourings of the Spirit, and this not only on additional people who had not yet received the Spirit, but also on the same people on whom He had already been poured out. The Holy Spirit as the One who has been given never ceases to be the Lord on whose coming man must depend Concerning the same people who had received the Holy Spirit at Pentecost the Book of Acts reports again later, "They were all filled with the Holy Spirit and spoke the Word of God with boldness" (Acts 4:31). Of the same Paul who was filled with the Holy Spirit at his conversion (Acts 9:17), it is reported again later that he was filled with joy and with the Holy Spirit (13:52). The coming of the Holy Spirit is a constantly new divine coming and working. The same is true of every baptized person. Even though the Spirit has been poured out on him through Baptism, he must continue to depend on the Spirit's coming. The outpouring of the Spirit is the beginning for a life in expectation of further activity of the Spirit. Thus the Spirit who has been given is the "guarantee of our inheritance" (Eph. 1:14), the "first fruits" of the coming redemption of our bodies (Rom. 8:23), the "guarantee" that what is mortal will be swallowed up by life (2 Cor. 5:4 f.). What is here said about the future consummation applies also to the earthly course of life toward this consummation. With the outpouring of the Holy Spirit the guarantee has been given for further gifts of the Spirit, gifts which the baptized is permitted to pray for and receive for his service in the church and to the world. It would be wrong to attempt to derive the immediate possession of all gifts of the Spirit from the reception of Baptism, even though the baptized has been assigned to the sphere of the Spirit's influence. The Spirit bestows His gifts in His freedom, when and to whom He will. Hence Baptism is the *beginning* of the reception of His gifts.

b. Effects of the Spirit in connection with Baptism

All New Testament writings share the common conviction that

all who believe in Jesus Christ and are baptized in His name receive the Holy Spirit. However, in distinction from the baptismal statements of the epistles and John's Gospel, the act of Baptism and the reception of the Spirit do not coincide in the accounts of Baptisms in the Book of Acts.

The Pentecost story indeed reports the temporal association of the act of Baptism and the reception of the Spirit. Peter had told the assembly, "Repent, and be baptized every one of you in the name of Jesus Christ for the forgiveness of your sins; and you shall receive the gift of the Holy Spirit. For the promise is to you and to your children and to all that are afar off, every one whom the Lord our God calls to Him" (Acts 2:38-39). This did not remain only a promise on that day but was fulfilled. When it is said of the baptized that they "were added," this means that through Baptism they became members of the church on which the Spirit of Pentecost was poured out and that the promise of Joel 3 has now been fulfilled also for them. It is altogether unlikely that only in Acts 4:31 Luke reported the fulfillment of the promise announced by Peter.

The Baptism of Cornelius and his house, however, followed after the Holy Spirit "fell" on all who heard Peter's sermon (Acts 10:44; cf. 11:15). Yes, Peter commanded these people to be baptized *because* they had received the Spirit (10:47 f.; cf. 11:16 f.). Of Apollos too it is reported that he was "fervent in spirit," even though he had not yet received Christian Baptism. (18:25)

In reverse order the first Christians in Samaria did not receive the Holy Spirit until some time after their Baptism, even though it had been administered in the name of Christ. They received the Spirit through the prayer and laying on of hands by Peter and John, who had come to Samaria from Jerusalem (Acts 8:17). Baptism and reception of the Spirit are here separated in such a way that not only an interval in time but also different persons were involved: the Baptism was performed by Philip, while the Spirit was imparted through the laying on of hands by Peter and John.

It is clear that in none of these different accounts of the temporal relationship between Baptism and the reception of the Spirit these are torn apart or made independent of each other. The opposite is the case. *Because* Cornelius and his household received the Spirit, they were to be baptized. *Because* the Christians in Samaria were baptized, it was impossible that they would remain without the reception of the Spirit. Concerning Apollos it is not expressly stated that he was baptized in the name of Christ because of the Spirit working in him, yet it is reported as something unusual that he was "fervent in spirit," even though "he knew only the Baptism of John" (Acts 18:25). Also the account of the Baptism of the disciples in Ephesus (Acts 19:1 ff.) supports the idea that the connection between Baptism and reception of the Spirit was regarded as necessary. Since they had thus far received only the Baptism of John but not the Holy Spirit, ". . . they were baptized in the name of the Lord Jesus. And when Paul had laid his hands upon them, the Holy Spirit came on them, and they spoke with tongues and prophesied" (5-6).[47] Even though the act of Baptism and the gift of the Spirit do not always coincide in time, according to the reports in the Acts, they are so intimately related that the baptized cannot remain without the effects of the Spirit and the one filled with the Spirit cannot remain without Baptism. Even though the Spirit is not in every case given to the believer *through* Baptism, He is nevertheless given in a necessary association *with* Baptism.

At the same time these reports call attention to an interval in time which is missing in the rest of the New Testament references to Baptism. This interval dare not be overlooked in any treatment of the doctrine of Baptism.

The peculiarity of these Lukan statements has been interpreted in a variety of ways. Since A. Seeberg the temporal differentiation of Baptism and reception of the Spirit has often led to the conclusion that Baptism was originally understood only as an act of the forgiveness of sins and only later as an act of the impartation of the Spirit. This is, however, contradicted by the fact that the oldest statements about Baptism in the New Testament, namely the Pauline, presuppose the unity of Baptism and reception of the Spirit as self-evident. It is doubtful whether Luke had access to still older baptismal traditions. It is clear, however, that Luke himself was not concerned about presenting a development of the understanding of Baptism. In his very first account of Baptism (Acts 2:37 ff.) the unity of the baptismal act and the impartation of the Spirit is presupposed.

An attempt has been made, furthermore, to clarify the distinction between Baptism and the reception of the Spirit by pointing to Luke's conception of the ministerial office, that is, that the Spirit "is imparted only by the apostles and their authorized emissaries and successors" (E. Käsemann).[48] Yet, in spite of his great interest in the association of all churchly activity with the apostolic circle in Jerusalem, at the very least Luke did not consistently carry through such a conception — if indeed he entertained it at all. Thus, for example, it cannot be assumed in the case of Paul's Baptism by Ananias that the latter had a special apostolic commission. On the contrary, he acted on the basis of a direct mission from the Holy Spirit.

But Luke's controverted relationship of Baptism and reception of the Spirit becomes clear in the light of the special character of his concept of the Spirit. In distinction especially from Paul's letters, the Acts do not deal with the inner operations of the Spirit in the recipient. The interest is centered entirely on what the Holy Spirit achieves through the recipient in public. Luke does not designate faith as an effect of the Spirit but rather regards faith as precondition for the reception of the Spirit. Not even the fraternal fellowship of the believers is identified as an effect of the Spirit, but rather it is presupposed already before the outpouring of the Spirit at Pentecost (Acts 2:1). Furthermore, Luke does not mention sonship, the being in Christ, the Abba-prayer as effects of the Spirit. Above all, the reception of the Spirit signifies the origin of boldness for public witness, the gift of prophecy, speaking in tongues, the authority for deeds in divine power. This concept of the Spirit, which in its peculiarity was first clarified by Hermann Gunkel,[49] is still quite close to the Old Testament statements about the effects of the Spirit.

These differences between Luke's and Paul's understanding of the Spirit cannot be ignored. There is, however, a certain similarity in the specific Pauline statements about the charismatic gifts, particularly the spiritual gifts of prophecy and speaking in tongues. Paul too does not say that the charismatic gifts are necessarily imparted in Baptism. Rather, the one who in Baptism has been "washed, sanctified, justified" by the Spirit receives the gifts which the Spirit desires to give to all. Also according to Paul, the Spirit sovereignly determines the moment in which the gift of the Spirit is imparted. Thus the apostle exhorts the members of the church who have already received the Spirit through Baptism to strive after the gifts of the Spirit. In contrast to Paul, however, Luke hardly seems interested in the indwelling of the Spirit as such, that is, in the renewal of the sinner through the Spirit. Luke's interest is concentrated entirely on the public manifestations of the Spirit's activity, that is, specific charisms and services in the Pauline sense.

In the development of his special theme, namely the presentation of the story of the Gospel's advance from Jerusalem to Rome, Luke maintained this concept of the Spirit. Indeed, from the perspective of this theme it seems natural to allow the activity of the Spirit on the individual recipient to recede into the background and not to reflect on the reception of the Spirit as first fruits of further gifts and work of the Spirit and as guarantee of the believers' future transformation. The Book of Acts is concerned about the storm that is rushing across the earth and about the attack of the Spirit on the state of this world, an attack that takes men everywhere into its service. It has correctly been pointed out again and again that the Book of Acts reports the temporal interval between Baptism and reception of the Spirit at precisely such historic moments as are of basic significance for the advance of the message and for the growth of the church in new areas. This is immediately apparent in the account of the Baptism of Cornelius. This was the decisive step toward the Baptism of Gentiles. The preceding outpouring of the Spirit laid the basis for this step. In the case of Samaria, where in reverse order the Spirit was imparted after Baptism by the laying on of hands, a decisive step was likewise involved, namely, the advance of the message concerning Christ into an heretical land that had separated itself from Jerusalem centuries before. By the act of the laying on of hands by the delegation from Jerusalem (Peter and John) the fellowship of the Jerusalem congregation with the Christians in Samaria was established, and the unity in the Spirit's operation of those baptized in the name of Christ became a reality. On the one hand, the Cornelius episode cannot lead to the conclusion that Baptism was administered only where the Spirit had already been poured out, and on the other hand, the account of the first church in Samaria cannot lead to the conclusion that the Holy Spirit was imparted not by Baptism, but only by the laying on of hands — or even only by the laying on of hands on the part of the apostles. Luke is concerned with special steps in the history of salvation which are of far-reaching significance as a matter of principle, namely, the overcoming of ancient and profound antitheses which opposed the growth of the church. This concern does not refute the witness of other New Testament texts according to which

Baptism in the name of Christ is at the same time Baptism with the Spirit. Yet in a radical way this concern excludes the misunderstanding which suggests that the Spirit establishes merely a personal relationship between the baptized and Christ. On the contrary, the Spirit places the baptized into the service of progressive subjugation of the world under the exalted Lord. This is the concern also of the rest of the New Testament, especially in the Pauline assertions about the gifts of the Spirit, among which prophecy is mentioned first after the apostolate (1 Cor. 12: 29; cf. Eph. 4:11). It is indeed true that Paul's understanding of the Spirit shows many differences.[50]

These incidents in the Book of Acts further exclude the misunderstanding that the Holy Spirit is imparted *only* through Baptism. He bestows His gifts of grace when and how He wills. The reference to Apollos being fervent in spirit before he knew of Christian Baptism is also to be understood in this sense. This gift of the Spirit, too, served the missionary advance. (Acts 18:25-28)

In the two incidents in the Book of Acts (9:17; 19:6) that speak of a laying on of hands in connection with Baptism, neither the specific historical situation of these Baptisms nor Luke's special concept of the Spirit may be disregarded. The point in Acts 9:17-20 is Paul's cure of his blindness and his being filled with the Holy Spirit, and Acts 19:5-7 deals with the impartation of the Spirit to the disciples in Ephesus who had received only the Baptism of John but neither Baptism in the name of Christ nor the Holy Spirit. In addition Acts 8:16 reports the laying on of hands and the bestowal of the Holy Spirit on the people in Samaria who had been baptized earlier. These cases of laying on of hands must indeed be distinguished from the commission to a specific concrete service (like that of Paul and Barnabas, Acts 13:3) and inauguration into an office (like that of Stephen and others, 6:6), but these too are concerned with effects of the Spirit which receive public expression. Bearing in mind Luke's particular understanding of the Spirit, the few passages in Acts do not allow the conclusion that in the early churches the Holy Spirit was received not through Baptism but through the laying on of hands. Also in Paul's understanding, Baptism and the reception of concrete gifts of the Spirit do not necessarily coincide in time. The fact that charismatic gifts are imparted in different ways does not contradict the certainty expressed in the epistles and in John's

Gospel that the Holy Spirit is active through Baptism. In expounding the three texts mentioned above it should also be observed that from the early Christian era a variety of acts have been handed down, such as commissions and healings, which were performed with prayer and the laying on of hands.[51]

c. The gift of the Holy Spirit and the admonition to walk in the Spirit

Baptism with the Holy Spirit is an act of God. Through the Spirit He assigns the believer to Christ, and through the Holy Spirit Christ takes the believer into His dominion. Thus the Holy Spirit is active as the Spirit of the Father and the Son, and He imparts Himself to the believer by implanting him in Christ and making him a child of God.

Here too the activity of the Holy Spirit, who is imparted to man through Baptism, cannot be separated from the imperative with which God confronts the baptized. If the imperative is not drawn into the doctrine of Baptism, a magical misunderstanding of the Spirit's activity and of Baptism all too easily results.

Paul did not only assure his congregations that "the Spirit of God . . . dwells in you" (Rom. 8:9), but he also commanded them to walk by the Spirit and not by the flesh (Gal. 5:25). The same baptized people who have received the Spirit are told to "sow to the Spirit" by performing deeds of love and humility (Gal. 6:8). The imperatives, which we noted above [52] on the basis of the assignment to Jesus Christ taking place in Baptism, apply here in like measure to the basis of the reception of the Spirit. Here too there is a summons to decision in a battle, the battle between flesh and Spirit. Here too life is promised to those who renounce the flesh, even though that life is already presupposed as the effect of the Spirit on the basis of Baptism. "He who sows to the Spirit will from the Spirit reap eternal life." (Gal. 6:8)

Just as the outpouring of the Holy Spirit after Jesus' exaltation was not a onetime event but rather an initial one, so also the gift of the Spirit which is imparted through Baptism is not only a onetime gift, but an initial one, a first fruit, a down payment, the beginning of a spiritual activity and of a giving of self. The new life of the baptized is not only a life proceeding from the gift of the Spirit, but it is also a life with a view to further gifts of the Spirit. To the indicative, "you have the

Holy Spirit," is added the imperative, "do not quench the Spirit" (1 Thess. 5:19), "earnestly desire the spiritual gifts" (1 Cor. 14:1; cf. 12: 31). Those who have received the Spirit are to live by the received Spirit and reach out for the charismatic gifts that are needed for service in the church and to the world. Beyond this is the command to wait for the future consummation of the Spirit's activity through which the mortal body will be transformed into the likeness of the resurrection glory of Jesus Christ.

As a gift that has been received the Holy Spirit never ceases to be the Giver. He is Gift and Lord at the same time. The baptized will never lord it over the Spirit. As the One who has been imparted and who dwells within man, the Holy Spirit continues as the One who encounters man. He is active not only as a power but as a person. Since the coming of Jesus, the Spirit is active as the "other Paraclete." He guides into the truth, He makes Jesus' Word and deed present, He sends men out to service and meets them as the Master. Thus the imperative to obey the leading of the Spirit is joined to the reception of the effect of the Spirit that has already taken place.

Here too, the imperatives do not annul the indicative which is valid because of Baptism, but they rather unfold it. The gift of the Spirit is their antecedent. Even though they demand decisions and deeds from men, they do not demand works that would cause the Spirit to be imparted. Rather, they unfold the activity of the Spirit that was begun in Baptism. They demand that the baptized make room in his life for the activity of the Spirit to whom he has been committed. Thus these imperatives are also consoling exhortations of the Gospel.

It is true, these exhortations also become warning, threatening, judging, when the baptized resists the Spirit who has been given to him. Since the Spirit who dwells in man is the Lord, the warning is issued to the baptized not to "lie" to the Holy Spirit (Acts 5:3), or "resist" Him (Acts 7:51), or "outrage" Him (Heb. 10:29). The serious warning about the sin against the Holy Spirit presupposes the reception of the Spirit. The gift of the Holy Spirit may turn into a judgment if the rule of the Spirit is disregarded. The disobedience of the baptized does not refute the activity of the Spirit in Baptism. But the activity of the Spirit refutes disobedience. It is impossible to boast of Baptism and the possession of the Spirit and be disobedient at the same time.

d. The danger of restricting the activity of the Spirit in the understanding of Baptism

Just as it is highly significant, in view of the name of Christ in which Baptism is performed, that the name be not used as a mere formula and that attention be focused not only on the exalted Christ, but also on the earthly One together with His death, so it is decisive in view of the Spirit's activity in Baptism that in distinction from the onetime incarnation of the Son of God the Holy Spirit be taken seriously as the One who always comes down again and again. As was the case in the Pentecostal event, so the Holy Spirit does not come in Baptism once for all, but initially so as to be expected again and again and to bestow additional gifts. In Baptism the Holy Spirit is received as down payment for further activities of the Spirit. Indeed, the Spirit's activity precedes Baptism in so far as He creates faith and the desire for Baptism through the Gospel.

The history of the doctrine of Baptism repeatedly shows the danger of overlooking this freedom of the Spirit's activity, that is, the freedom in which the Holy Spirit enlists and guides the further life of the baptized in new acts of coming and of granting charismatic gifts and directives. There is a frequent tendency to link the statements about the Spirit so closely with Baptism that His activity appears to be encapsulated in the Baptism event and that the result of Baptism is pictured as being the possession of the Spirit or of a spiritual character in place of the ongoing activity of the Spirit. As the giving into Christ's death takes place in Baptism definitively once and once for all, so also the activity of the Spirit in Baptism is understood as something once for all and definitive, and the first-time and down payment character fades away. Indeed, the more the understanding of Baptism is separated from the history of Jesus Christ, the greater the danger becomes of practically limiting the Spirit's activity to the baptismal act and thus running counter to what the New Testament says.

But such an approach at the same time impinges on the exhortation earnestly to desire the spiritual gifts and to pray for them. The forward look is turned back to the reception of the Spirit that happened in Baptism, and the confidence that God will grant the ever-new petition for the gifts and guidance of the Holy Spirit is replaced by the fear of a culpable loss of what has been received. A variety of motives induced

Eastern Christians in the 4th century to postpone Baptism—a tendency opposed by the great Cappadocians. The more the gracious activity of God through the forgiveness of sins and the gift of the Spirit was understood as the onetime and definitive effect of Baptism—as it is in fact the assignment to Christ—the greater the dread of receiving Baptism had to become. In part this misunderstanding is also responsible for the criticism of infant Baptism. But Christ rules over His own by constantly forgiving them their sins and by reendowing them through the Spirit.

But if the activity of the Spirit is limited to the Baptism event in such a manner, then the inevitable reaction will be a spiritualism which disparages Baptism and rests its certainty on "Baptism in the Spirit" and other experiences apart from Baptism. Then Baptism is no longer understood as a "washing of regeneration and renewal in the Holy Spirit" (Titus 3:5) but in any case as something that points to regeneration, or water Baptism is omitted entirely and regeneration is expected exclusively as the result of enthusiastic experiences. This spiritualistic tendency is present not only among the Quakers but accompanies all of church history.[53] It follows as a necessary reaction to a one-sided, Hellenistically suggested understanding of the Holy Spirit as a force and substance imparted in Baptism, whereas the Spirit is at the same time Giver and Gift, Lord and power, and this in the freedom of His activity.

3. Reception into the Church

a. Baptism as incorporation into the people of God, the body of Christ, and the spiritual temple

Through Baptism in the name of Christ the believer becomes a member of the church. Just as the church did not come into being because men joined together and founded the church, so it is at no time within man's power to become a member of the church. The church is called "church of God," not because at the time of their alliance men gave themselves this label, but because God has here gathered men and joined them together. Just as the origin of the church was God's deed, so every subsequent membership in the church results from God's deed. Man does not make himself a member of the church, but he is made a member. He does not join the church, but he is received into the church. In this sense Paul spoke of being "baptized into one body"

(1 Cor. 12:13) and Luke of a "being added" to the church through Baptism. (Acts 2:41)

Concretely, reception into the church means reception into the worshiping assembly, not only admittance to hearing the proclamation and participating in prayer but also to the Lord's Supper. Thus, according to the baptismal orders of the ancient church, first Communion was associated with Baptism. This may be assumed also of the earliest churches. It is from this worshiping assembly that the church gets her name. As assembly of the people of God she is the *ecclesia*. Because of the reception of the body of Christ in the Lord's Supper she is the body of Christ. As the fellowship of praise and adoration she is the temple of the Holy Spirit. It is not as if the church existed only in the event of the worshiping assembly. But this assembly is the center of all churchly life. It is this center which defines the concepts of church, the body of Christ, and the spiritual temple.

In the worshiping assembly God serves the assembled and makes them His servants.[54] The proclamation is here not only a remembrance of the saving deed which God accomplished in the sacrifice and resurrection of Jesus Christ, but through this proclamation God acts as the One who is present and grants participation in Christ's death and resurrection. Furthermore, the proclamation not only establishes the prospect of Christ's coming, but through this proclamation the Coming One acts as the Present One and grants participation in the life to which the believers look forward. This applies in a similar way to the Lord's Supper. It not only reminds of Jesus' death on the cross, but the Crucified One is present as the Exalted One and in the consecrated bread and wine He gives Himself, His body and His blood. Also the Lord's Supper not only points to the coming meal in the kingdom of God, but Christ is here present as the One who has come and the One who is coming, and now already grants those who wait for Him participation in the future "marriage feast of the Lamb" with the church. As the assembled believers proclaim Christ's death and await His return, God is at work in Christ and through the power of the Holy Spirit, justifying, sanctifying, vivifying. Through Baptism the sinner is taken up into this constantly new saving activity with which God serves the assembled believers. He is at the same time taken into the service by which the congregation responds to God, namely, in the common confession of sins and of faith and in the common prayer and

73

intercession, thanksgiving, and adoration through which the congregation offers itself to God as a sacrifice.

By uniting the assembled believers with Himself, God is also uniting them with each other. In the fellowship of the Word, the Lord's Supper, and prayer the fellowship of the baptized with each other grows at the same time. "Communion of saints" means, first of all, fellowship in the reception of holy gifts, but as such a fellowship it is at the same time the mutual fellowship of those who have been sanctified by God. As the members of the church are in the worshiping assembly called out of the world again and again, they are the new people of God in whom the cleavages of this world have been overcome. "There is neither Jew nor Greek, there is neither slave nor free, there is neither male nor female; for you are all one in Christ Jesus" (Gal. 3:28). As they partake of Christ's body in the Lord's Supper, they are built up as a body in which every member is joined to the other for service in love. As "living stones" they are fitted together and built up into a "spiritual house," a "temple of the Holy Spirit." The New Testament witnesses are one in the conviction that the Holy Spirit is given to all members of the church. Paul in particular asserts that each member of the church receives a special gift of the Spirit for service in the church and to the world. Through the variety of the spiritual gifts Christ manifests His presence in the church. Paul has set forth the variety of spiritual gifts so much as a principle that his statements cannot be restricted to the congregations in Corinth and Rome. This variety belongs to the essence of the church in all ages and it keeps breaking forth where it has been concealed. Through Baptism the believer is taken into this fellowship of charismatic gifts and services and is himself placed into service to his brothers.

Even though reception into the church is always concretely a being added to a specific worshiping community, there is more involved than reception into the local congregation. In the New Testament the word *ekklesia* means both the local congregation and the whole church on earth. In the same way the body of Christ and the temple of the Spirit are not only applied to the local church but also to the universal church (especially in Ephesians). The basis for using the same terms for the local assembly and the people of God scattered throughout the world is that in every worshiping assembly the same Christ is present. The body which He gave on the cross, the body in which He grants participation in the Lord's Supper, is one and the same body wherever the meal is celebrated. In the same way the same Holy Spirit bestows His gifts wheresoever the message concerning Christ is heard and the meal is received. Since one and the same God in Christ through the Holy Spirit has mercy on His own in all places, God unites those assembled locally not only with each other but with all believers on earth. The local church is not only a part of the total church, and the total church is not only the sum of the local churches, but in each of the local churches the whole church manifests itself through the presence of the one Lord. Thus the relationship of the universal church to the many local churches is not one of addition but of inclusion. For that reason Baptism means reception into the "one, holy, catholic, and apostolic church." (Nicene Creed)

However, the one church into which a man is baptized is not only the fellowship of all believers who live on earth at the same time but also the fellowship with the fathers who have preceded us in faith. It is at all times the one Lord by whose grace the believers live, the same Lord who acted upon the fathers and is today acting upon us, in order to act as the Coming One upon them and us together. This fellowship with the fathers is not merely a historical remembrance of those who have gone ahead and through whose service we were brought to faith, nor is it merely that in our worship we preserve their teaching and approach God with their prayers. We have fellowship with them as with those who are alive even though they died. They have been assigned to the same risen Lord whose own we too have become. The people of God on the earthly pilgrimage and the people of God arrived at the goal are one and the same people, even though this cannot be seen. Through Baptism one is brought into this one people of God which He gathers at all places and times and will one day present visibly in the "Great Supper."

The church of which Baptism makes one a member is not an end in itself, but she is the instrument of Christ's pervading dominion over the world. "All authority in heaven and on earth" has been given to the Risen One; all men have been put under Him, whether they know it or not, whether they acknowledge it or deny it. Through the church Christ exposes the fact that the world is under judgment and proclaims salvation to the world. Through the church's message God calls men to repentance and faith and thus reaches out to them in order to save them. Hence the church is not only the fellowship of contemporaries, nor only a fellowship with those who have preceded in faith. Rather, the church is directed toward fellowship with those who are still afar off and will come to faith. Not for one moment can the church stand still. She is the people of God on pilgrimage, the people rejected by the world. She is the growing body of Christ, the growing temple — growing both in people and in gifts, permeating and filling the world more and more. This is not to say that only this growth makes the church a complete entity. Since Christ, the Head of the body, the "Cornerstone" of the building (Eph. 2:20), is set as Lord over "all," the church is "catholic" from the start. As a complete entity which in Christ and the Holy Spirit is already a reality the church grows into the all to the measure determined by God.

Here the way which is prescribed for the church is none other than that of the earthly Christ. "A disciple is not above his teacher, nor a servant above his master; it is enough for the disciple to be like his teacher, and the servant like his master" (Matt. 10:24-25a). If the message of the apostles led to strife, slander, and persecution, and if Christ manifested His glory precisely in these sufferings of theirs, this applies to the way of the church in all ages. The church is directed to regard the enmity of the world as the normal state of affairs, rather than the approval of the world. Yet amid all earthly uncertainty she has the promise that "the powers of death shall not prevail against" her (Matt. 16:18). This does not mean that the church will always confront the world with the same degree of clarity and power as Christ's summons, since there are also periods of eclipse and weakness. Nor does it mean that the church will always grow at the same rate, since there are periods of retrogression and decay. But God will always renew the church and reenlist her for service to the victorious course of the message of Christ. Hence to be baptized means to be received into the flock of those who have received the promise of the Good Shepherd, "they shall never perish, and no one shall snatch them out of My hand." (John 10:28)

Thus in Baptism the believer ceases to be an individual. As such he approaches Baptism, for he follows a call that snatches him from the ties of his former life. But as one who has been baptized he is no longer an isolated individual but a member of the people of God in which God at all times unites the believers in Christ through the Holy

Spirit. Through Baptism he has been drawn into a dynamic which permeates world history from beginning to end. Not Christ by Himself but Christ and the church, Christ and the new humanity, are the mystery of world history. Through Baptism man is given into the manifestation of this mystery. This mystery is so great that it cannot be defined but only attested. It is no accident that the New Testament describes the church by means of some eighty concepts and pictures. This description contains greatly differing relations between the church and God, Christ, and the Holy Spirit — as well as differing relations between the church and the old covenant, and also between the church and Christ's return. It is not possible at this place to enter into a discussion of the questions which are thereby posed for the doctrine of the church. Within the framework of the doctrine of Baptism we must confine ourselves to ecclesiological indications. Four basic ecclesiological concepts of the New Testament which do not coincide were employed. Let the fact that we declined to make them coincide in a systematic way serve to point to the mystery which embraces and bears the baptized.

As the statements about Baptism by the Spirit in the last analysis only unfold what happens when the baptized is assigned to the living Lord, so the statements about reception into the church ultimately add nothing new. They only unfold what is given with the assignment to Christ through the Holy Spirit. Jesus Christ cannot be parted from those who were crucified and raised with Him. Christ and the church belong together. To be in Christ means to be in the sphere of Christ's rule, in the body of Christ, in the church.[55] Therefore Baptism into Christ is in its essence reception into the church at the same time. Also the statements about Baptism by the Spirit are merely unfolded by the ecclesiological explanations. In essence the Spirit creates fellowship with Christ and with all who are in Christ. It is only because this being added to the church is self-evidently given together with the assignment to Christ and to the activity of the Holy Spirit that the New Testament affirmations make comparatively little explicit mention of this fact.

b. Incorporation into the church and commissioning for service to the world

It is important also for understanding the ecclesiological significance of Baptism that the divine act of being received into the church is not separated from the divine command under which the church stands together with each of her members. If God's deed were separated from God's command, both Baptism and church would immediately be misunderstood.

The church is the nation of God's children called out of the world and the nation of prophets, priests, and kings sent out into the world. The church lives in the world in an elementary double movement of life: as being summoned by God out of the world again and again and as being sent back to the world again and again. Both movements belong inseparably together. Both have their center in the worshiping assembly. Here God again and again gathers those who are scattered in the world, unites them, and makes them one with Christ. Here at the same time God sends the assembled into the world and authorizes them for service to the world. The response of the congregation to the service which God performs for it in the worshiping assembly cannot consist only in the witness, prayer, and confession of worship, but must move out of the assembly and advance in intercession for the world and in witness before the world. The sacrifice of praise offered to God by the church cannot be confined to the worshiping assembly but must find expression in service to those who stand afar off. The church is the summons of Christ, the instrument of Christ the Lord, the voice of the herald who proclaims to the world its only Savior. Mission work is not some sort of churchly activity among others, but it belongs to the essence of the church. Both movements, being saved from the world and being sent into the world, necessarily belong together. If the church can no longer be called out of the world, her service to the world will lead to secularization. But the church becomes a part of this world also when she becomes introverted and withdraws herself from service to others.

Thus the imperative linked with incorporation into the church receives the following explication:

Since God has made him a member of the church through Baptism, the baptized stands under the command to attend the worshiping assembly. As a member of the people of God he is now to live with the other members in the joint reception of the gifts which God grants His people every day anew through Word and meal. For God desires to continue and complete for every one what He has begun in Baptism. Since God is here serving the baptized, the latter is to serve his brothers

78

with the gift he has received and thus in participation in the charismatic gifts offer God the sacrifice of praise which responds to the sacrifice on the cross. Since the believers have been incorporated into the one body, the command of love to the brothers applies. Since they have been built into the same spiritual building, the imperative is addressed to them, "like living stones be yourselves built into a spiritual house, to be a holy priesthood, to offer spiritual sacrifices acceptable to God through Jesus Christ" (1 Peter 2:5). Such imperatives are not the demands of a law that cannot be fulfilled. On the contrary, they are based on God's gracious deed and give expression to this deed.

Since God through Baptism places him into His people, every baptized person stands under the command to let himself be sent by God as a member of the nation of prophets, priests, and kings. God's deed through the Holy Spirit includes the command of service, not only in the fellowship of the believers among each other but of service to the world. Every baptized person is sent by God to be a witness in his place in accordance with the guidance and gift of the Holy Spirit which he has received. This imperative, too, is a command of grace which demands nothing that God has not already granted. But it is God's will that the one who has received these gifts affirm and grasp them and manifest and put them to work in the witness to Christ. In the decision to serve, the baptized must provide room for the gift.

Since God preserves men in spite of their rebellion and their being under the judgment, and lets His sun shine on the good and the evil, the baptized has also been placed under the command of preservation. The baptized must serve not only the saving activity of God through the Gospel but also His preserving activity. The paradox must be taken seriously that God preserves those who are under judgment, even when they refuse Christ's rule. This paradox obligates the church not only to proclaim the message of Christ but also to become involved in righteousness and peace for the world. But above all the church must proclaim the message of Christ and witness to men concerning the peace of God. The specific promise given the church's service is not the preservation of man but his renewal.

But where the fact of incorporation into the church is isolated from these imperatives, and where the baptized thinks he can be sure of his salvation through Baptism even when he refuses obedience in the midst of the people gathered and sent by God, the same thing will happen as in the case of the Old Testament covenant people on their way through the wilderness. Even though "all were baptized into Moses in the cloud and in the sea" (1 Cor. 10:2), many of them were overthrown in the wilderness because they rebelled against God's mission and guidance. "These things happened to them as a warning [τυπικῶς, as a type], but they were written down for our instruction" (v. 11). The witness that the Savior of God's people does not cease to be the judge of the saved is not limited to the Old Testament. It is very important for the ecclesiological understanding of Baptism not to isolate the New Testament statements concerning the unity of Christ and the church. Although the church is one body with Christ, He Himself remains the Head and continues to confront the church as the Lord. He is able to condemn not only individual members but entire churches. "Would that you were cold or hot! So, because you are lukewarm, and neither cold nor hot, I will spew you out of My mouth" (Rev. 3: 15b-16). Christ is set as Judge not only of the world but also of those who are called by His name.

c. The danger of reducing the understanding of Baptism to external church membership

The church consists of true and apparent, living and dead members. She includes believers and hypocrites, penitent and impenitent. To her belong such as are elected by grace and such as will be rejected because of their guilt. Thus the church on this earth is a mixed fellowship, and the reformers, following older distinctions, differentiated the "church in the proper sense," that is, the true church of the believers, and the "church in the broader sense." At the same time they agreed with Augustine's anti-Donatist decisions in explicitly declining to separate the true church from the broader church. They left this separation up to God's final judgment. Thus the boundaries of the true church are hidden until the Day of Judgment. But the reformers taught that this hidden "church in the proper sense" is a reality and is to be recognized by the preaching of the Gospel and the distribution of the sacraments.

The antecedent for all statements in this chapter is *faith*. The doctrine of Baptism must indeed say something about what unfaith receives in Baptism. But this question has thus far been consciously pushed into the background. This chapter is concerned first of all with what the believer receives through Baptism; for that reason we shall at once summon to faith in the saving action of God in Baptism. If we remain with this antecedent, we must reject most emphatically the idea that through Baptism we have only been incorporated into the external church fellowship but not into the church in the proper sense. In view of the large number of baptized who are members of the church only outwardly and withdraw themselves from God's activity in proclamation and Lord's Supper, one is tempted to separate the understanding of Baptism from the New Testament understanding of the church as the people of God, the body of Christ, and the temple of the Holy Spirit. This may be done either by reducing the significance of Baptism to a mere offer of grace and by leaving membership in the church up to the use which the baptized will make of this offer, or by understanding Baptism from the start as only a reception into the external church fellowship and avoiding assertions about membership in the body of Christ. Yet even though the separation between the "church in the proper sense" and the "church in the broader sense" is still in the future, the believer may be certain that he has been incorporated into the true church through Baptism — just as he can be certain of his justification by faith while he is still waiting for the coming Judgment.

This certainty of incorporation into the body of Christ may, furthermore, not be called into question by pointing to God's hidden decree of election. Although the elect will not be separated from the rest until the final Judgment, God's decree of election does not remain hidden until then. On the contrary, this decree becomes evident already now through the call to faith and it is realized in the believer through God's gracious activity. The certainty of this activity of God through Baptism dare not be called into question as a result of brooding over God's hidden decree of election. On the basis of God's call and Baptism we can be certain of our election. "Blessed be the God and Father of our Lord Jesus Christ, who has blessed us in Christ with every spiritual blessing in the heavenly places, even as He chose us in Him before the foundation of the world, that we should be holy and blameless before Him." (Eph. 1:3-4)

4. The New-Creating Deed of the Triune God

a. Baptism as the deed of God in Christ through the Holy Spirit

Through Baptism God makes the believer Christ's own, gives him the Holy Spirit, and receives him into the church. In this way God through Baptism accomplishes man's regeneration and makes him a new creature.

Even though the concept of regeneration was taken up only as the Gospel advanced into the Hellenistic environment, where it was well known in the language of the mystery religions, and then quickly became a central idea in the baptismal teaching of the ancient church, this concept cannot be called the result of a Christian-Hellenistic syncretism. Rather, this is a different way of witnessing to God's new-creating deed which already the prophets had proclaimed and the pious of the old covenant had prayed for. "Create in me a clean heart, O God, and put a new and right spirit within me" (Ps. 51:10). As the author of the new creation God now fulfills the promise, "a new heart I will give you, and a new spirit I will put within you; and I will take out of your flesh the heart of stone and give you a heart of flesh" (Ezek. 36:26). The new creation of man in Christ through the Holy Spirit is called regeneration. Beyond this, the idea of new creation also has a cosmic horizon in the expectation of the new earth and the new heaven.

The new creation is distinguished from the first creation, the *creatio ex nihilo*. As the new birth presupposes the birth from the womb, so the new creation presupposes the first creation. Those who have already been created and born are created and born anew. But that does not make this new creation any less a sovereign deed of God than the creation out of nothing. Also the new creation is not the product of cooperation between God and someone already there. In no way can man recreate and renew himself or give himself a new birth. The more he tries to free himself of himself the more he falls back upon himself. In spite of all yearning to be different from what he is, he struggles against the end of his old life. Even while he yearns to be different, he desires to have control over himself. But God new-creates man in spite of his rebellion against Him and in spite of the failure of his endeavors. In the new birth God produces what is simply impossible for man. "How can a man be born when he is old? Can he enter a second time into his mother's womb and be born?" (John 3:4). In fact *he* cannot do it. Thus the sovereignty of God's activity and the passivity of the believer on whom God acts are very strongly emphasized in these New Testament passages on Baptism. "He saved us, not because of deeds done by us in righteousness, but in virtue of His own mercy, by the washing of regeneration and renewal in the Holy Spirit." (Titus 3:5)

The new creation has begun in Jesus Christ. By "sending His own Son in the likeness of sinful flesh" (Rom. 8:3) God has in Him assumed the old man. Thus the incarnation of the Son of God is the hidden beginning of the new man. For that reason the fathers of the ancient church brought Baptism into a causal relationship not only with Jesus' death and resurrection but also with His birth. Our new birth is based on the birth of the Son of God from the Holy Spirit and Mary.[56] In the resurrection God revealed Jesus as the first fruit of the new humanity. The Risen One is the same one who had before walked on this earth in the flesh, but He now lives with God in a totally different mode of existence as of the One glorified in the Spirit, removed from the restraints and limitations of the flesh.

God new-creates the sinners by making them Christ's own through the Holy Spirit, giving them into Christ's death and resurrection, and making them His members. As God thus brings about the death of the old man and the life of the new, He creates the new humanity in Christ, the growing people of God, the growing body of Christ, the growing spiritual house. The church, then, has a significance that goes beyond men, a significance that permeates the all. The church is "the fulness of Him who fills all in all." (Eph. 1:23)

This new fellowship brings to realization what God the Creator had in mind for man at the beginning. God had created man in sovereign love and made him in His image. In a love like God's, man was to honor the Creator by loving God who had first loved him; in a fellowship like God's, men were to love each other; in a dominion like God's, men were to be God's representatives on earth. To such obedience God had promised eternal life. Men failed in this destiny and became subject to death. But Jesus Christ realized this destiny. He is the new Man who lives with God forever. In Him God grants life to those who failed in their destiny. In Christ God new-creates men through the Holy Spirit so that they might live as His image.

This new creation is still hidden under sins, weaknesses, and trials—under the suffering and dying of those who have been translated into life. The new creation is still hidden in the dialectic of present and future. It still confronts men in the double form in which God addresses the regenerated, in the promise of salvation and in the demand to lay hold of this salvation. And yet the new creation is already a reality by faith.

As we compress the New Testament statements about God's activity through Baptism in the concept of the new creation, more precisely God's new creation in Christ through the Holy Spirit, we must realize that such a statement is not the last word. What we have done is to take one of the many concepts used to depict God's activity through Baptism, to expand its specific meaning beyond its original import among many other New Testament concepts, and to elevate it to the position of an over-arching concept. Such a concentration of the Biblical variety in a few concepts always results where the faith is formulated in a creed—in dogma and in dogmatics. The concept of new creation has the advantage in that it involves the totality of man who is touched by Baptism and the totality of human history which has reached its end and its new beginning in the new man Jesus Christ. It likewise involves the relationship between the individual who is baptized and the consummated new humanity of the future. This concept also witnesses to the activity of the Holy Spirit. However, it does not give explicit expression to the forgiveness of sins, the justification of the sinner, his dying with Christ, and other New Testament assertions, nor does it allow the variety of New Testament relations between Baptism, the old covenant, the history of Jesus, and the *eschaton* to assert themselves. If the concept of new creation is not understood as an indication of the New Testament variety but rather as a reduction of that variety, it must lead to an impoverishment of the doctrine of Baptism. In the history of theology such a one-sided emphasis on regeneration has not infrequently had this result. Since every dogmatic expression of ideas involves a free choice, the possibilities among which the choice is made must be borne in mind and constantly given expression. This means the obligation to remain conscious of the limits of formulations for the purpose of teaching and to keep basic dogmatic concepts open for supplementation and correction by the Biblical witness which is not explicit in them. Without such an awareness and openness the ecumenical dialog on Baptism has no prospect of success.—But in whatever thought patterns and in whatever salvation-history context

84

the doctrine of Baptism is concentrated, it is decisive to establish the point that in spite of all their variety the New Testament texts bear witness to an *activity of God* through Baptism. In this chapter we could not deal with all the individual exegetical questions posed by these texts. There is some debate about many of the details. But it is clear that exegesis in our time has reached an astonishingly large consensus, a consensus running diametrically across all churches, that Baptism in the New Testament not only points to God's saving action but that God's saving action takes place in the event of Baptism.

b. The name of the Father and of the Son
and of the Holy Spirit

With one exception, namely that of the baptismal command, the New Testament texts speak of Baptism only upon (in) the name of Jesus Christ. The formula "in the name of the Father and of the Son and of the Holy Spirit" may represent a later development, a formula that was at first used alongside the name of Christ and then supplanted it. On the basis of the New Testament witness concerning God's activity through Baptism the later triadic formulation of the name may be understood as a proper interpretation of the name of Christ. By means of the name of the Father and of the Son and of the Holy Spirit the act of God which He does in Baptism in the name of Christ is recognized. Hence the trinitarian formula says nothing new over against the Christological formula.

The certainty, that God acts through Christ and the Holy Spirit and that assignment to Christ is at the same time assignment to the sphere of the Holy Spirit's activity, is already present in early baptismal texts of the New Testament. Thus Paul reminded the Corinthians of Baptism when he said, "You were washed, you were sanctified, you were justified in the name of the Lord Jesus Christ and in the Spirit of our God" (1 Cor. 6:11). Now one cannot say that in this passage Paul "gave God-consciousness its trinitarian formulation" (A. Schlatter).[57] Paul is not speaking here specifically either of a "threeness" in God or of the unity of Father, Son, and Holy Spirit. Yet there is here already an important supplement to the name of Jesus, which may perhaps be understood as a binitarian formula and as a transition to the later trinitarian formula. On the basis of the peculiarity of the Christian Baptism event the addition of the Spirit of God to the name of Jesus

85

seems just as natural as the addition of the Father's name. For Jesus Christ in whose name one is baptized is confessed as the Son of God. This unfolding of the name of Jesus became all the more necessary the more the Gospel advanced beyond Palestine to other areas where faith in the one God was unknown. To this fact the amplification of the confession to Christ by the addition of the confession to God the Creator and the Holy Spirit corresponds also.

In the triadic formulation of the name Father, Son, and Holy Spirit are named side by side, but the double "and" which connects them is not further defined in its significance. The same is true of other triadic statements of the New Testament, as, for example, the benediction, "The grace of the Lord Jesus Christ and the love of God and the fellowship of the Holy Spirit be with you all" (2 Cor. 13:14). The oneness of Jesus Christ, God, and the Holy Spirit is not stated explicitly but only indicated by means of the "and" of coordination. It is presupposed that God's love, the grace of Jesus Christ, and the fellowship of the Holy Spirit are imparted together and that the activity of Jesus Christ, of God, and of the Holy Spirit constitute *one* activity. There is a coordinated series also in Eph. 4:4-7: "There is *one* body and *one* Spirit, just as you were called to the *one* hope that belongs to your call, *one* Lord, *one* faith, *one* Baptism, *one* God and Father of us all, who is above all and through all and in all." Here too the unity of the Spirit, the Lord, and God the Father is not explicitly stated, but it is implied in the repeated emphasis on the oneness and uniqueness of each and of His activity as well as in the preceding admonition to the church to be at peace. Thus the "name of the Father and of the Son and of the Holy Spirit" is to be regarded for the first as triadic but not yet as trinitarian. It is to be noted, however, that Baptism is here commanded "in *the name* of the Father and of the Son and of the Holy Spirit." Baptism is performed not in three names but in *one* name.

The "and" in the triadic name is made more precise by the question as to *who* assigns a person through Baptism to the one Lord. We would not do justice to the New Testament statements concerning the lordship of Christ and the activity of the Holy Spirit if we were to limit ourselves to the answer that God assigns the baptized to the Lord Christ through the Holy Spirit. If the exalted Christ is the Lord to whom God has subjected all things, then He is not only the One to whom God assigns a person through Baptism. As the Lord He is Himself at work, He draws the baptized to Himself through the Holy Spirit, and He gives Himself to the baptized. In Baptism God the Father and Jesus Christ act through the Holy Spirit. But we cannot be content with saying that the Holy Spirit is the power and instrument of God and Christ. He is not only the organ through which the Father and the Son act in Baptism. The Holy Spirit is at the same time instrument and actor, gift and giver, the one who is sent and the one who sends. Through Baptism the Holy Spirit implants men in Christ and makes them God's children. Thus Father, Son, and Holy Spirit are active through Baptism: justifying, sanctifying, saving, and making alive. Correspondingly, the ancient church spoke of God the Father as well as the exalted Christ as well as the Holy Spirit as the subject of the saving action in Baptism. Yet there are not three Lords at work here, but one Lord, and the baptized is not assigned to three Lords but to one Lord when he is assigned to the Father and the Son and the Holy Spirit.

For the sake of the unity of name and the unity of action the church has called the formulation of the name in the baptismal command not only triadic but trinitarian.[58] From what happens in Baptism in the name of Christ, according to the New Testament, the trinitarian understanding of the name of Christ follows so cogently that a rejection of the trinitarian name would also mean rejection of the name of Christ.

These points do not, of course, exhaust the full content of the dogma of the Trinity. In Baptism we are dealing with the historical reception into the sphere of the dominion of Father, Son, and Holy Spirit. If the triadic name does not explicitly state the historical unity of Father, Son, and Holy Spirit, it does so even less with regard to the eternal unity of God in the eternal differentiation of Father, Son, and Spirit. Nevertheless, the doctrine of Baptism may not push the eternal immanent Trinity aside as a product of metaphysical speculation. On the contrary, the acknowledgement of the eternal unity and distinction of God the Father, God the Son, and God the Holy Spirit is a necessary consequence of praising and *worshiping* God the Father and Jesus Christ and the Holy Spirit on the basis of their historical saving activity.[59] In the doxology God is praised on the basis of His historical activity as the One who is one and the same in His historical action and in His eternal reality. To that extent the trinitarian dogma is contained in a nutshell in the triadic name of the baptismal command, even though the dogma was liturgically and dogmatically fixed at a much later time. Thus the church baptizes in the conviction that the eternal triune God, who has created us and has turned toward us sinners in the incarnation of His Son and in the outpouring of the Holy Spirit, makes us participants in His eternal life in Baptism.

c. The interaction of Word, washing with water, and God's saving deed

For faith, which acknowledges God's new-creating action through Baptism, immersion in water (or washing), pronouncing the name, and the new-creating activity of God are inseparable and constitute *one* divine deed.

Thus the New Testament bears witness to God's saving activity through Baptism in part directly by naming God as the One who is acting (e. g., Titus 3:5), in part indirectly by expressing in the passive voice what the baptized experienced in Baptism (for example, Rom. 6:4, "We were buried with Him by baptism into death"). As this passage indicates, Baptism can be called the instrument of the divine action, but it can also be referred to as the subject of the saving action. "Baptism . . . now saves you . . . through the resurrection of Jesus Christ" (1 Peter 3:21). Such a statement does not contradict the acknowledgment that *God* saves through Baptism, but because God saves through Baptism, because through Baptism one is assigned in a saving way to the exalted Christ, it is also proper to say that Baptism saves "through the resurrection of Jesus Christ, who has gone into heaven and is at the right hand of God." The action of God, the presence of Jesus Christ, the operation of the Holy Spirit, and the baptismal event are so intimately conjoined that they are interchangeable in the affirmations of faith, and each separate statement bears witness to the totality of the baptismal event, namely the gracious action of the triune God through Baptism. The same can be said for the statements about washing and about the name. Thus one can speak of the forgiveness of sins not only through Baptism, but also of the reception of forgiveness "through His name" (Acts 10:43), "in which the Name is probably used *a parte potiori* (chief part for the whole) for the baptismal act as a whole." [60] "Just as the acquisition of salvation can be attributed to Baptism, so it can also be attributed to being 'called,' without any substantial difference in meaning." [61] This is true since the call leads to reception into the church through Baptism. On the other side, in view of the washing with water one can also speak of a "washing away of sins" (cf. Acts 22:16; 1 Cor. 6:11). Just as salvation by God and salvation through Baptism are not in opposition to each other, so also forgiveness of sins "through His name" and through the washing are not in opposition, but God forgives sins through the washing and through the name, and in each case the entire baptismal event is designated. As a rule, however, Baptism and the name are mentioned together, and Eph. 5:26 might well be understood in this sense. Christ has cleansed the church "by the washing of water with the Word." But whether the New Testament mentions the name, or the washing, or even only the effect, its interest is always concentrated on the saving activity of God through Baptism. There God's deed, the Word event, and the washing take place in *one* act. The New Testament does not separate Word, washing, and God's deed from each other, nor does it provide a theoretical definition of their relationship in a way that would indicate what the Word does in Baptism in distinction from the water or what the water does in distinction from the Word or, again, what God does in distinction from the water and the Word. Such questions came up much later. In spite of the Hellenistic influences discernible in the history of primitive Christian Baptism, this conjunction and interaction of Word, washing, and God's deed cannot be derived from intrusion of Hellenistic elements. On the contrary, we must think first of all of the Old Testament statements about the name of Jahweh as Jahweh's present reality and about the Word of God as God's creative act.

This concentration of the New Testament statements on what God does with the baptized in Baptism corresponds to their peculiarly small interest in describing the baptismal rite as such. In the epistles this interest is lacking altogether. Furthermore, it is in line with the concentration on God's activity that the New Testament baptismal statements show hardly any interest in a symbolical interpretation of the baptismal process, that is, immersion or the washing or the water. There are indeed occasional metaphorical echoes of the baptismal act in the statements about God's activity, for example, when mention is made of the washing away of sins or cleansing. However, it is to be doubted whether Paul saw the dying and rising with Christ symbolized by the immersion and emersion in Baptism. R. Schnackenburg tries to show "to what extent Paul gave consideration to the *rite* as the external demonstration of the inner saving process." [62] The raising of such questions probably belongs to a later period. More to the point is Albert Schweitzer's observation:

Paul "does not refer to the symbolism of the act for an explanation of the process. He does not reflect on it." "For him Baptism is a being buried and a rising with Christ, because it is administered upon the name of Jesus Christ." [63] It is completely improbable that Paul found the being clothed with Christ (Gal. 3:27) pictured "through plunging in the baptismal water." [64] All interest is centered on God's action in Baptism, not on the correspondence between that action and the baptismal rite, although there are in fact some correspondences. Again, the New Testament says nothing to describe what the baptized experiences in the act of immersion. In the place of symbolical interpretations of the baptismal rite there are comparative references to the great deeds of God: creation, the deliverance of Israel through the Red Sea, and other unique and foundational saving deeds which determine the future.

If we try to sharpen the New Testament statements by means of concepts which play a big role in the current discussion and if we ask whether Baptism is there understood in a causative (effective) or cognitive sense, we shall find that this alternative proves to be improper. One can indeed call the New Testament understanding of Baptism causative, since God saves through Baptism. But this is not opposed by a cognitive understanding as an alternative. Rather, the latter rests on the former. In this sense the New Testament exhortations are based on God's saving deed in Baptism, bring it to remembrance, and demand a life in conformity with it. "Do you not know that all of us who have been baptized into Christ Jesus were baptized into His death? . . . Let not sin therefore reign in your mortal bodies" (Rom. 6:3 ff. and 12 ff.). The cognitive significance of Baptism must by no means be underestimated. It determines our whole life, but it is not brought into relationship to an act of God that is distinguished from Baptism, but to an act of God that took place in Baptism. Likewise the question whether Baptism in the New Testament is understood "sacramentally" or "symbolically" poses a false antithesis. The question is unclear, on the one hand, because "symbol" can signify the present reality of what is pictured and, on the other hand, the concept of the "sacramental" need not necessarily contain the impartation of grace. If, however, a symbol is understood merely as a sign pointing to grace while a sacrament is understood as a means of grace, then the New Testament understanding of Baptism must be labeled sacramental. The New Testament does not permit us to separate Baptism as a mere sign from God's action. Such a conception of sign can claim the support of neither the Pauline statements concerning the "likeness" of Christ's death, with which we are planted together in Baptism (Rom. 6:5),[65] nor the succession in which Heb. 10:22 speaks of the sprinkling of the hearts and the washing of the body with water. We are dealing here with *one* event which provides the basis for the exhortations that follow. On the other hand, to the extent that Baptism is the sign by which we recognize the new-creating act of God it may be called a symbol.

We cannot here pursue in detail the further history of the understanding of Baptism up to the dogmatic definitions of the various churches. Here we must confine ourselves to listing the most important steps from systematic points of view.

The history of the understanding of Baptism in the second century has been transmitted to us largely in the form of descriptions of the baptismal act (the *Didache,* Justin Martyr, Tertullian, Hippolytus), and less in the form of doctrinal presentations. The variety of New Testament statements about the effect of Baptism continues. Some New Testament statements are ignored while others are added. Thus the Pauline material about dying with Christ receives little emphasis, although there is some reference to the cross of Christ (Barnabas 11, for example). In addition to the forgiveness of sins second century authors now accent regeneration,[66] illumination, sealing, and the idea of Baptism as a consummation. The great variety of these statements finds expression in the liturgical development of the baptismal act which is coupled with anointing and the laying on of hands. There are some attempts to ascribe specific saving effects to each one of these liturgical acts,[67] but in general the unity of the baptismal act together with its effects is preserved. In the understanding of the name there are some shifts in so far as the name is related not only to the person who is baptized in the name of Christ or of the triune God but also to the water as such, which is consecrated for baptismal use through the name or the invocation of the name. There are also shifts away from the act of Baptism, which is soon viewed more strongly in its symbolism, to reflection on the water and its suitability for accomplishing regeneration. Thus Tertullian [68] speaks in detail about the inner relation of water to the Spirit, a relation which existed from the beginning of creation (Gen. 1:2), its generative power, etc. He does this in order to prove that the water was suited to becoming, through the invocation of God, a sacrament of sanctification and the impartation of life. But in spite of these and other shifts the interplay of Word, washing, and God's gracious activity is safeguarded. Without the pre-supposition of this interplay the development of the baptismal liturgy in the ancient church would be simply unintelligible. The fact that Baptism together with the Holy Spirit and the church was then con-fessed as part of the faith in the Nicene Creed is to be understood only on the basis of the certainty of God's activity through Baptism. These statements about God's saving activity are affirmations made in faith and a summons to faith. Baptism is considered in faith, and the catechumens and the baptized are called to faith. The problem con-cerning what unbelievers receive in Baptism does not yet determine the structure of the statements about Baptism.

A theological reflection on the relationship between the adminis-tration of Baptism and God's new-creating action does not arise until later, and it proceeds along different lines and different concepts in *Eastern* and *Western theology*. But in both areas concepts of Platonic and Neo-Platonic philosophy were employed to define the relationships, especially the distinction between the visible and the invisible, type and essence, symbol or sign and reality. By adopting the term *mystery* to designate Baptism, as well as the Lord's Supper and other churchly acts, Eastern theology departed from the usage of the New Testament, where the term mystery is used above all to witness to God's saving plan and its historical realization in Christ and in the church. Origen indeed safeguards the relationship in so far as the mystery of Baptism is based on the mystery of Christ and points to it. He was concerned not only with defining the relationships between water Baptism and baptismal grace, but also with the relation of both to the historically unique Christ event and the Old Testament prehistory which points to the Christ event in a typological way. Over against a ritualistic-magical understanding Origen pointed from the visible, external Baptism event to the spiritual, inner event — from the external image to the spiritual reality — from the symbol to the mystery. But these conceptual distinctions did not con-stitute a separation. In the symbol of Baptism the believer participates in the mystery, and in that sense Baptism is not only called type or symbol but the mystery itself. In distinction from pre-Christian Baptism which was only a symbol, Christian Baptism is "the Spirit-filled and savingly effective symbol," [69] which is "at the same time realization with refer-ence to the Old Testament sign, and sign with reference to the future realization." [70] Thus the visible in Baptism is not only a reference to the mystery of dying and rising with Christ, but in Baptism the giving into Jesus' death, regeneration, takes place, and the beginning of the future consummation is imparted. Baptism is at the same time representation and bestowal of the mystery. "It is almost impossible to determine what in the writings of the oldest fathers is, in fact, 'symbol,' and what is 'reality' in the sacraments. They scarcely regarded these two terms as being antithetical." "Quite generally the opinion prevailed that the sacraments are 'means' of salvation." (F. Kattenbusch) [71]

This is true also of the *Western* fathers. It is true that in distinction from the term "mystery" there is no direct support in the New Testament for the term, *"sacrament,"* which has been applied to Baptism since Tertullian. In the usage of the ancient church there was indeed an assimilation in content to the Greek concept of mystery, but as a whole the sacrament was less seen as something representing the realization of the historical Christ-mystery than as an implementation of the same. Hence the problem of the relation of "visible" and "invisible," of "sign" and "matter" remained in the narrower sense the problem of the relation of the washing with water and the divine grace. But the differences in East and West understanding of Baptism became more profound because of the varied treatment of *heretical Baptism.* While Cyprian agreed with most Eastern churches in rejecting heretical Baptism as invalid, Pope Stephen acknowledged its validity. In contrast to Cyprian, Augustine also did this in his conflict with the Donatists and answered the hitherto unanswered question about what the validity of heretical Baptism means and what the nonbeliever receives through Baptism.

The concepts which Augustine used to answer these questions were not new. Already before his time, and also in Eastern theology, Word, water and grace, "sign" and "matter" had been distinguished. What was new was the consistent antithesis of *sacramentum tantum* (Word and element) and *virtus sacramenti* (grace), sacrament and effect, benefit and use of the sacrament, sacrament and forgiveness of sins, visible Baptism and invisible sanctification, sign of salvation and salvation itself, etc. The believer receives both, the unbeliever only the "bare," "visible" sacrament, "the form of the sacrament," but not "the form of righteousness." The question about what is imparted to the recipient in Baptism without grace must be considered later. In the context of this chapter it is, however, of great significance that the distinction between sacrament and grace was maintained by Augustine also in his statements about the believing reception of Baptism. The sacrament is sign and pledge of grace but is not identical with grace. The external sacramental event and God's gracious activity are, in a certain sense, independent, even though they are conjoined for the believer, and finally for the elect. In Augustine's definition of the relations of Word, water, and grace an important structural shift over against the New Testament baptismal statements becomes evident. While the New Testament statements were determined in their structure by the act of a believing reception of Baptism, a reception to which they summon and which they call to mind, the statements of Augustine are made from a perspective in which he reflects on a believing and a nonbelieving reception of Baptism. While the New Testament starts with the act of believing reception and believing remembrance and does not proceed to any theoretical analysis of the relation of water, Word, and God's grace, such a result was inevitable as soon as one reflectively stepped outside of this act. This was true especially when—in distinction from the New Testament—heretical Baptism had become a problem and had been acknowledged as valid. This reflective stepping outside of the basic statements, which are made in the summons to a believing reception and to a believing remembrance, happened even before Augustine, when Platonic concepts were employed. Yet in the distinction of visible and invisible, in spite of many variations in detail, the presence and the sharing of the invisible in the visible had been taught, and the nonbelieving reception of Baptism had remained a peripheral problem which did not determine the texture of the doctrine of Baptism as a whole. But this did happen in Augustine's teaching on Baptism. While in the understanding of Baptism as a mystery there was a union of the external and the spiritual event and the mystery of the historical and the eschatological Christ, Augustine created a conceptual structure of the doctrine of Baptism which could be applied equally to the church's Baptism received in faith and to heretical Baptism, a structure in which sacrament and grace were not only distinguished but even separated. To be sure, with the sacrament the believer also receives grace, and in his later statements during his anti-Pelagian battle Augustine even emphasized this conjunction very strongly. Hence, in spite of the separation, Baptism is a means of grace for the believer, and this is where Augustine saw the decisive difference between Christian Baptism and the Old Testament rites as well as the Baptism of John.

Nevertheless, we dare not overlook the exceedingly important structural shift of his statements and the separation of the baptismal act and God's gracious activity in principle. Both have become extremely significant for the further history of the understanding of Baptism in the West. At any rate the structural shifts referred to had given rise to theological problems which had not been previously considered and which could now be further elucidated in quite different ways. The definition of the relationships between Word, water, and grace has remained a basic problem that cannot be lost sight of.

Subsequently the *West* generally appealed to Augustine — in very different ways, to be sure, depending upon whether one took his point of departure from the basic separation of the reception of the sacrament and of grace, or from the conjunction of both in the believing reception. The latter approach was preferred and developed further in the direction of seeing Baptism as an efficacious bearer of grace, a vessel of grace, and the like. In opposition to views of an immanence of grace in Baptism (for example, Hugo of St. Victor), Bonaventure appealed to Augustine and insisted that grace was in the soul, not in the visible sign. Also Thomas rejected the idea of grace being contained in Baptism as in a vessel and understood Baptism as an instrument to which God imparted effective power only in passing. Thus Thomas mediated between both conceptions by distinguishing between God as the active primary cause and Baptism as the instrument employed by God concretely. He incorporated into an Aristotelian context of form and matter the Augustinian statements about the Word which makes the water a sacrament. The Franciscan schools of the Scotists and Occamists placed more emphasis on the gap between the sacramental sign and the spiritual reality.

In their struggle against the scholastic doctrine of Baptism all reformers appealed to Augustine and made use of his terms. At the same time, all of them manifest shifts over against his views. Especially Augustine's sentence, "when the Word is added to the element, it becomes a sacrament," [72] was cited frequently. But while Augustine probably thought primarily of the Word of God by means of which the *water* is consecrated and made ready for the baptismal act, the reformers understood it above all as the Word of God which confronted the *person* to be baptized together with the water — the Word which conveyed God's promise through Baptism, as well as the baptismal sermon. In their elaboration of the Augustinian concepts, sacrament-grace and sign-reality, the Reformation views on Baptism differ considerably from each other.

At this place we cannot enter into the differences between Luther's early baptismal statements in opposition to high scholasticism [73] and his later ones against the "Enthusiasts." In the definitive form of his teaching on Baptism, as it appears in his catechisms and was taken over into the Confessions of the Evangelical Lutheran Church, the Word of God appears in a threefold meaning: first, as "God's Word and command which have instituted, established, and confirmed Baptism";[74] second, as the name of God, for "to be baptized in God's name is to be baptized not by men but by God himself," [75] and third, as promise, which here means more than a mere offer and proclamation; rather, through the promise God produces in the believer what the promise declares: forgiveness, life, salvation. In this threefold significance God's Word is constitutive for Baptism. "Baptism is not merely water, but it is water used according to God's command and connected with God's Word." [76] The "nucleus in the water is God's Word or commandment and God's name." [77] Water and Word are so intimately conjoined that Baptism is defined both as the water in God's Word and as God's Word in the water. Luther is emphatic in saying that "these two, the Word and the water, must by no means be separated from each other." [78] Similarly Luther can speak of faith both as a clinging to the Word and as a clinging to the water. God grants forgiveness, deliverance from sin, death, and devil, salvation, life, and regeneration not only through the Word, but through Word and water — through the water in the Word and through the Word in the water. For faith there is here presupposed a complete interpenetration of Word, water and salvation — of the baptismal event and God's new-creating activity. Because *God* is active through Baptism, Luther can also say that *Baptism* "effects forgiveness of sins, delivers from death and the devil, and grants eternal salvation to all who believe, as the Word and promise of God declare." [79] Because God's Word and the water are *united* in this activity, Luther can call Baptism a "divine, blessed, fruitful, and gracious water," "a gracious water of life and a washing of regeneration in the Holy Spirit," "a divine water." [80] Not as if the baptismal water were of itself saving, apart from the Word and without faith. But the position from which Luther makes these statements is that of hearing and receiving by faith. The aspects which had been separated by reflection are here brought together again, and Luther witnesses to this interplay by using concepts which in Augustine's reflection had been separated.

d. The danger of letting the statements about the Word, the washing with water, and God's saving deed fall apart

The unity of the baptismal act and God's deed, recognized and proclaimed in faith, has not always and everywhere been maintained in the history of the theology of Baptism. This unity has been loosened or dissolved in quite different ways, and thereby the opposite directions in which this happened qualified or confirmed each other, as, for example, the magical misunderstanding of Baptism and Zwingli's refusal to regard Baptism as a means of salvation. In what follows we shall not present the history of how the statements about Word, water, and grace were separated, but we must confine ourselves to employing a sort of ideal-typological concentration and indicating the most important approaches.

(1) If the statements about the effect of Baptism are separated from faith in God who acts in freedom, a *magical* misunderstanding of Baptism results.

The concept of magic is ambiguous and controverted. As a rule magic and religion [81] are distinguished. Magic is understood as an action by means of which man thinks he can bring about a helpful or a destructive effect, without having to depend on a deity that is to be invoked. "We are dealing here with a purely objective act where a higher being, whose will was being influenced, is not involved at all. The only presupposition is that certain modes of action be followed by certain results, or, more correctly stated, where such actions directly produce such results. In contrast to the attempt to arrive at the goal by exerting pressure on the free will of a supernatural being, everything is here geared to the automatic effect of a specific kind of action" (A. Bertholet — C.-M. Edsman). [82] In a magical understanding, therefore, Baptism would have a cleansing, life-giving, and protective effect simply through the use of the baptismal formula and the water, independent of the invocation of God and His concrete activity.

However, in the history of religions magic is found not only in distinction from religion but also in conjunction with it. In this case there is indeed reference to the action of God or the gods, but the aim is to induce, or even compel the divine action by means of specific practices as such. Magical practices may be imported by a religion, but invocations of God and sacramental actions can also degenerate into magical practices. One such magical misunderstanding of Baptism would be the expectation of salvation from a Baptism separated from penitence, faith, and prayer.

There is no question that both kinds of magical understanding of Baptism[83] have appeared in the course of church history and may still be found today. It is equally clear that such misunderstandings have been promoted by theological formulas. This is true, for example, of the medieval sentence, "the sacraments contain grace." As it stands this sentence says nothing about faith as a condition for the reception of Baptism. Hugo of St. Victor explained it by saying that grace was enclosed in the water as in a vessel. Bonaventure emphatically rejected this interpretation; in no sense was grace in its essence contained in the sacraments. Also the later Franciscans rejected this view. The formula, *"ex opere operato,"* in fact also promoted a magical understanding of Baptism in the sense that Baptismal grace was imparted by a mere performance of Baptism. A magical understanding of this formula suggests itself in so far as the words themselves do not speak of God as acting and faith as receiving, but only of the act of Baptism itself. For that reason the reformers decisively rejected this formula. This is true, similarly, of the formula, *"non obex,"* used already by Thomas Aquinas and especially by the Scotists and Nominalists. The formula expresses the view that every one receives the baptismal grace who does not intentionally put an obstacle in the way. This formula was likewise rejected by the reformers since grace is received solely by faith.

Although formulas of this kind have in fact promoted a magical understanding of Baptism, it is nevertheless necessary to examine these formulas critically and in detail to determine whether in their original theological intention they were really an expression of magical thinking. Even those who, like Hugo of St. Victor, make much of the formula, "the sacraments contain grace," do not dispense with God's activity. On the other hand, Bonaventure did not simply reject this formula, but he could affirm it in the sense that the sacraments designate the grace that is effective—not indeed in the visible sign but in the soul—as the sacrament is received. Thomas also used the formula and explained that the sacraments contain grace only in so far as God makes use of them as

98

means of His grace. Luther's statements about "the gracious water of life" can, of course, also be misunderstood magically if they are isolated from the context of his baptismal theology. Even the formula, *"ex opere operato,"* cannot uncritically be called magical. In its historic original meaning it was not directed against God as the One acting through Baptism but against man. Baptism derives its efficacy not *"ex opere operantis,"* that is, not from the man who administers or receives Baptism, nor from man's ethical presuppositions, but solely through the divine institution and the divine activity. Moreover, this formula is not primarily concerned with the grace that is received through Baptism but with the validity of Baptism. It is possible within Roman Catholic theology to interpret this formula in such a way that Christ Himself establishes the effect of a sacrament and that therefore in the application of the sacrament every human manipulation of grace is excluded. According to this understanding the sacraments do not seize control of grace, but on the contrary the sacrament is always the sign of Christ's efficacious deed. "Thus in the last analysis this concept is praise and acknowledgment of the absolute transcendence of God who distributes His grace when and where He wills, and the acceptance of this grace is at His disposal alone." (Karl Rahner)

(2) On the front opposing every form of magical understanding of Baptism Calvin went beyond Augustine and loosened the connection between the baptismal event and the divine activity. Indeed in connection with Rom. 6:3 ff. Calvin could say "that through baptism Christ makes us sharers in his death," and he added the reference to Col. 2:11-12, "we 'were buried in Christ through baptism.' " [84] He could say occasionally that God "leads us [through Baptism] to the present reality and effectively performs what it [Baptism] symbolizes," [85] and he adds that "it is not my intention to weaken the force of baptism by not joining reality and truth to the sign, in so far as God works through outward means." [86] From this one could conclude that Calvin understood the forgiveness of sins, dying with Christ, regeneration, and incorporation into Christ's body as the effect of Baptism.

But in the great majority of his statements the activity of God through Baptism is restricted to a "signifying" *(significare)*, a "promising" *(polliceri)*, a "sealing" *(obsignare)*, a "representing" *(figurare)*, a "showing" *(ostendere)*, a "testifying" *(testificare)*, and the like. Even from Rom. 6:3 ff. and Col. 2:11 ff. Calvin simply deduces that "the free pardon of

99

sins and the imputation of righteousness are . . . promised us."[87] Hence through Baptism God points in an exhibitory, promising, confirming, sealing way to the saving deed in Christ and through the Spirit, but this saving deed is clearly distinguished from the act of Baptism. Correspondingly, the ever-recurring designations of Baptism as "sign" *(signum)*, "seal" *(sigillum)*, "portrait" *(pictura)*, "image" *(imago)* indicate that Baptism is understood as something that is differentiated from grace, the "matter" *(res)*. According to all of these ever-recurring statements Baptism is not the means of God's action which forgives, gives into Christ's death, and renews, but it is the sign through which God makes the believer sure of this saving activity.

Now this cognitive significance of Baptism dare not be underestimated. Calvin very strongly emphasizes its significance for the confirmation and strengthening of faith and in this respect he speaks of the power of Baptism. But the acknowledgment of this faith-strengthening power is coupled with a pointed rejection of the idea that Baptism saves. This rejection not only teaches that God alone saves but that the baptismal act and God's new-creating activity are two separate events which need by no means coincide in time. Calvin frequently calls God's new-creating activity upon a concrete human being the antecedent for Baptism (especially in establishing the basis for infant Baptism), but this divine activity may also be postponed until later in life. This temporal disjunction between the baptismal act as sign and the divine deed signalized by Baptism applies not only to the special case of an unbelieving reception of Baptism in which only the sign but not the grace is received. Accordingly Calvin sees no essential difference between Christian Baptism and the Baptism of John, which promised the Baptism in the Spirit but did not impart it. Contrary to Augustine, Thomas, and Luther he fails to see the depth of the difference between Christian Baptism and Old Testament rites.

The fact that, in spite of his preponderant recognition of no more than a cognitive significance of Baptism, Calvin occasionally makes remarks about God's activity through Baptism — this might be explained by the consideration that he sets his doctrine of Baptism not only against Roman Catholic teaching but also against the baptismal understanding of Zwingli and the Anabaptists. But in the full compass of his doctrine of Baptism his occasional statements about Baptism as a means of salvation must be interpreted in the light of his statements about the cognitive significance of Baptism, and not vice versa. To this corresponds the way in which the teaching on Baptism in the Heidelberg Catechism consistently parallels the baptismal event and God's activity by means of the formula, "just as — so also" (and similar expressions); thereby the connection between both acts is noetic but not effective-temporal.

Just as the connection between Baptism and God's gracious activity has been loosened by Calvin in his doctrine of Baptism, so also the connection between Word and water. He indeed speaks repeatedly of God's promise in Baptism and mentions proclamation and sacrament side by side as equally significant and necessary, but in other statements Baptism is understood purely as an "appendix" to the Word, and the Word is not understood as the Word of God which finds expression in the baptismal act itself, or as the name of God, but as the preceding and following proclamation. The accent shifts from the water enlisted by the Word to the water, or the act of the washing with water, which joins the preceding proclamation as a sign of confirmation. In these contexts the sacramental concept as such is determined above all by the external sign.

(3) In a completely different way the divine activity and Baptism were separated by Zwingli and the Anabaptists. In contrast to the tradition following Augustine Baptism was here understood not primarily as the God-given sign of grace, but as the commanded sign of *human* obedience. On the basis of the grace previously received the believer puts himself under obligation through Baptism.

Thus in his "Commentary on True and False Religion" (1525) Zwingli understood Baptism as a sign of obligation, of recognition, and of confession. He had proceeded from the ancient secular Latin meaning of sacrament as pledge, oath, military oath, and on this basis interpreted Baptism as a confession by means of which the baptized person obligates himself in the presence of the congregation. "In the hands of Zwingli the New Testament sacraments as means of the divine application of grace become acts of confession which make one's own personal faith visible; the divine gift becomes a human act in which *I* obligate myself to obedience to the command of Jesus. This is Zwingli's revolutionary reinterpretation of the sacraments. For him they are acts of the believer. Not what we receive but what we do constitutes the sacraments" (Fritz Blanke).[88] This understanding of Baptism not only conflicted with that of the ancient church, the scholastics, and Luther, but it also could not be affirmed by Calvin. Even when Zwingli, in the course of his argument with the Anabaptists, acknowledged Baptism not only as a sign of obligation established by the person baptized but also as a sign of the church whereby she designates the baptized as her member, he did not assign any saving significance to Baptism. On the contrary, he understood it as the believing man's response to God's preceding saving deed. It is true that Zwingli did not remain with this understanding in his last writings.[89] Already Usteri in his "Darstellung der Tauflehre Zwinglis" [90] and, more recently, Blanke have pointed out that here Zwingli grants that Baptism can be advantageous for faith through influence on the soul. But here too he does not understand Baptism as a means of grace but rather as pointing to grace. "For him the sacraments are not instruments which convey grace to faith. They are merely intuitive means which point to grace; they represent grace but do not grant it." [91] These late statements made it possible for Zwingli's successor, Bullinger, to negotiate with Calvin in 1549 and achieve the *Consensus Tigurinus.*

The movement of the first Anabaptists arose in the circle of Zwingli's friends in 1525 and appealed to his understanding of Baptism. They agreed with Zwingli in acknowledging Baptism as a sign of duty for faith and in rejecting Baptism as a means of grace. Their common opinion of what constitutes a sacrament becomes especially clear in a comparison between Zwingli's theses in his writing, "Of Baptism, of Rebaptism, and of Infant Baptism" (1525), and the Anabaptist document, "Hubmaier's Remarks on Zwingli's Book on Baptism" (1526).[92] Both denied that Baptism can wash away sins; both understood Baptism as a sign of duty. Apart from the problems of infant Baptism there were no differences in their understanding of the essence of Baptism. At most there was a shift in accent in that Zwingli speaks of the duty-sign of the people of God, while Hubmaier is speaking of the duty-sign of the individual believer. Konrad Grebel shared this understanding of Baptism. In his letter to Thomas Muentzer, Grebel wrote: "Thus the water does not confirm and increase faith, as the scholars in Wittenberg are saying . . . nor does the water save." On the contrary, Baptism is "a sign of the fact that one has died to sin and must have died to sin, that one must walk in newness of life, and that one will surely be saved if one conforms to the proper sense of faith through the inner Baptism." [93] Hence Baptism is the sign by means of which the believer pledges himself to obedience over against the New Testament imperative, and he does so on the basis of the Baptism of the Spirit which has gone before.

Consequently the divine saving deed, the Baptism in the Spirit, is separated from Baptism. Zwingli also makes the distinction between Spirit Baptism and water Baptism.

The understanding of Baptism set forth by the rapidly spreading Anabaptist movement, associated in part with spiritualistic tendencies, but in part also repudiated, has not yet been uniformly [94] and sufficiently examined. In their writings the questions concerning the church, church discipline, relationship toward the state (for example, oaths and military service) often take up more space than a presentation of their understanding of Baptism. We cannot here pursue the later history of Anabaptism, which is variable and theologically not unequivocal. But through all variations the understanding of Baptism has maintained itself as an act of confession and obligation on the part of the person who has come to faith and has been reborn and baptized by the Spirit beforehand. Only in a peripheral way have statements been made in the course of the history of Anabaptism concerning an effect of Baptism that strengthens faith or even transmits grace. Such remarks have never determined the Baptist understanding of Baptism as a whole. Thus, for example, it is in character that the original form of a statement in the Berlin Baptist Confession that had been formulated under pietistic-Lutheran influences was deleted five years later. The sentence read, "We believe that Baptism is not a mere sign but that, under the proper presuppositions, it really grants and produces as means of grace what it signifies, that thereby we are transported from the old Adam into the new Christ, incorporated into His visible church on earth, and made partakers . . . of the Holy Spirit." [95] It is quite significant, however, that several Baptist exegetes of our time have again recognized the New Testament witness to God's activity through Baptism.[96] Thus, for example, Beasley-Murray rejects the alternative between a symbolical interpretation and the acknowledgment of spiritual effects produced by Baptism — although "evidently no Baptist before the year 1925 had claimed that the Holy Spirit is imparted to the believers in Baptism." [97]

In his 1943 lecture on "The Teaching of the Church Concerning Baptism" Karl Barth had in essence held to Calvin's teaching on Baptism, although he reached different conclusions with regard to infant Baptism. While at that time Barth had opposed the Roman-Catholic, Lutheran, and Anglican teaching, in his *Church Dogmatics,* Vol. IV, 4, which appeared in 1967, he also parted company with Calvin and his own earlier work on Baptism, and he himself stressed his nearness to Zwingli and especially to the Baptists and Mennonites.[98] While acknowledging the connection between Baptism in the Holy Spirit and water Baptism, Barth distinguishes them very strictly, to such an extent that "we are dealing with completely different activities of two permanently different subjects: On the one side, the activity of *God* directed toward man, and on the other side, an activity made possible and evoked by God, but an activity of *man* toward God. On the one side, it is the *word* and *command* of God, expressed by means of his *gift;* on the other side, it is the *obedience* of man's *faith,* imposed on him as *recipient* of God's gift and obligating him to comply." [99] The idea of Christian Baptism as a means of grace is firmly rejected. "Baptism refers to the one divine deed performed in Jesus Christ, the one word of God spoken in him, but Baptism is no such work and word. It is the work and word of men who have become obedient to Jesus Christ and put their hope in him. Baptism is performed as water Baptism, proceeding from Spirit Baptism and looking toward it, but as such it is not also Spirit Baptism; it is and remains water Baptism." [100] For New Testament support Barth goes not so much to the baptismal material in the epistles which, he concedes, do not in every case exclude the possibility of a sacramental understanding, but primarily to the Baptism of John the Baptist. With it he equates Christian Baptism in essence, as Zwingli and Calvin did, in spite of admitting some differences. Although Barth rightly assigns to John's Baptism a fundamental and paradigmatic significance for establishing the basis for Baptism, he strangely does not incorporate in his understanding of Baptism the fact that John's Baptism was changed and fulfilled by the descent of the Holy Spirit at Jesus' Baptism.

(4) The more strictly Spirit Baptism and water Baptism are separated and the more strongly the accent is placed on the experience of Spirit Baptism, of dying and rising with Christ, and of regeneration, the more water Baptism in general is questioned. It is true, the Baptists very strongly insisted on water Baptism as a necessary act of obedience toward the baptismal command. But if the experience of Spirit Baptism is separated in a spiritualistic way from the external Word, the idea also suggests itself to separate this obedience from the directives of Scripture and hence from the baptismal command and to rely on the immediate guidance of the Spirit. Thus in the 16th century many Baptists adopted the position of such spiritualists as rejected water Baptism. George Fox

likewise rejected water Baptism, and there is already a dilution of this position when a modern Quaker adds: "It is indeed true that a special external act can be helpful for many people in bringing this inner experience to maturity and expression; but this does not happen then because through this act a special 'grace' is imparted by divine command. Rather, it happens because it enables the baptized by means of the normal psychological process to have a lively awareness of his belonging to Christ in the Christian fellowship." [101]

5. The Necessity of Baptism

Apart from the most intimate circle of disciples, who according to the Pentecost account in Acts received the Holy Spirit without Baptism (cf. also John 20:19 ff.), all members of the primitive Christian church are reported by the New Testament to have received Baptism. From the beginning the proclamation of the Gospel was not only a call to repentance and to faith but also to Baptism, and the exhortations of the New Testament letters to the members of the congregations have from the beginning made reference to Baptism; the exhortations are based on what God has done with the Christians through Baptism. "That baptism is the indispensable condition for admission to the Congregation and for participation in salvation is self-evident, and is at least indirectly expressed in Acts 4:12." [102] This generally attested fact that the members of the church were baptized would be unintelligible, in view of the fact that Jesus Himself did not baptize, if Baptism had arisen and established itself only gradually in the history of the primitive church—whether because of a resumption of John's Baptism, now, of course, in the name of Jesus and in expectation of the Holy Spirit—or because of the direction given by primitive Christian pneumatics. The most obvious source of this practice of Baptism observed from the beginning is the command of the Risen One which had been handed down, even though this source cannot be historically verified, since we lack analogies from our own sphere of experience.

On the basis of the command of the Risen One, transmitted in Matt. 28:19 f. and Mark 16:15 f., and the general primitive Christian practice it has become the custom to speak of the necessity of Baptism and to distinguish between the necessity of the command (*necessitas mandati sive praecepti*) and the necessity of salvation (*necessitas salutis*). The statements about the necessity of Baptism are all the more important since we are here not dealing with Baptism as such in its isolation, but with admission to the Lord's Supper made possible by Baptism and with the total gracious activity of God in the church through the word, through answers to prayer, and through the charismatic gifts. In general the distinction between the necessity of command and the necessity of salvation is determined by the question whether salvation may be obtained even without Baptism.

Depending upon the basic types of the understanding of Baptism, as discussed in the preceding paragraphs, the answers to the question concerning the necessity of Baptism will vary.

The question is answered negatively by consistently spiritualistic movements and by the Quakers.

But even for those who answer positively the necessity of salvation does not mean the same things everywhere. It makes a difference whether this necessity is understood from the perspective of viewing Baptism as a means of grace necessary for the reception of grace, or whether it is understood from the perspective of viewing Baptism as a duty-sign necessary for obedience. The answer will again be different, if Baptism is understood as a sign of grace but not as a means of grace.

Depending upon the understanding of Baptism, also the necessity of the command does not mean the same thing. If one believes in God's new-creating activity through Baptism, then this command is the invitation and the permission to receive grace. If, on the contrary, Baptism is understood as the believer's sign of duty and confession, then the necessity is not so much invitation as it is demand for an obedient fulfillment of what has been commanded.

The necessity of Baptism for salvation can be spoken of in the proper sense only if Baptism is understood as God's saving action. But if it is understood as the sign of man's duty, then it stands in any case in an indirect relation to salvation. This is the case in so far as a refusal to obey the baptismal command places in question the regeneration which has already taken place before Baptism, because this regeneration must manifest itself in works of obedience. Yet even where Baptism is understood not as a means of grace but only as a divine sign of assurance, one cannot speak of the necessity of Baptism for salvation with the same definiteness as one can where Baptism is acknowledged as a means of grace.

In practice these differences manifest themselves in that the

106

Baptists reject infant Baptism, while Calvin rejects emergency Baptism, especially in the case of children. He regards it as superfluous, since God "adopts our babies as his own before they are born." [103] On the contrary, where Baptism is viewed as a means of grace, emergency Baptism is administered to children and adults in danger of death.

If in agreement with the New Testament statements we are certain of the new-creating activity of God through Baptism, then there is no alternative between the necessity of the command and the necessity of salvation. The command of Baptism is combined with the promise, "he who believes and is baptized will be saved" (Mark 16:16). This is not a command of the Law but a call of the Gospel. It does not summon us to the performance of a rite but to the reception of grace. We would not be grasping the essence of Baptism if we were to speak only of a *necessitas mandati* or *praecepti*. For it is here a matter of an invitation to the reception of grace and at the same time it concerns the necessity of salvation. Here *necessitas mandati* and *necessitas salutis* are intertwined, so that the saving will of God is the inner basis of the command to receive salvation in Baptism. Thus the baptismal command participates in the structure of New Testament exhortation which is command, admonition, and consolation at the same time.

We can, of course, speak of a necessity of Baptism for salvation only as we call to a reception of Baptism, but not if we establish theoretically that salvation is impossible without Baptism. If statements about the necessity of Baptism for salvation are no longer made within the structure of invitation and exhortation but rather in the structure of judicial establishment, this procedure will lead to questions and answers that will lead astray. This has indeed not infrequently been the case in the history of theology, for example in the discussion of the question whether the salvation of unbaptized children who died was possible. Thus in his later expressions Augustine denied this, while others looked for a milder form of purgatory for such children. The concept of the necessity of Baptism for salvation is vitiated when God's final judgment upon the unbaptized is anticipated. To use the concept in a determinative rather than an admonitory way also has in it the danger that the baptized become certain of their salvation in a false way. Such generally formulated dogmatic sentences as, for example, that of Thomas Aquinas that "without Baptism there is no salvation for men," [104] must be retranslated into the structure of invitation in order to be valid.

No church has in fact drawn out the full conclusions from that sentence. No church teaches an absolute necessity of Baptism for salvation. Already the ancient church acknowledged the "Baptism of blood" of the catechumens in part as a substitute for water Baptism, in part even as surpassing Baptism. Beyond this, the desire for Baptism (*votum baptismi*) was acknowledged either as a complete or as a still incomplete substitute for Baptism, and this not only in times of persecution. Thus also Thomas qualified that general sentence with the explanation: "The sacrament of Baptism may be wanting to some one in two ways. First, both in reality and in desire; as is the case with those who neither are baptized, nor wished to be baptized . . . . Secondly, the sacrament of Baptism may be wanting to anyone in reality but not in desire . . . . Such a man can obtain salvation without being actually baptized, on account of his desire for Baptism . . . ." [105] The general thesis concerning the necessity of Baptism for salvation is dissolved even more when the concept of the *votum baptismi* is enlarged in such a way that an unconscious desire for Baptism is imputed even to pious heathen who have heard nothing of the Gospel and of Baptism. If Baptism is equated with a conscious or unconscious desire for Baptism, the necessity of Baptism for salvation is still affirmed only apparently. Here there is even danger that the act of Baptism will experience a debasement contradictory to the doctrine of Baptism.

The necessity of Baptism for salvation cannot be maintained as a general theoretical affirmation. God's freedom over against the saving means given by Him — the freedom of His grace — must be respected. One cannot get control of this freedom by formulating exceptions concerning a conscious or an unconscious *votum* — nor by setting up antithetical statements like: only faith is necessary for salvation but not Baptism — or — only the proclamation but not the sacraments. On the contrary, we must respect God's freedom by urgently calling every one to repentance, to faith, and to Baptism. With the same urgency we must warn against a contempt of Baptism. "Whoever rejects Baptism rejects God's Word, faith, and Christ, who directs us and binds us to Baptism." (Luther) [106]

CHAPTER THREE

The Administration and Reception of Baptism

1. The Single Reception of Baptism

Every person may receive Baptism only once. The single reception is everywhere presupposed in the New Testament. It was maintained even in the serious discussions of the ancient church on the question of the readmission of apostates following the persecution of Christians. The concern was solely with the problem of penitence, absolution, and reconciliation — but not with a repetition of Baptism. Also in the controversies about heretical Baptism none of the contending parties were concerned with a repetition of Baptism but solely with the question whether a Baptism administered by heretics or other gross sinners was to be considered valid. Thus Cyprian denied that the Baptism administered to previously baptized heretics upon their return was a rebaptism, since heretical Baptism could not be recognized as valid. This is true, correspondingly, of the baptismal practice of the Donatists. The Baptists, too, teach the single application of Baptism and refuse to be named rebaptizers. If people who were baptized as infants later submit to Baptism as adults, this should not be called rebaptism since [according to their teaching] infant Baptism is not a Christian Baptism.

By its one-time application Baptism is distinguished from the preaching of the Gospel and the administration of the Lord's Supper. The Gospel must be preached to man again and again — as assurance of the saving deed which God has done in Christ and will do one day, and as admonition to live in conformity with this saving deed. The congregation is to assemble again and again for the Lord's Supper — for the reception of the body of Christ and for building up as His body especially through this reception. However, Baptism occupies a special position because of its single administration.

This special position does not mean that in the church's activity or in theological thought Baptism may be isolated from preaching and the Lord's Supper. For Baptism follows on the basis of the heard Gospel and leads to participation in the worshiping assembly and thus to a constantly new hearing of the Gospel and a constantly new reception of Christ's body and blood. Baptism, Gospel, and Lord's Supper belong together in the most intimate way. Wherever the Gospel is proclaimed it calls to a reception of Baptism. Proclamation and Baptism belong together so intimately that regeneration can be said to be effected either through Baptism or through the Word (1 Peter 1:23; James 1:18). The acceptance of the Word is consummated by the approach to Baptism. Again, the Gospel brings the already received Baptism to remembrance, since the imperatives of the Gospel are based on the divine deed that was done to man through Baptism. But also the celebration of the Lord's Supper retains its relationship to Baptism in so far as Baptism is the way of access to the Lord's Supper. Thus in a sense Baptism is included in all the repeated proclamations and in all the repeated celebrations of the Lord's Supper. This applies also to absolution, ordination, and other acts in which the church has further unfolded the promise and the task of the Gospel—whether these developments are called acts of blessing, commissions, or also sacraments. *All* churchly activity comes from Baptism and points back to Baptism.

Since proclamation, Baptism, and Lord's Supper cohere so intimately, we must ask wherein the particularity of Baptism consists—in relation to the different forms of the preached Word and of the Lord's Supper.

The answer to this question appears easy if we look at the special manner in which God's gracious activity meets man: In the sermon God acts through the Word alone, in Baptism through Word and water, in the Lord's Supper through Word, bread, and wine. To these differences corresponds the special manner in which man here receives grace: through the sermon by means of believing hearing, through Baptism by means of believing hearing and being immersed or having the water poured over him, through the Lord's Supper by means of hearing and oral eating and drinking. In the sermon God acts through the promise concerning Christ's death and resurrection, in Baptism through assignment to the name of Christ, and in the Lord's Supper through the gift of Christ's body and blood. The differences between Baptism and Lord's Supper in word and action cannot be overlooked.

110

Baptism has no words of distribution corresponding to the words of distribution in the Lord's Supper. The water of Baptism is not Christ's blood. What Luther says about the baptismal water can be said only in a figurative way. Faith

> . . . sees the cleansing fountain, red
> With the dear blood of Jesus,
> Which from the sins, inherited
> From fallen Adam, frees us,
> And from our own wrongdoings.[1]

The answer to the question regarding the particularity of Baptism becomes more difficult, however, when we ask about the specific gift and effect which is imparted to man by means of this special way of God's activity. The connection between Baptism, Gospel, and Lord's Supper was not created by the church but is given in Christ. One and the same name of Christ is proclaimed through Gospel, Baptism, and the Lord's Supper. It is the same Crucified and Risen One whom the Gospel proclaims, in whose name Baptism is administered, and whose death is proclaimed in the Lord's Supper. Proclamation, Baptism, and Lord's Supper are based on the same victory of Jesus Christ on the cross, and this saving deed is their content. Through preaching, Christ's death and resurrection are proclaimed to us as having happened for us. Through Baptism we are given into Christ's death and resurrection. In the Lord's Supper the Risen One gives us His body that was offered on the cross and His blood of the covenant. Gospel, Baptism, and Lord's Supper not only proclaim Jesus Christ, but He, the proclaimed Christ Himself, is active through them as the present Lord. Through preaching, Baptism, and Lord's Supper the name of Christ is not only proclaimed, but in that name "forgiveness of sins, life, and salvation" (Luther) are given us. Both through the proclamation and through Baptism as well as the Lord's Supper God justifies, sanctifies, renews the sinner, grants him the life of the Son, and transforms him into His image. Thus Baptism, Gospel, and Lord's Supper not only belong together, but they interpenetrate each other and must be understood as the unity of God's gracious activity. In the sense of this interpenetration Baptism and the Lord's Supper are to be called "visible Word," and the preached Word "audible sacrament." Hence preaching, Baptism, and Lord's Supper are to be recognized as different forms of the same saving activity of God.

But if proclamation, Baptism, and Lord's Supper belong together and interpenetrate each other on the basis of the identity of Giver and gifts of forgiveness, life, and salvation in this way, the question arises: Does not the believer participate in Christ's body and blood also through Baptism? Does not Baptism, as a being given into the historical event of Christ's death, at the same time grant participation in the very Person who died on the cross and is now living? Indeed, does not the believer receive participation in Jesus' body and blood already through the proclamation? For the Gospel is not only the report of a past event, but it is the efficacious Word through which God promises and gives us what He has done for the world in Jesus' death and resurrection! The person of Jesus Christ, His corporeality, and His historical career cannot be separated from each other. But then the further question arises: Why have Baptism at all? Why not simply a first Communion? Indeed, why have Baptism and Lord's Supper at all? Why not simply the proclamation of the Gospel? In what respect do preaching, Baptism, and Lord's Supper differ from each other? What constitutes the particularity of Baptism?

These questions lead us to the mystery of the riches of God's gracious activity. God takes man into the one saving deed which He accomplished in Jesus' death and resurrection, and He does so by means of several acts and thus embraces man's existence in various ways. This activity of God is characterized by a superabundance and extravagance which strangely eludes a rational coordination of one method with another.

We would surely not do justice to God's gracious activity toward man if we were to view the proclamation of the Gospel purely as invitation and command to receive forgiveness, life, and deliverance in the sacrament.[2] The Gospel is God's new-creating word-in-action. Through the Gospel God produces what the Gospel promises. The riches of God's gracious activity are likewise misunderstood when, conversely, the saving deed is expected of the preaching of the Gospel, while the sacraments are acknowledged only as signs which merely confirm and guarantee the forgiving, saving, vivifying activity of God which takes place through the sermon.[3] Nor is it proper to affirm that through the sermon God acts only on the human spirit and not on man's totality, including his corporeality. This He does only through Baptism and especially through the Lord's Supper.[4] On the contrary, by means of the promise and address of the proclamation God reaches out for the whole man. All such distinctions are rationalizations which attempt to establish a systematic order at the expense of this or that manner of God's gracious activity. In a variety of ways God grants participation in the same riches of His grace. We would fail to appreciate these riches of God's gracious activity if we would isolate the gifts from each other or even reduce them to a single one, since God grants participation in Jesus Christ also in the others. These riches should rather be manifested in further acts, as this is in fact done by all the churches in one way or another.

In a certain respect the conjunction and interpenetration of proclamation, Baptism, and Lord's Supper can be elucidated by an analogy from the doctrine of God's attributes. Each of the divine attributes must be acknowledged as God's perfection. This perfection does not consist in the sum of the attributes, but in each one of them the others are also present. Thus God's love is at the same time almighty, just, wise; His omnipotence is at the same time loving, just, wise, etc. Yet we can recognize, praise, and teach the divine perfection in no other way than by listing God's attributes one by one. But no enumeration can lay claim to completeness, since God's perfection is infinite. Yet in each attribute God's infinite perfection is acknowledged.

To be sure, this analogy clearly has its limits. It is true that also the knowledge of God's attributes rests on God's historical revelation, for the love of God has appeared in Jesus Christ. God's eternal attributes, His eternal divine essence, are praised on the basis of His revelation. The doctrine of proclamation, Baptism, and Lord's Supper, however, is not only based on God's historical saving deed, but it is the doctrine concerning God's historical activity through Word and sacrament. All curious questions about why Baptism and Lord's Supper have been instituted in addition to preaching and how their gifts are related to each other are thrown back upon the historical task which Jesus Christ has given and the command to act in accordance with this task in the historical life of the church by preaching and hearing the Gospel and administering and receiving the sacraments. We cannot in a speculative way derive these different forms of God's gracious activity from God's eternal love. Nor can it be deduced from Christ's death and resurrection that Baptism and Lord's Supper are necessary alongside the message. Nor

113

can we derive this variety from man's weakness and his dependence on the different senses of hearing, seeing, tasting, etc. But we must open ourselves to the riches of God's gracious activity by obediently following the historical commission and faithfully using proclamation, Baptism, and Lord's Supper as forms of God's gracious activity—forms which cannot be exchanged or replaced, forms which cohere and interpenetrate each other.

Since Baptism is assignment to Jesus Christ and thus the death of the old man and the start of the new life, it is the access to the riches of God's gracious activity. Therein its particularity consists. On this rests the onetime administration of Baptism. The fact that one can be baptized only once does not yet follow cogently so long as Baptism is regarded primarily as the confessing act and deed of man, rather than as God's deed to man. Furthermore, the onetime application of Baptism must become subject to question when its significance is found in the intensity of religious experience. Baptism is a onetime act as God's new-creating deed. Hence it is not unique in the sense of other events which disappeared in the past and which we recall as past events, but it is unique in the sense of a happening which determines and embraces the entire subsequent life. The same "once for all" (ἐφάπαξ) applies to Baptism as to Jesus' death and resurrection. Just as Jesus died and rose again not only "once" but "once for all," so also through Baptism man is given into Jesus' death and resurrection once for all. But through Baptism the sinner is once for all made the property of the crucified and risen Lord in order to live by the Lord's strength henceforth. Just as the age following Jesus' death and resurrection is different from the preceding age because it is already bracketed by His victory on the cross and His return, so also the period of a man's life after his Baptism is different from the time before. "The old has passed away, behold, the new has come" (2 Cor. 5:17). Hence the ancient church regarded Baptism as *the* sacrament.

2. The Administration of Baptism

a. The baptizing church

In distinction from Jewish baptisms, Christian Baptism from the beginning was not self-administered. The fact that one person administers Baptism and another receives it conforms to God's activity through Baptism. As the Gospel is proclaimed and heard, so Baptism is administered and received. Of course, where Baptism is no longer understood as God's deed to man and as God's sign for man, the question might be raised whether Christian Baptism could not also be self-administered. But apart from some extremely rare exceptions, also the Baptist movement in its Biblicism has steadfastly conformed to the New Testament accounts of Baptism and insisted on Baptism as an act to be administered by a baptizer.[5]

According to the New Testament, Baptism was administered exclusively by members of the church. They accepted the candidate's confession of faith and his desire for Baptism and performed the baptismal act. The administration of Baptism is ascribed to apostles and their co-workers, but also to those members of the church concerning whom no special "office" may be presupposed on the basis of the texts. In every case, no matter who did the baptizing, no matter what words were used, it involved the same faith in Christ which the church confessed and the same Baptism by means of which all believers had been assigned to Christ and made members of the church.

Since, therefore, the baptizer does not act as an individual but as a member of the church and in the fellowship of the church, we may also say: the church baptizes. The church proclaims the Gospel, calls to Baptism, tests the desire for Baptism, and by her Baptism consigns the believer to Christ as to the Lord, and thus receives him into her fellowship — the fellowship of the Word, the Lord's Supper, and prayer. In this way the church is the "mother of the believers." She gives birth to the believers through her proclamation and her baptizing. The church is not only the goal of Baptism but also its antecedent, since her preaching and her call to faith and to Baptism precede the administration of Baptism. The conception of the church as mother has its origin not only in Old Testament statements about God's people as Jahweh's bride and wife, but also in Galatians (4:25-31) and in Revelation (12). The ancient church further developed this idea and the reformers, especially Luther, took it over.

The order of the catechumenate, which soon became necessary, led to the result that admission to Baptism was combined more closely with the church's office than had been the case in the primitive church. Also the essential connection between Baptism and the unity of the church makes it easy to understand why the administration of Baptism soon became the task of the bishop and the co-workers authorized by him. Thus, for example, Tertullian declared: "The supreme right of giving it belongs to the high priest, which is the bishop; after him, to the presbyters and deacons, yet not without commission from the bishop, on account of the church's dignity: for where this is safe, peace is safe." [6] By the fact that the leader of the congregation, whose office was understood at the same time as the bond of unity among the members, performed Baptism, the unity of Baptism in its connection with the unity of the church was made manifest. The more consciously the church's office was understood as the bearer of the apostolic tradition, the more Baptism became evident as transcending reception into the local parish and as being at the same time reception into the universal church which encompasses time and space.

b. The church as instrument of the baptizing God

In the New Testament baptismal texts it is noteworthy at the same time that there is very little if any interest in the person of the baptizer. Although the accounts in Acts repeatedly mention the name of the baptizer, it is clear that neither his person nor his status in the church has any significance for the validity and effect of Baptism (apart from the special problems connected with the account in Acts 8:12-17). In the frequent references of the epistles to Baptism as antecedent for exhortation, the person of the baptizer plays no role whatsoever. When various factions developed in Corinth and appealed to those who had baptized them, Paul condemned this attitude in the strongest terms. ". . . each one of you says, 'I belong to Paul,' or 'I belong to Apollos,' or 'I belong to Cephas,' or 'I belong to Christ.' Is Christ divided? Was Paul crucified for you? Or were you baptized in the name of Paul? I am thankful that I baptized none of you except Crispus and Gaius; lest any one should say that you were baptized in my name. (I did baptize also the household of Stephanas. Beyond that, I do not know whether I baptized any one else.)" (1 Cor. 1:12-16). So little did Paul think of Baptism as being determined by the person or office of the baptizer that he added, "for Christ did not send me to baptize but to preach the Gospel" (v. 17). This sentence does not justify the conclusion that Paul disparaged Baptism or was ignorant of a tradition of the baptismal command, but it does suggest that he usually left the baptizing to the congregations. The name of the baptizer is immaterial, the name of Christ means everything. The baptizer is only an instrument.

116

If the church is spoken of as the baptizing church, "the mother of the faithful," then she must also be spoken of as only an instrument. Like every individual baptized by her, the church herself was created by the Spirit of God. Not only her members, but the baptizing church herself has been baptized, as Eph. 5:25-32 uniquely states. By giving Himself up for the church Christ did it "that He might sanctify her, having cleansed her by the washing of water with the Word, that He might present the church to Himself in splendor, without spot or wrinkle or any such thing, that she might be holy and without blemish." The church's holiness and glory are those of the Christ who is active and gives Himself to her. Only as the one baptized by Christ is the church the organ of His baptizing, His cleansing, sanctifying, glorifying. Only because of the Head is the church the body of Christ growing in all dimensions—growing toward Christ, growing in the fellowship of her members with each other, growing in the advance of the message into the world and through the addition of those who stand afar off. As the one baptized, the church by her baptizing is the growing body of Christ whose fullness permeates all things and is the new all in all.

The fact that God Himself is the baptizer and the church and her members are only His instruments was maintained only at the cost of severe conflicts. If the concern in Baptism is with the incorporation into the body of Christ by means of the service of members of this body, a problem arises when Baptism is administered by people who, while belonging to church outwardly, live in gross sins and have become dead members of the body of Christ. This problem was not in principle dealt with until the controversy concerning heretical Baptism and the discussions surrounding the Donatist schism, but it was in existence even before then, and in fact the Donatist separation had its roots in the divergent answers given to the problem. The controversy between Cyprian and Pope Stephen I concerned itself primarily with the validity of heretical Baptism, but Optatus of Mileve, around 370, furnished the basic answer to the internal problem of the church. His answer was that the church's holiness does not rest on the holiness of her members but on the holiness of the sacraments, and that the sanctifying effect of the sacraments does not depend on the holiness of the administrators but on the saving activity of God. Neither the church nor her members are lords over the sacraments, but rather their servants. This basic clarification was of lasting significance for posterity.

117

The reformers, too, maintained it. "Although the Christian church, properly speaking, is nothing else than the assembly of all believers and saints, yet because in this life many false Christians, hypocrites, and even open sinners remain among the godly, the sacraments are efficacious even if the priests who administer them are wicked men...." (Augsburg Confession, VIII). Yet tendencies to make the effect or even the validity of Baptism depend on the holiness of the administrator have repeatedly again manifested themselves.

Also in another respect the purely instrumental significance of the baptizer has been maintained in theology and canon law. Even when the authority of the episcopal office was further strengthened in connection with the development of a comprehensive church order and the free service rendered by the charismatic gifts was further de-emphasized, the possibility of a valid Baptism administered by *laymen* continued to be recognized. At times there was indeed some uncertainty in the recognition of such Baptisms. Tertullian, for example, opposed Baptism by women.[7] Augustine, however, accepted as valid the Baptism by every layman that was administered in conformity with the church's rule; and yet such a Baptism was to be performed only in special emergencies. In support of this position Thomas stated that in Christ, the true baptizer, there was no difference between male and female.[8] The fact that generally such emergency Baptism needed subsequently to be approved by the bishop does not vitiate the fact that the general priesthood of all believers continued to be recognized here as an active service and not just as a concept. Recognition of lay Baptism confirms in a special way that the baptizer is only an instrument of the baptizing God and that the person and status of the baptizing Christian mean nothing, while the person and name of God mean everything. Here Calvin occupies a peculiar position of his own. He rejects emergency Baptism on the ground "that it is wrong for private individuals to assume the administration of Baptism; for this as well as the serving of the Supper is a function of the ecclesiastical ministry. For Christ did not command women, or men of every sort, to baptize, but gave this command to those whom He had appointed apostles."[9] Thereby Calvin demonstrated a more exclusive understanding of office than the Roman Church. But the question needs to be asked to what extent his understanding of the office was really the determining factor, rather than his understanding of the sacrament, which made an emergency Baptism unnecessary.

c. The administration of Baptism separated from the church

Closely connected with the problem of Baptisms administered by sinful members of the church is the problem of the validity of Baptisms that were performed outside the church. This problem did not arise in connection with all rites that resembled Baptism, but it did arise where schismatic and heretical communities likewise baptized into (or in) the name of the Father and of the Son and of the Holy Spirit. In favor of rejecting such Baptisms seems to be, first of all, the unity of the church which is at the same time unity of faith, of Baptism, and of the Lord's Supper. But what is the relationship between the unity of the church and the unity of Baptism? Is Baptism administered only if this is done by a church, or is not rather the unity of the church the result of the one Baptism? Is Baptism the work of the church, or is the church the product of Baptism? In the second century heretical Baptism was considered invalid in most of the areas of the Eastern Church and in the church of Africa. When the heretic entered the Catholic Church he was rebaptized. Cyprian of Carthage had defended this practice by insisting that the unity of the church and of the Holy Spirit could not be separated from the unity of Baptism. He was opposed by Pope Stephen who upheld the validity of heretical Baptism and received heretics into the Catholic Church simply by an act of reconciliation and the laying on of hands. Hence the prerequisite for acknowledging validity was not the consensus in doctrine but only the *de facto* agreement with the baptismal ritual of the Catholic Church. In the controversy of that time the question as to what the baptizand received in heretical Baptism that could be acknowledged as valid was not clarified. It is clear, however, that Stephen in fact assigned priority to the power of the divine name invoked in Baptism over the orthodox or heretical prerequisites of the baptizer and his fellowship. In the fight against the Donatists the African church also acknowledged heretical Baptism, and Augustine thought through the problem of what the heretic receives in his Baptism and developed the formulas, referred to above,[10] which became decisive for the entire systematic structure

119

of his teaching on Baptism. Western Christendom, including the churches of the Reformation (apart from some Baptists), has generally acknowledged heretical Baptism. Most Eastern churches hesitated much longer before they admitted such Baptisms. Their recognition was based not so much on doctrinal principles as on the accommodation of love.

Of course the act of acknowledging heretical Baptism in no sense means approval of the schism or the heresy, but it does mean acknowledgment of the sovereignty of God who acts also through baptizing schismatics and heretics if they do the same as the church does. Recognizing this divine activity, which transcends the church's boundaries, includes the thought that the call to unity meets the schismatics and heretics not as a call coming only from the outside, but as a call founded in their Baptism. If God in His faithfulness stands by His name, even when it is invoked outside of the church, then the obligation follows for all the baptized to seek the unity of the church—tne unity of confession of faith, of the Lord's Supper, and the commonality of the church's offices. In this way the decision of the ancient church in the controversy about heretical Baptism became an exceedingly important starting point for the ecumenical endeavors for unity in our time.

The ultimate inference from the recognition of the sovereignty of the baptizing God and the purely instrumental significance of the baptizing man was drawn when discussing the question whether even a pagan could validly baptize, if he did it in conformity with the church's order. Augustine wavered in his answer to this question, but Thomas regarded as valid a Baptism performed by one not baptized, if it is done according to the church's rules. He reasoned as follows: "The man who baptizes offers but his outward ministration; whereas Christ it is Who baptizes inwardly, Who can use all men to whatever purpose He wills. Consequently, the unbaptized can baptize. . . ." [11] Such considerations appear to have very little practical value and may strike us as highly sophistical, and yet they furnish an impressive witness to the fact that in the doctrine of Baptism all glory belongs to God as the Savior.

3. The Reception of Baptism

a. Faith in Jesus Christ

Baptism is to be received by faith in Jesus Christ. This faith rests on the Gospel of Jesus Christ and is the obedient acceptance of this Gospel.

The Gospel is the message concerning the historical man Jesus and His career. It proclaims Jesus as the Christ promised in the Old Testament and His historical death and His resurrection as man's only salvation. Jesus endured the divine judgment upon sinners and in His resurrection is revealed as the Righteous One in whom God has reconciled the world unto Himself. However, the Gospel is not only the report of the history of Jesus, but it is at the same time the Word through which the risen Christ is Himself present and active and proves Himself to be the Lord. "The Gospel of Jesus Christ" means not only the message which has Jesus Christ as its content, but it is the message which comes from Jesus Christ, not only in the sense of a historical tradition but in the sense that it proceeds from Jesus Christ as the present Lord. As the Gospel proclaims that Jesus Christ has taken the world's sin upon Himself, the Crucified One offers Himself to the hearers of the Gospel as the One crucified for them. As the Gospel proclaims His resurrection, He Himself calls the hearers from death to life. Jesus Christ Himself confronts the sinner in the human word which bears witness to Him and calls the sinner to faith. Through the Gospel Christ informs the world that the people have become His property and summons them to submit themselves to Him as the Lord.

When the Gospel is received by faith this happens in contrast to what is perceived by the senses. The person addressed by the Gospel sees and hears a man who addresses him. He hears the story of a man whose impotent death on the cross is apparent but whose resurrection escapes every analogy with human experience of life. Faith clings to the Gospel in contrast to what it sees and hears. Faith is not indignant over God's hiddenness in the humiliation. Faith is offended neither by the insignificance of the human words nor by Jesus' impotence and failure on the cross. Nor does faith seek God's glory on a higher level beyond this lowliness which alone is visible. But in the lowliness of Jesus on the cross, faith lays hold of the divine salvation. In the insignificance and unverifiability of the human words faith grasps the Savior who meets him in those words.

Where the Gospel is received by faith, this includes acknowledgment of the sentence upon the sin of men, which God has pronounced on the cross. For as the message of the judgment which God executed

121

upon Jesus on the cross, the message concerning Christ is the Word of salvation. The Gospel reveals the hearer in his contradiction against God and shows him that he has come under judgment. The Gospel uncovers man's concrete transgressions against God and his fellowmen, yes, it reveals him not only as the one who has sinned but as the one who is a sinner, who has not only heaped guilt upon himself but who is enslaved by sin and has become guilty of death. God's saving deed on the cross is recognized only as man recognizes his own righteousness as unrighteousness, his own wisdom as folly, and his self-chosen ways as the ways of perdition. Accepting the Gospel means abandoning one's own righteousness, one's own wisdom, one's own self-understanding, one's boasting of oneself. Faith in the Gospel is always at the same time repentance.

The faith which accepts the Gospel agrees with the No which God says to sin but clings to the Yes which God has spoken to the sinner in the sacrifice of Jesus. As faith agrees with God in His wrath against sin, it clings to Jesus Christ who has endured the sinners' God-forsakenness and death — to Jesus Christ who died not only through us but for us men and who now intercedes for us as the Exalted One. The believer not only leaps over the insignificance of what he perceives with the senses as he hears the Gospel but also over what has become visible and palpable for him under God's Word as his own human reality. In spite of being confronted with the sins which have been laid bare by the Word of God, he believes in the promise of righteousness: "Jesus Christ was put to death for your trespasses and raised for your justification." The believer believes in the love of God which is revealed in Jesus Christ precisely in God's wrath against sin.

This faith in the Gospel cannot remain mute. For by faith the sinner knows himself to be addressed not only by the man who proclaims the Gospel to him but by God who grants him the saving deed in Christ. Through the Gospel the Crucified One Himself confronts him as the living Lord. The call of the Gospel demands the response of faith. In the hearing of the Gospel the personal encounter of the Lord with the hearing man takes place, and faith in the Gospel is faith in the present Christ and God active in Him. The responses of faith in prayer and witness are manifold. But all of them are concentrated in confession. In confession faith says Yes to the message it has received. By means of this Yes, faith submits itself not only to the Gospel but to Jesus Christ

122

Himself whom the Gospel proclaims. But whether the believer confesses Christ in his own words or in the words of others, he does not remain an individual by himself, but by means of this Yes he joins in the confession of those who have come to faith before him. He becomes part of the confessing church. In this confession of faith the confession of sins is always included at the same time.

If the Gospel is received by faith, it cannot be done without a desire for Baptism. For the Gospel concerning Jesus Christ is also the call to Baptism in the name of Christ. In the approach to Baptism the obedience of faith toward the Gospel is realized. At the same time faith in Christ and the approach to Baptism are not side by side without relation to each other. Just as faith in the Gospel that is heard is faith in the Christ who confronts him in the Gospel, so also Baptism is to be desired by faith in the saving activity of Christ through Baptism. The believer takes no offense at the insignificant action with water and human words, he does not look for Christ's glory beyond this event, but he receives Baptism in the expectation that through this action God assigns him, the sinner, to Christ, and thus separates him from his guilty past and takes him into the sphere of Christ's spiritual power. The confession of faith impels to the act by which Christ makes Himself known to us. The submission to Christ as the Lord, a submission that is expressed in the confession, impels one toward acceptance by this Lord Himself. This does not mean that Baptism is to be made a second means of appropriating salvation alongside faith, but faith and Baptism belong together. Thus in Baptism the salvation "through the resurrection of Jesus Christ" is the answer to the "appeal to God for a clear conscience." (1 Peter 3:21)

Yet everything that was said about the faith in which Baptism is to be received would be misunderstood if the leap over the perceivable, the clinging to the Gospel, repentance, prayer, the confession to Christ, and the desire for Baptism were urged as man's activity valid before God. Even though faith is accomplished in man's activity, it is not man's work. As faith holds to the Gospel, grasps it, clings to it, relies on Christ, and opposes His death to the verdict of the Law—it is not man who effects salvation but God who in His mercy reaches for man and takes him up into His gracious activity. In spite of all daring, leaping, clinging, faith in its proper sense is not a human act but the reception of divine grace. Not only what we receive but the act of receiving is God's gift.

123

Not only God's address in the Gospel, but also the act of hearing the Gospel as God's address, is God's grace. No matter in what conflicts man may have come to the certainty of faith, the believer will always confess that he came to certainty, not through his own wrestling and striving but by grace alone. Faith too and the desire for Baptism are God's saving deed done to men. In the reminder to the Colossians that they were buried in Baptism and raised "through faith in the working of God" (Col. 2:12), the reference is hardly restricted to faith *in* the working of God but includes the idea of faith created *by* the working of God who raised Christ from the dead.[12] The Gospel is the power of God and faith is the work of the Holy Spirit who acts through the Gospel. The confession is also a gift of the Holy Spirit. It is not man's work but the end of man's own works in the self-surrender to Jesus Christ.

Just as faith is passive reception in spite of all activity, so also the approach to Baptism is the end of all human activity. For man comes to an act in which he himself is not the actor but one who is surrendered to the activity of another. In its essence Christian Baptism is not self-administered but received passively, and already the summons to Baptism, "let yourself be baptized" (Acts 2:38) does not put the stress on "let" but on being baptized, "be baptized." [13] Through Baptism man is rendered powerless and consigned to death. The passivity of reception cannot be questioned by reinterpreting it into an activity, as, for example, Johannes Warns does. "The person to be baptized is not only active in causing Baptism, but he must cooperate in the immersion, he must suppress the resisting impulses which every one experiences involuntarily as he is plunged backward into the water." [14] It is true that the reception of Baptism presupposes the desire for Baptism and thus the Yes to one's own death. But since it is the Yes to death and surrender to the new-creating activity of God, man's activity cannot be urged here, although man submits himself to being baptized. By the very essence of Baptism every boasting in man's own activity is excluded.

b. The threefold connection between faith and Baptism

Since God's act through Baptism takes place once for always and thus determines the entire subsequent life, the relationship between faith and Baptism transcends the baptismal act itself and endures until the end of life. It is not accidental that the New Testament passages speak less frequently of the faith that precedes Baptism than they do of the faith that is to be referred back to Baptism. Most of the baptismal statements are used as basis for admonition to the baptized. These are admonished to live in accordance with the saving deed that was done to them in Baptism. Hence the connection between faith and Baptism may not be restricted to the temporal sequence: faith — Baptism, but the connection must be maintained also in the reverse order: Baptism — faith. Altogether a threefold connection between faith and Baptism must be distinguished.

1. Baptism is to be received by faith in Jesus Christ. This faith is awakened through the message of Jesus Christ as an operation of the Holy Spirit. The faith in Jesus Christ which desires Baptism does not only confess in general that Jesus Christ is Lord, but it is at the same time the expectation that Jesus Christ as Lord will act on the believer through Baptism, receive him for His own, and grant him participation in His dying and living.

2. Since Baptism is one of the ways in which God has mercy on man, we must not expect less of Baptism than of the proclamation of the Gospel. If the Gospel is the power of God by which faith is created, then faith is to be expected also as a result of the administration of Baptism. Also through Baptism God is active in the power of the Holy Spirit. Not only is Baptism to be desired in faith, but the strengthening of faith is also to be expected of Baptism. The reference of Hebrews to the enlightenment which the members of the church had received may perhaps be understood in this context. They are "those who have once been enlightened, who have tasted the heavenly gift, and have become partakers of the Holy Spirit, and have tasted the goodness of the Word of God and the powers of the age to come" (Heb. 6:4-5). Through Baptism man receives his sight and he is enabled to see the light which has dawned in Christ. It is no accident that the concept of enlighten-ment, which was familiar from the Hellenistic mysteries, played an important role in the ancient church's doctrine of Baptism.

3. Since in Baptism God embraces the entire life of man in a saving way, the baptized must ever anew lay hold of this saving deed by faith and draw his life from that deed. The baptized no longer only goes to meet the coming death and the coming resurrection, but he already comes from his death and his resurrection. Through his being given

125

into Christ's death the life with Christ has already been opened up for him. Thus the Christian lives not only in a hurrying forward to ever new hearing of the Gospel and to ever new reception of the Lord's Supper, but at the same time he hurries back ever again to his Baptism through which he has been given over to the dominion of Christ. The New Testament admonitions are thus based primarily on Baptism; they call it to mind and exhort the baptized to draw his life ever anew from the source of his being a Christian. You "must consider yourselves dead to sin and alive to God in Christ Jesus" (Rom. 6:11). This imperative, which lays the foundation for the individual concrete exhortations, is the summons to faith in the saving deed which God once performed for each member of the church through Baptism. This summons applies to the whole life. Thus Baptism is not only the beginning but the firm and abiding basis upon which faith must establish itself again and again. Baptism is not only the means by which God once acted on the baptized, but it is at the same time the weapon for the fight of faith. At a time when many postponed the reception of Baptism for fear of losing again the receiving baptismal grace because of sin, Gregory of Nazianzen, in his great "address on Holy Baptism," [15] praised especially Baptism as the best weapon of faith against all the onslaughts of the devil and demonstrated this in connection with the most varied kinds of temptations. In this way the onetime Baptism is to be used constantly by faith. By faith one must constantly "crawl back" to Baptism (Luther) in order to find there the deliverance from the onslaughts of the powers of perdition. The Christian's repentance is to be performed by thinking back to one's Baptism in which "forgiveness of sins, life, and salvation" were imparted.

Thus the church summons to a believing reception of Baptism and to a believing remembrance of Baptism and expects the creation and strengthening of faith from Baptism no less than from the preached Gospel.

c. The reception of Baptism separated from faith

Faith and Baptism can become separated in the reception of Baptism as well as in its administration. Baptism can be received hypocritically or with unbelieving expectations. But an apostasy from faith is also possible after a believing reception of Baptism. Even if the baptized himself then regards his Baptism as a meaningless external rite, the question concerning the significance of such a Baptism has not yet

126

been answered for him. In spite of the difference in individual cases and in the answers given, the church has burdened the unbeliever with the fact that God has acted on him through Baptism and that he is now not the same as he was before.

The danger of disobedience, of indifference, and of apostasy on the part of the baptized has been with the church from the beginning. Thus Paul warned the Corinthians by pointing to the passage of the fathers through the sea and the Baptism which followed "into Moses in the cloud and in the sea" (1 Cor. 10:2): "Now these things are warnings for us, not to desire evil as they did. Do not be idolaters as some of them were; as it is written, 'The people sat down to eat and drink and rose up to dance.' We must not indulge in immorality . . ." (6-8a). Paul warns against putting God to the test (v. 9) and grumbling (v. 10) like the fathers, and announces God's judgment upon them as it had also struck the fathers. The severity of the judgment corresponds to the greatness of God's saving deed. Just because the baptized have been saved by Christ they will be judged if they fall away from Him. However, the last word is here not the announcement of the judgment but the call to return and the offer of the promise, "God is faithful, and He will not let you be tempted beyond your strength, but with the temptation will also provide the way of escape, that you may be able to endure it" (v. 13). Also the warnings of Hebrews must be understood as the ultimate call to return. "It is impossible to restore again to repentance those who have once been enlightened, who have tasted the heavenly gift, and have become partakers of the Holy Spirit, and have tasted the goodness of the Word of God and the powers of the age to come, if they then commit apostasy, since they crucify the Son of God on their own account and hold Him up to contempt" (Heb. 6:4-6; cf. 10:20-23). Here the church that has grown weary is recalled to faith by framing an apodictic statement about the impossibility of a second renewal. The endangered members of the churches are reminded of what they received in Baptism once for all. In these and other New Testament admonitions Baptism as the one-time deed of God is presupposed, a deed that remains determinative for the entire life of the baptized. Unbelief does not turn Baptism into a nothing. It remains as the basis for judgment on the apostate and as power for the penitent in their battle against temptations.

The fact that Baptism is already requested and received in unbelief,

127

perhaps for the sake of some external advantage, did not become a more widespread danger until the church began to receive public acclaim, and membership in the church brought advantages or even formed the prerequisite for the attainment of civil rights. The proclamation met this danger by the call to repentance and the threat of judgment, as already the Acts report Peter as having done over against the deceitful request of Simon Magus for the laying on of hands and the reception of the Spirit (Acts 8:18-24). The question about what the unbeliever receives in Baptism did not become a theme for theological reflection until the controversy regarding heretical Baptism. This question was not yet explored in the controversy between Pope Stephen and Cyprian but received systematic treatment in the conflict between Augustine and the Donatists.

According to Augustine the nonbeliever receives only the baptismal sacrament but not the baptismal grace. What significance, then, does the validity of this Baptism have? Although the nonbeliever does not receive grace, he does not remain untouched by Baptism and is not the same after Baptism as he was before. For through Baptism the "distinguishing mark of the Lord" has been stamped upon him similar to the "royal mark" that was given soldiers, or the impress of a coin or seal. The nonbeliever, too, has been made Christ's property. Already before Augustine Baptism was called a seal and impress according to the image of Christ, and this sealing was understood as an operation of the Holy Spirit and as a pledge of eternal life. But Augustine separated the seal from the reception of the Holy Spirit, just as he separated the concept of a sacrament from grace. Augustine spoke of the abiding "character" which the nonbeliever receives as well as the believer and because of which he is distinguished from the unbaptized as one who belongs to the Lord. If he later comes to faith he must not be rebaptized, but he is assured of the forgiveness of sins by the laying on of hands, and now the grace of Baptism becomes effective.

The concept of the character which is imparted also to the nonbeliever through Baptism was more carefully defined by Thomas. Here too it does not mean character in the present sense, but it signifies that the soul has been stamped in an objective way, a process that is differentiated from grace. Through Baptism the nonbeliever receives only the *character dominicus*, while the believer also receives grace. Here the character is understood as a sealing for enlistment, as being stamped

128

for priestly service. The sacramental "character is a kind of seal by which the soul is marked, so that it may receive, or bestow on others, things pertaining to divine worship."[16] Together with the character also the ability to fulfill the obligation is imparted,[17] but this capacity is distinguished from the reception of grace. Since Christ's priesthood is eternal, the sacramental mark, this being stamped for priestly service, is ineradicable in the soul.

Luther likewise granted unbelief merely the reception of the sacrament but not the reception of grace. Where "faith is lacking, it remains a mere unfruitful sign."[18] But he was less concerned about what happened to the nonbeliever in Baptism than about what God has placed at the nonbeliever's disposal through Baptism. His statements about this problem have less the structure of positing facts than of invitation. From this point of view we must understand his reference even to the Baptism of nonbelievers as a "treasure." It is "not the treasure that is lacking; rather, what is lacking is that it should be grasped and held firmly."[19] In the use of this term Luther distinguishes less strictly between the valid sacrament and grace than [is done] in the Thomistic distinction between character and grace. Luther uses the word "treasure" to designate both the Word in Baptism,[20] as well as the benefit of Baptism,[21] as well as the Baptism that was received without faith and benefit.[22] In the act of proclamation it is not the theoretical clarification of what the nonbeliever receives in distinction from the believer that is in the foreground, but rather the call to repentance and the invitation to make use of the proffered treasure and to receive the promised grace by faith. It is not the enlistment of the nonbeliever as a result of Baptism that stands in the foreground, but the promise which has been made also to him, although a Baptism without faith is a treasure that is not used and hence leaves the person under God's judgment.

The various answers to the question concerning the significance of Baptism for the nonbeliever have this in common: He is no longer in the same situation in which he was before. There is no return of the baptized to the status of the pagans. The baptized stand under God's judgment and God's grace in a special way. Even though the New Testament does not so directly express a warning against a Baptism to judgment as it does a warning against eating and drinking the Lord's Supper to judgment, the concern in both cases is with the reality of the divine activity.

All of these statements about Baptism presuppose their acknowledgment of Baptism as the promise, sign, and deed of God. If, on the contrary, Baptism is viewed merely as an act of human obedience, a Baptism received without faith cannot logically be regarded as valid. It must be repeated when it is requested in faith.

Of course it must be borne in mind that the concept of faith is not always the same in these various answers. For Augustine faith meant also love to the believers and thus membership in the community of the Catholic Church. He denied baptismal grace even to those who believed in Jesus Christ but did not become members of the Catholic Church. Luther's understanding of faith as trusting reception burst through this limitation. He reckoned with the reception of baptismal grace even outside the Reformation churches. In the Roman Church an important break-through in the Augustinian boundary of the church was achieved in the "Dogmatic Constitution on the Church," of Vatican II. Emphatic reference is there made to "elements or endowments" which exist also outside the Roman Catholic Church. In this connection Baptism is mentioned especially, but not only with reference to its validity. "They also share with us in prayer and other spiritual benefits. Likewise, we can say that in some real way they are joined with us in the Holy Spirit, for to them also [Christians separated from the Roman Church] He gives His gifts and graces, and is thereby operative among them with His sanctifying power. Some indeed He has strengthened to the extent of the shedding of their blood." [23]

4. Infant Baptism

In view of what has been said about the relationship between Baptism and faith it is not self-evident that the church baptizes children, and even infants. The term "infant Baptism" is imprecise and subject to misunderstanding, for the church does not baptize all children. As a rule the concern is with the children of baptized parents who bring them to Baptism and also the children of unbaptized parents who desire Baptism for themselves and their children, and occasionally orphaned children who are adopted and reared by Christians. In all these cases we are therefore dealing with such children as will grow up within the sphere of the church. Hence, infant Baptism does not mean the Baptism of children in any case, but of such children as have already been born within the sphere of the church. Thus the term infant Baptism is narrower than it sounds. Yet even with this qualification, the fact remains that infants cannot make a decision of faith, they cannot make a confession of sin and of faith, they cannot come of their own accord but must be carried to Baptism. But a distinction between infants and children who can at least perceive the baptismal act or even give their consent to it plays no role in the customary practice of infant Baptism.

The problem of infant Baptism is a problem of the proper order in the administration of Baptism. To that extent this matter belongs in the last chapter of this doctrine of Baptism which treats of the "form of the baptismal act." Now every question of church order is a dogmatic question at the same time. But this is especially true of infant Baptism. Here all problems involved in the understanding of Baptism are concentrated in a peculiar way. Here we are dealing not only with the relationship of faith and Baptism, but also with the relationship of Baptism and God's deed, as well as Baptism and church. For that reason we shall separate infant Baptism from the treatment of the other problems dealing with the form of the administration of Baptism. We shall discuss it as the conclusion of the interrelated chapters two and three, that is, as conclusion to the teaching of God's saving deed through Baptism and the teaching of the administration and reception of Baptism.

a. The origin of infant Baptism and its rejection

There is dispute about the time when infant Baptism originated. In historical-critical scholarship, at the beginning of this century, the conviction was widespread that the primitive church did not practice infant Baptism, but since the 20s this opinion was shaken by Albrecht Oepke,[24] Johannes Leipold,[25] Joachim Jeremias,[26] and Oscar Cullmann.[27] In a most comprehensive way J. Jeremias advanced the arguments in favor of assuming the practice of infant Baptism in the primitive church and maintained the thesis that from the beginning children born before the Baptism of their parents were baptized together with their parents, although this did not yet apply to children born of Christian parents. In testing the individual arguments of Jeremias, Kurt Aland[28] came to the conclusion that the primitive church baptized no infants, and that the Baptism of children did not arise until the 2d century, while the Baptism of infants was not practiced until about 200.

We are interested especially in the origin of infant Baptism. Following the method of Aland we shall begin with the first witnesses and look for earlier traces from there.

(1) The earliest reliable attestations to infant Baptism appear around 200.

In his treatise, "Against Heretics," (after 180) Irenaeus explains the statement that Jesus "came to save" by adding, "all, I say, who through Him are born again to God — infants [*infantes*], and children [*parvulos*], and boys, and youths, and old men." [29] The fact that the context speaks of Jesus "sanctifying every age by that period corresponding to it which belonged to Himself" cannot be exploited against the fact that to be "born again" *(renasci)* is a technical term for Baptism.[30] The conclusion is valid that in the area of the Gallican church infants were baptized already in the 2d century.

The church order of Hippolytus, which originated in Rome about 215, contains the directive: "First the little ones should be baptized. All who can speak for themselves should speak. For those however who cannot, their parents or another who belongs to their family should speak." [31] These sentences appear in both the Latin text and in the Eastern translations of the church order. Since infant Baptism is attested also elsewhere for the same period, it is not likely that we are dealing with an interpolation from a later date.[32] In view of the character of a church order it must be regarded as plausible that infant Baptism had been practiced for a considerable time before Hippolytus. For the church orders of that period as a rule did not impose new orders, but made adjustments to their time primarily through the manner in which they brought existing orders together.

It is clear from Tertullian's treatise on Baptism that infants were baptized in the area of the African church around the year 200. Tertullian opposed this practice: "Let them (children) 'come' therefore when they grow older; let them 'come' when they are able to learn, when they can be instructed whither they should 'come'; let them become Christians when they can know Christ." [33] Hence the chief reason for his warning is the inability of children to understand and make their own decision. Tertullian further urges against infant Baptism, "Why does the age of innocence hasten to the remission of sins?" [34] This sentence seems to contradict what Tertullian said in his writing, "On the Soul," that "practically no birth is pure." [35] Perhaps this contradiction could be resolved if in this writing only pagans were referred to, while in the treatise on Baptism the children of Christian parents were meant, children whom Tertullian regards as sanctified on the basis of 1 Cor. 7:14.[36] A further argument against infant Baptism is the danger for the sponsors, who may be prevented by an untimely death from keeping their promise or be disappointed in the way the growing children develop.[37] Tertullian also advises virgins and widows to postpone Baptism because they are endangered through temptations. But Tertullian does not say one word to suggest that his opposition to infant Baptism rests on its being an innovation. His opposition seems rather to foretell an ethical rigorism which subsequently led Tertullian into Montanism. He understood Baptism not as an aid in the battle against temptations but rather as a "heavy burden." [38] It is important to note that in spite of all his criticism, Tertullian in no way contested the validity of the Baptism of infants; he merely regarded postponement as "more beneficial." [39] One cannot gather from his remarks that the failure to practice infant Baptism led to a separation from the church. Obviously at that time infant Baptism had not yet become obligatory in Africa. As such it appears in the days of Cyprian. In his letter to Fidus, Cyprian refers to a synod of Carthage around 251 which decreed that the children should be baptized right after their birth, not on the 8th day.[40]

About 240, Origen in his homilies on Luke and his commentary on Romans mentions the Baptism of infants three times.[41] Whereas Hippolytus designated his church order on the whole as apostolic, Origen made this claim specifically for infant Baptism: The "church received a tradition from the apostles to give Baptism to infants too." [42] Origen also points out that even a day-old human being is not free from sin. From this argument it is not at all necessary to conclude that infant Baptism was only beginning to assert itself in his time. Even long-standing church practices may one day become the object of theological reflection — for a variety of reasons. Since the writings of Origen referred to were composed in Palestine, it is debatable whether his statements about infant Baptism refer only to this area or also to other regions of the church visited by him. The latter is more probable since he appeals to apostolic tradition.

Thus infant Baptism from ca. 200 has been documented from greatly different areas of the church. It is remarkable how much this practice is regarded as self-evident. Nowhere is there a reference to the counter argument that infant Baptism was an innovation. It is certain that this practice did not arise only about the year 200. Even Tertullian acknowledged this Baptism as valid, although he warned against it. Yet it cannot be assumed for that period that this practice was spread equally in all areas of the church. In particular, it cannot be presupposed that this practice was obligatory everywhere. In Africa at any rate such a firmly established order does not become evident until Cyprian's letter to Fidus.[43] From Byzantium and Cappadocia we have the tradition that even in the second half of the 3d century the children of Christian parents were by no means generally baptized. In this postponement of Baptism it is debated,[44] however, whether infant Baptism had not yet established itself or whether in opposition to an already established practice people subsequently had doubts similar to those of Tertullian. The admonition of Gregory of Nazianzen might point in this direction. He suggested that Baptism be deferred to the age of 3 years when children are able to perceive the baptismal act. Yet when in danger of death the infant was to be baptized at once. The immediate Baptism of the children of Christian parents and the postponement of Baptism occurred side by side in the same church. In contrast to Tertullian the great Cappadocians argued against postponement by insisting that Baptism is not a gift that is endangered and must be anxiously guarded but an aid in the ethical conflict. In the controversy between Augustine and Pelagius infant Baptism was already a general assumption, accepted by both sides.

(2) If we move back from these certain witnesses into the 2d century we find no convincing support for the practice of infant Baptism. What is said about Baptism in the *Didache* and the first *Apology* of Justin makes no mention of infant Baptism, although it does not exclude it. The same is true of the remaining baptismal texts of the postapostolic and early patristic period. An exception is the *Apology* of Aristides, but from it we can gather with certainty only that children were baptized in an age when they could already be taught.[45] The statements of Polycarp and other Acts of the Martyrs, concerning the large number of years during which these witnesses served Christ from childhood on, do not permit any sure *a posteriori* conclusion that they were baptized already as infants. Just as little do the inscriptions offer any reliable support. On the other hand, it cannot be cogently inferred from the development of the catechumenate that the special case of infant Baptism was excluded.

Nor does the New Testament contain any explicit statements for or against the Baptism of small children. We can only draw *a posteriori* conclusions. Of special significance are the statements of Paul (1 Cor. 1:16) and of Luke (Acts 11:14; 16:15, 33; 18:8) concerning the Baptism of an entire "house." But the word "house" in both Old and New Testaments can mean such different things [46] that it is not proper to speak of an established "oikos-formula." [47] These passages do, however, make clear that the totality of the family is involved, and this in principle includes children, the slaves, and their children. But of course the texts do not say that there were children or, indeed, infants in the families mentioned by Paul and Luke. The unity of the family in Christ is the concern also of the tables of duties, especially in the "deutero-Pauline" letters, with their admonitions to husband and wife, parents and children, masters and slaves. But these do not indicate to us whether or when the children were baptized. Nevertheless, the presupposed understanding of the family as a fellowship in Christ is so important for our question that it is difficult to rule out the possibility of infant Baptism in primitive Christendom.

Even more uncertain are the conclusions drawn from proselyte Baptism which included the children. On the one hand, it cannot be proved beyond a doubt that this Baptism was already a widespread practice at the time when the first Christian community arose, and on the other hand, it cannot be demonstrated conclusively that the Christian church took over the practice of infant Baptism from that of proselyte Baptism. No conclusions can be drawn from the initiation rites of the mystery cults because they did not involve infants. Other arguments drawn from the New Testament are not convincing either, as, for example, reference to the correspondences between Matt. 18:3, Mark 10:15 (Luke 18:17), and John 3:5,[48] or the interpretation of Acts 2:38 f., applied to the children of the people addressed,[49] while precisely in Luke's thought this may well refer to the succession of generations. Nor can the primitive Christian practice of infant Baptism be cogently derived from the fact that the word "hinder" is found in various New Testament reports of Baptism as well as in the Synoptic tradition of Jesus' blessing of the children,[50] even though there might be the use of a formula here. And 1 Cor. 7:14 cannot be used as an argument for infant Baptism, since the passage speaks not only of a sanctification of children but also of the pagan husband. This text involves

135

an additional concept of a sanctification which is not only imparted through Baptism, and therefore speaks against infant Baptism rather than for it.

Thus on the basis of the New Testament infant Baptism can neither be excluded nor proved, and the question remains whether the fact that we have no reliable witnesses to this baptismal practice until about the year 200 is to be explained by the late origin of this practice or by the late beginning of theological reflection on this practice or by the accident of sources that have been preserved. It is certain that the Baptism of little children was already common in the 2d century without being a generally obligatory arrangement.

(3) Tertullian's warning against infant Baptism and the postponement of Baptism in the 4th century as reported from Byzantium and Cappadocia are fundamentally different from a rejection of the validity of infant Baptism and the demand to rebaptize those who had been baptized as children. This rejection cannot be documented with certainty until the 16th century. It is one of the most important characteristics of the Baptist movement which spread from Zurich and then, after the early extermination of its leaders, continued among the Mennonites and later, in a quite different way, in the Baptist bodies. These movements made their appeal not only to the New Testament and the early church,[51] but also to later separations from the great church, especially the Albigenses and the Waldensians. However, the Albigenses rejected water Baptism altogether, and the Waldensians, to the extent that they denied the validity of Baptisms performed by the Roman Church at all, may have been influenced by Donatistic motives which were not specifically directed against infant Baptism. The prehistory of the Baptist movement is difficult to elucidate since the documents of the various ancient and medieval separations from the imperial church were mostly destroyed. There is much, however, in favor of the idea that the rejection of infant Baptism as a matter of principle arose only in the 16th century as a result of a new understanding of the individual person and his responsibility for sanctification.

b. Individual theological arguments for and against infant Baptism

The question concerning the theological basis for infant Baptism must be distinguished from the historical question concerning its origin. Even if it could be proved historically that infant Baptism was practiced in primitive Christendom, this would not yet constitute a theological basis for the practice. But even the fact that infant Baptism became universally established in a few centuries cannot take the place of a theological basis. Time-bound sociological factors may have been at work, factors which do not permit universally valid basic conclusions. Nor is it a convincing argument to assert with Luther that God put up with infant Baptism for so long a time [52] and that "God at all times has given great and holy gifts to many who were baptized as children, and has enlightened and strengthened them with the Holy Spirit and the understanding of the Scriptures." [53] For these spiritual effects might also have been imparted through the Word of God and the Lord's Supper in spite of infant Baptism. On the contrary, the fact that infant Baptism established itself universally in the first centuries only by a gradual process is no proof against its legitimacy. Even if it could be proved that in the missionary situation of primitive Christendom children were nowhere baptized, this would not refute the legitimacy of infant Baptism. There have been other questions of order, for example, questions pertaining to worship and the church's offices, in which the church had to make changes to do justice to new situations and new tasks. For this reason we must ask about the theological arguments advanced for or against infant Baptism.

In the history of the theology of Baptism it is surprising how late and how sparsely theological arguments in favor of infant Baptism appear in the documents. The conclusion is obvious that infant Baptism was so self-evident and unproblematical that any justification of the practice was superfluous. Irenaeus asserted the sanctification of all ages of life by Jesus, and Origen pointed to the apostolic origin of infant Baptism and to the fact of sin in support of it. But not until the time of Augustine, in his controversy with Pelagius, was there a more comprehensive argumentation, and even here it is a question whether Augustine was primarily concerned with establishing and defending infant Baptism or whether he made use of the universal practice of infant Baptism as an argument against the Pelagian denial of original sin. In his brief comments on infant Baptism, Thomas Aquinas refrained from individual arguments from the New and Old Testament (for example, the Baptism of houses and circumcision) and confined himself essentially to references to original sin and the faith of the church.[54] He answered the question concerning the faith of children by distinguishing between *"habitus fidei"* and *"actus fidei."* [55] Not until the debates between the reformers and the Anabaptists is there a heaping up of individual arguments in support of infant Baptism. This was the case especially with Luther's writing "To Two Pastors Concerning Anabaptism" [56] and Calvin's *Institutes*.[57]

We cannot here offer a historical presentation of the individual theological arguments which have been advanced by the various fronts for and against infant Baptism. In what follows we shall from a systematic perspective limit ourselves to some of the most commonly used Biblical references.

In favor of the Baptism of little children the baptismal command of Matthew 28 has been cited again and again. This command is universal. The Risen One sends out His disciples to make disciples of the Gentile world, "all nations." No exception is mentioned. Hence the inference that children are included in the baptismal command. This "making disciples" is to be done by means of Baptism and teaching. This sequence has also led to the conclusion that Jesus' commission includes the Baptism of infants with whom instruction must follow Baptism. However, in the baptismal command the children are explicitly excluded as little as they are explicitly mentioned. The sequence baptizing—teaching need not be understood as a temporal sequence. Even though the teaching is to follow Baptism, the proclamation preceding Baptism and the believing acceptance of this proclamation might as a rule be presupposed.

In support of infant Baptism the story of Jesus blessing little children (Mark 10:13-16; cf. Matt. 19:13-15 and Luke 18:15-17), the so-called "children's Gospel," is frequently adduced—in part also in the baptismal liturgy. The account concerns little children who are carried and whom Luke expressly calls "infants." The word of Jesus, "to such belongs the kingdom of God," should perhaps be construed as a synthetic rather than an analytic judgment, that is, Jesus awards these children the kingdom of God and through His "blessing" grants them participation in it (Mark 10:16). Since reception of the kingdom of God and fellowship with Jesus cannot be separated from each other, the inference is drawn from this text that if Jesus had the children brought to Him and gave them participation in the kingdom of God, the church has the right and the duty to make the infants Christ's own through Baptism. But the text contains neither an order to the disciples to con-

138

tinue in the blessing of children nor a command to baptize the children. The text says nothing *directly* about Baptism.

A reference to circumcision plays an important role especially in the Reformed tradition. Col. 2:11 ff. indeed calls Christian Baptism a circumcision. In Christ "also you were circumcised with a circumcision made without hands, by putting off the body of flesh in the circumcision of Christ; and you were buried with Him in baptism. . . ." Yet it is not yet such a New Testament metaphor but primarily the understanding of the unity of the Old and the New covenant, as well as the identity of the divine promise given in circumcision and Baptism that leads to the inference: if circumcision was applied to infants in the Old Covenant, then the church has the right and the duty to baptize the children born in her midst. Since there is a difference between circumcision and Baptism only in the ceremonial form but not in the divine covenant promise, also conclusions by analogy with regard to the time of circumcision and the time of Baptism are permitted and even demanded.[58] But it is beyond doubt that the difference between the New and the Old Covenant as well as the Pauline antithesis between Baptism and circumcision have not been sufficiently noted. Luther rightly employed the argument of circumcision only in a very peripheral way in view of the difference between the two Testaments and their signs. Thomas Aquinas does not use this reference at all. While he acknowledged the preparatory and typical significance of circumcision, he emphasized the newness of Baptism, given by Christ's coming, over against circumcision.[59]

Since in Calvin's view the "external form, economy, and administration," but not the "substance" of the Old Covenant was changed in the New Covenant,[60] the Old Testament may be used also in another respect to support infant Baptism. From the doctrine of the unity of the covenant the inference is drawn that since the children of the Old Covenant were a holy seed, also the children of Christians are regarded as holy, and therefore they may not be deprived of Baptism, the sign of the New Covenant. If "the covenant still remains firm and steadfast, it applies no less today to the children of Christians than under the Old Testament it pertained to the infants of the Jews. Yet if they are participants in the thing signified [namely, on the basis of their descent from Christian parents] why shall they be debarred from the sign [namely, Baptism]?"[61] Calvin presented this argument in great detail. In this connection he also considered 1 Cor. 7:14. Like the children of the

Jews "the children of Christians are considered holy; and even though born with only one believing parent, by the apostle's testimony they differ from the unclean seed of idolators." For that reason the covenant is to be "sealed" in the children of Christians through Baptism.[62] Calvin is here arguing not on the basis of physical descent from Christian parents as such, but on the basis of the covenant promise which God gave His people for all generations. Nevertheless the physical descent in fact receives here a sanctifying and renewing significance that is foreign to the New Testament understanding of the church as the people of God called out of this world. Furthermore, this physical descent seems to leave nothing for Baptism but the significance of a confirmation and sealing of the sanctification that was already received by birth.

Against infant Baptism the primary argument is that in the New Testament accounts repentance, faith, and the desire for Baptism precede Baptism and that the candidate must himself take the initiative in coming to Baptism. Beyond this, the experience of Baptism in the Spirit is not infrequently demanded as a prerequisite for the administration of water Baptism. Even though in the accounts in the Book of Acts acceptance of the Gospel and therewith repentance and faith preceded the reception of Baptism, yet allowance must be made for the fact that in the New Testament epistles' numerous baptismal statements, seldom is reference made to the faith that precedes Baptism, and hence to the faith – Baptism sequence. They rather recall God's saving deed in Baptism and summon to a life flowing from faith in this foundational deed. They are here not concerned with the baptismal experience as such, but rather with God's new-creating deed that was accomplished once for all and that must be taken seriously in faith and conduct ever again. Moreover the New Testament accounts of Baptism mention the gift of the Holy Spirit only very rarely as having preceded Baptism. As a rule this gift is attested as an effect of Baptism.

Against infant Baptism it is also urged that it is generally administered in Western Christendom by pouring or sprinkling but not by immersion, and thus the act of being buried and raised with Christ is not demonstrated. But immersion in the primitive church cannot be generally assumed, because a sufficient supply of water cannot be presupposed everywhere in the East. Furthermore, the symbolical interpretation of the baptismal act probably did not play the role in the primitive church that is assumed here.

140

We could continue analyzing further individual arguments based on the Bible. But if the defense and the rejection of infant Baptism were to rely solely on such individual arguments, the justification of infant Baptism could be neither proved nor disproved. For such arguments in isolation are partly inadequate, partly irrelevant. In general, in the use of such individual arguments *pro* and *con* we must beware of a Biblicism which allows the Christian to do only what is expressly commanded in the Bible and which forbids everything that is not expressly commanded. Such a legalism would render the Christians incapable of performing their divinely appointed service in the course of history.

The decision for or against infant Baptism is to be made neither on the basis of the historical question about its age nor in the presentation of such individual arguments. We must rather go behind the individual arguments and search out the theological contexts within which these arguments become valid. The affirmation as well as the negation of infant Baptism is conditioned primarily by comprehensive insights and not by individual arguments of this kind. Which are these foundational presuppositions?

It may be assumed that in the battle over infant Baptism differences in anthropology manifest themselves, and this is partly the case. This is especially clear in the affirmation of infant Baptism by Origen, Cyprian, and Augustine in their reference to original sin, while Tertullian spoke of the "innocent age" in his criticism of infant Baptism.[63] Thus Aland finds in the historical development of the dogma of original sin the "inner motive" [64] for the spread and success of infant Baptism. But quite apart from the moot question whether and in what sense the idea of the children's innocence stands at the beginning of the history of Baptism,[65] anthropology cannot be acknowledged as the decisive prerequisite for the affirmation or negation of infant Baptism. Infant Baptism was practiced already before the doctrine of original sin had established itself, and Chrysostom still baptized children in the conviction that they were without sin. The doctrine of original sin never made its way in the East with the same consistency as in the West, and yet infant Baptism became general practice also in the East. On the other side, the denial of original sin is by no means characteristic of the Baptist movement. So, for example, Balthasar Hubmaier explicitly affirmed the doctrine of original sin,[66] even though he leaned toward Erasmus in the question of the freedom of the will. Pilgram Marbeck's "Epistle Concerning Five-fold Fruits of True Repentance" (1550) [67] shows how deep and comprehensive the understanding of sin was in Baptist circles. But above all the doctrine of original sin was recognized in its full severity at the origin of the English Baptists, who rejected infant Baptism on the basis of Calvin's doctrine of sin and predestination. This Calvinistic background operated also in the German Baptist position of Johann Gerhard Oncken.[68] It is true, in the history of the Baptist movement there have also been some Pelagian dilutions; but, as is known, such inclinations have appeared also in those churches which have maintained infant Baptism.

As important as the connections between Baptism and anthropology are, the decisive prerequisites for supporting or rejecting infant Baptism are to be sought in the understanding of Baptism itself and, very closely connected with it, in the understanding of the church. It is only in connection with these two prerequisites that the controverted question concerning the relationship of faith and infant Baptism can be answered. On the other hand, as long as the problem of infant Baptism is seen exclusively in the problem area of the temporal sequence of faith and Baptism, only the surface is being considered.

c. Inferences from the understanding of Baptism for the attitude toward infant Baptism

1. The fact that infant Baptism established itself so self-evidently in the ancient church, that it was felt so little as a problem, and that according to the sources it was never rejected in principle, that is, was never regarded as invalid and needing repetition, rests in the first instance on the certainty that God is graciously active in Baptism. There was no thought of the exceptional case of a heretical Baptism or of a deceitful reception of Baptism, but the concern was one of faith in the saving activity of God through Baptism on behalf of man in need of grace. People thought differently about the innocence and sin of children and therefore also about their being subject to judgment, and no clear distinctions were as yet made between man's sinful nature and his sinful decisions. Yet even before the doctrine of original sin was formulated, and at the same time as thoughts of the innocence of

142

infants were entertained, there was present a perception of the child's weakness and poverty, as well as of the temptations and dangers that would beset the growing child. In short, there was a realization that the child had to depend on the grace of God. Whether this dependence was understood only as a lack or as original sin and subjection to judgment—what is decisive for the practice of infant Baptism is the conviction that through Baptism God has mercy also on the children, makes them Christ's own, and transfers them by the Holy Spirit from the dominion of sin, death, and devil into the life of the children of God. No matter how different the statements about the saving activity of God through Baptism sound in detail, they are all concerned with the certainty of a onetime, foundational act of God's grace—an act which determines and embraces the entire subsequent life of the baptized. Also in later times the practice of infant Baptism was primarily supported by this certainty, and this certainty is rooted in the baptismal statements of the New Testament.

The more certainly Baptism is recognized as God's saving deed, the more certain it is at the same time that the baptized is purely the recipient. Repentance, faith, approach to Baptism, confession of faith, these are the end of self-activity, they are reception, and this reception is itself the effect of grace which enables us to recognize and confess God's saving deed. But if Baptism and faith are God's saving deed, then faith cannot onesidedly be demanded as precondition and prerequisite for the reception of Baptism. Faith can also be expected as the effect of God's saving activity through Baptism. If faith is understood as a conscious act of knowing, acknowledging, and trusting, an act that finds expression in the confession of faith, then the infant is capable of doing this neither before Baptism nor immediately after it. However, the reception of the saving deed which embraces man and his entire life until his death cannot be limited to conscious acts of faith, of repentance, and of confession. The saving activity of God cannot be made to depend on man's activity. The limit of man's psychic possibilities is not the limit of God's grace. By baptizing the children in the certainty that they receive not only a valid Baptism but also the baptismal grace, the church respects this mystery of reception, which is not accomplished only in conscious acts but which is already the precondition for conscious acts.

143

In the history of the doctrine of Baptism various groping statements have been made about this matter. According to Augustine,
in infant Baptism the sacrament itself takes the place of the missing faith
of the person to be baptized, and reference is made to the representa-
tive faith of the church. Knowing that infants cannot produce the act
of faith and of love, Thomas taught that the effect of their Baptism was
the habit of faith which subsequently makes possible the acts of faith
and of love when the children grow up—"thus also when a man is
asleep, though he may have the habits of virtue, yet is he hindered from
virtuous acts through being asleep." [69] Hence through Baptism the child
receives not only the "character" but also grace. In this connection the
nominalists occasionally spoke of an "infused faith" (*fides infusa*). In
Luther's close bracketing of faith and benefit of Baptism, infant faith
received special emphasis in the argument for infant Baptism. He too
knew that the infant could not produce acts of faith, and he did not
describe infant faith as trust, obedience, etc. He understood faith as
a pure gift of God, as operation of the Holy Spirit which is received
in a completely passive manner. "Luther indeed described infant faith
in connection with infant Baptism as a gift of God poured into the children through the 'Word,' but he never said that this faith is also a 'grasping' on the child's part of the promise in Baptism or a 'clinging' to the
water" (Karl Brinkel).[70] The child can decide neither for God nor for
an idol. "The Word of God really effects the little child's 'being addressed,' or, as Luther says, its 'hearing.' Thus in a little child infant faith
is identical with its being addressed by God's Word and for that reason
it is 'gift of God.'" [71] Even though this Word of God precedes Baptism
as sermon or exorcism, it dare not be separated from the promise that
is given expression to in Baptism. Thus also Luther teaches that the
child receives not only a valid Baptism but also the baptismal grace,
deliverance from sin and death, as well as regeneration and adoption
as God's child.[72] Also Zwingli and Calvin conceded the possibility of
the Spirit's activity in infants. Pointing to the Spirit's activity in John
the Baptist in his mother's womb (Luke 1:15) and to the conception of
Jesus by the Holy Spirit, Calvin rejects the idea "that infants cannot
be regenerated by God's power, which is as easy and ready to Him as
it is incomprehensible and wonderful to us." [73] It is true that Zwingli
and Calvin did not look upon this activity of the Spirit as an effect of
Baptism. But in any case God's gracious activity does not depend on

144

man's psychic presuppositions and concrete decisions. Neither the child nor the adult is capable of coming to faith by his own strength. Faith is the work of the Holy Spirit. However doubtful they may be individually, the considerations mentioned point to this mystery.

When Baptism is seen as God's saving deed, the second and third of the above mentioned relationships between faith and Baptism in infant Baptism move into the foreground. Faith is the effect of Baptism through which God imparts the beginning of the Spirit's activity, an activity of which the baptized later becomes conscious by faith and which becomes the response of the believer in the form of confession. At the same time the admonition applies to ever anew lay hold of the saving deed of God received in Baptism and to die with Christ in daily repentance.

2. However, if Baptism is not understood as God's saving deed for man but as man's act of obedience to God — not as a sign under which God acts in a forgiving and new-creating way, but as a sign by means of which man commits himself to God, then infant Baptism must be rejected, not only as a means of grace but also as a valid Baptism. Since the infant cannot obligate himself by his own act of confession, his Baptism is no Baptism. It must be repeated when the child has grown up and come to conscious faith and has become capable of approaching Baptism and making his confession by his own decision.

The more one-sidedly Baptism is viewed as man's deed, the less faith will be understood as reception, and the more it takes on voluntaristic and activistic characteristics. As man's decision faith now becomes the condition for the reception of Baptism. In the process it is not only faith that remains as the condition. Now everything that according to the New Testament may be expected of Baptism as God's gift can more or less explicitly be demanded as precondition for Baptism. It is true that the Schleitheim Confession only demands that Baptism "shall be given to all those who have learned repentance and amendment of life, and who believe truly that their sins are taken away by Christ, and to all those who walk in the resurrection of Jesus Christ, and wish to be buried with Him in death. . . ." [74] Yet in many Baptist texts down to the present the experience of having died with Christ, of Baptism in the Spirit, and of regeneration is already mentioned as precondition for Baptism. These experiences are understood in part as effects of the divine Word, in part also as immediate effects of the Spirit. From the perspective of such a view of faith Luther's statements about the faith of children, and indeed Calvin's statements about their spiritual rebirth must seem absurd. This aspect of experience may even recede entirely in the case of those who view Baptism as a confessional act on the part of man. Thus in his statements on Baptism, Zwingli referred less to the personal act of faith than to the content of the church's confession. With Karl Barth the decisive presupposition for the act of obedience in Baptism is the fact that in the onetime death of Jesus Christ all men have already died with Christ and are already justified; hence the Baptism in the Spirit which precedes Baptism primarily produces the recognition of this universally valid fact.

If Baptism is understood as man's act of obedience and sign of obligation, then the first of the above mentioned three relationships between faith and Baptism necessarily moves to the fore. The temporal sequence, faith — Baptism, has thus become for the Baptists an unalterable law and the norm for the validity or invalidity of Baptism. The third relationship, that of faith's reflection on Baptism, is indeed not missing, but it has a character different from that contained in New Testament exhortation. For the reflection is now concerned not with God's gracious deed in Baptism, but with the obligation discharged by means of Baptism.

3. Between these opposing conclusions arising from contradictory views of Baptism Zwingli occupies a position of his own, peculiar and self-contradictory. From his understanding of Baptism as sign of obligation and confession the rejection of infant Baptism follows logically, and before the appearance of the Anabaptists Zwingli was quite logically critical of infant Baptism.[75] Infants are not capable of confessing their faith. Yet he retained infant Baptism. Early Anabaptists rightly appealed to Zwingli's teaching on Baptism, and when he persecuted them they accused him of denying his own teaching. It is no accident that the Anabaptist movement originated in Zwingli's intimate circle of friends. Even though in his last writings Zwingli understood Baptism not only as an act of confession but also as representation of grace, this still did not justify infant Baptism, since he emphatically distinguished this representation of grace from an impartation of grace and because infants cannot recognize such a representation. It is true, between Zwingli and the Anabaptists, in spite of their common understanding of Baptism as an act of confession, there were differences in so far as Zwingli saw this

act of confession determined less by subjective experiences than by the objective content of the Creed. Furthermore, Zwingli was shocked by incidental enthusiastic claims concerning the sinlessness of the rebaptized, and in the insistence of the Anabaptists on the necessity of rebaptism he suspected the danger of a relapse into the view of Baptism an an *opus operatum*. But the real reason for his retention of infant Baptism is to be seen not in his understanding of Baptism as such but in the Anabaptists' calling the civil order into question and especially in their rejection of the traditional unity of the Christian community and the civil community. In favor of the view that Zwingli's retention of infant Baptism was based ultimately on his understanding of the church is also his increasing emphasis, in the course of his arguments with the Anabaptists, on Baptism as the sign of obligation on the part of the church, a sign by which she acknowledges the baptized as her member — and not only as the sign of obligation on the part of the believing baptized.

Calvin's teaching differs extensively from Zwingli's approach. Here Baptism, in its decisive aspect, is the sign which *God* gives in assurance of salvation. Calvin understood the confession of the baptized not only as precondition but also as a part of Baptism. It is "the mark by which we publicly profess that we wish to be reckoned God's people." [76] Thus Calvin incorporated Zwingli's perspective into his own definition of the essence of Baptism. But here the confession plays a decidedly inferior role over against the significance of Baptism which controls the whole, namely Baptism as the sign and seal of *God.* However, in Calvin's theology the few statements about Baptism as means of the divine saving action recede entirely behind the dominant understanding of Baptism as a means of providing assurance of salvation, so that the reception of salvation and the assurance of salvation are distinguished as separate acts and in general are separated also in time. Therefore the question arises here too, whether infant Baptism can be justified on the basis of such an understanding of Baptism. For the causative significance of Baptism has been so greatly weakened or rejected altogether and, on the contrary, the cognitive significance for the assurance of faith has been made so prominent that it does not seem logical to baptize children who are not yet competent to discern the divine sign. Even though Calvin teaches Baptism as a promise that is valid for the entire life of the baptized and says that the children should be baptized in view of their future

147

faith, it remains more consonant with his cognitive understanding of Baptism not to administer Baptism until the person is able to recognize the sign. It is true that in distinction from Zwingli's approach and that of the Anabaptists it does not follow from Calvin's teaching on Baptism that infant Baptism in invalid, but it does raise the question whether infant Baptism can be retained as the appropriate order for baptismal practice. These difficulties may help us to understand why in the last edition of his *Institutes* Calvin devotes more space to a defence of infant Baptism than to all the rest of his baptismal teaching, and this defence, as already frequently mentioned, is presented by heaping up individual arguments without much systematic coherence. A careful examination of these arguments makes clear that also Calvin's support of infant Baptism rests less on his understanding of Baptism than on his understanding of the church, or, more accurately, on his view of the identity of Old and New Covenants. But if Calvin's baptismal theology is viewed in isolation from his understanding of the church, it would seem that Karl Barth in *The Teaching of the Church Concerning Baptism* (1943), where in the main he supported Calvin's position, was right in drawing the inference that infant Baptism must not be regarded as the appropriate order of Baptism. "If it is to be natural, the candidate, instead of being a passive object of baptism, must become once more the free partner of Jesus Christ, that is, freely deciding, freely confessing, declaring on his part his willingness and readiness." [77]

But K. Barth did not remain with Calvin. In the last volume of his *Church Dogmatics* (IV, 4) he explicitly moved away from Calvin and his own earlier position on Baptism and taught that Baptism is the act of the obedience of faith, similar to the position of Zwingli and the Anabaptists. Now he rejected not only the saving activity of God through Baptism, but also Baptism as a divine sign of assurance. Must not this understanding of Baptism lead to the conclusion that infant Baptism is no Baptism, since in it there is no act of obedience and confession on the part of the. baptized? Yet Barth did not draw this conclusion. While he emphatically warns against infant Baptism, he rejects the rebaptism of those who were baptized as infants. "Their Baptism was administered in an extremely doubtful and questionable manner, because it was improper. Yet this does not yet make it simply invalid." [78] The reasons for this inconsistency are here too probably to be sought elsewhere than in the doctrine of Baptism as such.

However, there are difficulties and inconsistencies also within the Baptist communities where the more recent historical exegesis of the New Testament material on Baptism has led people to see again that there a new-creating divine activity through Baptism is affirmed. It is impossible to reduce the understanding of Baptism to an acknowledgment of previously received regeneration and to an obligation of the baptized to obedience. But the more the New Testament witness to God's saving action in Baptism is again perceived, the more difficult it becomes to maintain a rejection of infant Baptism as valid Baptism. So, for example, the Baptist New Testament scholar, George Beasley-Murray, was led by his New Testament sacramental understanding of Baptism to propose: "Where an applicant was baptized as a child and was later received in due form into membership of a church by confession of faith, no matter by what ritual, he should be received into a Baptist congregation as if he came from another Baptist congregation, that is, by transfer." [79] If Beasley-Murray will go no farther in his acknowledgment of infant Baptism, this would seem to rest less on his understanding of Baptism than on his membership in the Baptist communion.

d. Inferences from the understanding of the church for the attitude toward infant Baptism

With a discussion of the conclusions resulting from the understanding of Baptism with reference to the problem of infant Baptism, the moot question of the relationship between faith and infant Baptism can not yet be adequately clarified. For the concern in Baptism is not only with something that happens between God and the baptized — whether Baptism is understood as God's activity on behalf of the baptized or the activity of the baptized in obedience toward God — but also with something that happens between God and the church. The church administers Baptism by God's command, and through Baptism the person baptized becomes a member of the church. Therefore an understanding of the church is also of great significance for the question of infant Baptism.

1. If Baptism is understood as God's saving activity, the church confronts the baptized as an instrument of the divine activity. By acting in obedience to her Lord's command the church's action is God's action. The words, "he who hears you hears Me" (Luke 10:16), apply also to

149

Baptism. When the church baptizes, Christ is at work and the triune God is baptizing. Although regeneration is the work of God's Spirit, Paul could write to the Galatians that he had given birth to them and was again in travail with them (Gal. 4:19). In the same context he also called attention to the "Jerusalem above." She is "free, and she is our mother" (v. 26). "So, brethren, we are not children of the slave but of the free woman" (v. 31). The church is the divinely called community of believers and at the same time the organ through whose word God calls men to faith and through whose baptizing God makes the believers members of the body of Christ. In this sense the church exists before the individual believer. The church does not come into being by the association of believers but is created by God and grows as God through her service constantly adds more people and nourishes them by the Word and the Lord's Supper. In this sense also Luther called the church "the mother of the believers."

Baptism is administered by the local church, but the baptized thereby becomes a member of the universal church. Even though the local church is understood as the organ of God's saving action, we must look beyond the locality. The New Testament uses the same word, *ecclesia,* to designate both the local congregation and the universal church. The latter is present in each local church, for the same God gathers His people in every congregation. Furthermore, both the local church and the whole church on earth are called the body of Christ. For as the Giver of His sacramental body Christ is present in each local church. So also by the same Holy Spirit the individual Christian, as well as the local congregation, as well as the whole Christendom are the temple of God. The validity and effectiveness of Baptism do not depend on the smallness or dubious character of the local church; for through Baptism God makes man a member of the one holy, catholic, and apostolic church, the fellowship which embraces space and time and includes all those living at the same time and those who have in faith preceded them — the fellowship of the brothers and of the fathers. The universality which includes all churches on earth at the same time embraces the continuity of the people of God on pilgrimage through the centuries. The individual Christian is borne and nourished with all the gifts which God has granted the church in the past and in the present — not only by the local church but by the universal church.

Thus the church confronts the individual person to be baptized as the existing universal sphere of the power of Jesus Christ, as the building of God and body of Christ advancing into the cosmos and growing, yes, as the new creation which is already permeating, changing, and filling the universe. God has already made the whole creation subject to the exalted Christ, whether it acknowledges Him as Lord or not. With an irresistible dynamic this rule of Christ moves in on the world through Word and Sacrament. Taken into Christ's service as the vehicle of His rule, the church approaches the individual, embraces him with the love with which Christ has loved her, gives birth to the new man, and bears and nourishes him so that he may grow in the understanding of faith and likewise become an instrument of the Christ who is present and active. This understanding of the church forbids looking only at what the baptized may or may not be able to do in the moment of Baptism. It rather permits the confidence that God acts on the baptized in a variety of ways, not only at the moment of Baptism but also thereafter through the service of the church, through proclamation, instruction, the Lord's Supper, and intercession. Thus God strengthens, admonishes, and warns the baptized to recognize and confess the Lord whose own they have become through Baptism. In this way the individual is surrounded, borne, and guided by the faith of the church both in Baptism and after Baptism.

Also this understanding of the church, as the spiritual power sphere of the rule of Jesus Christ which is a given for the individual, as this concept is found already in the writings of Paul and especially in Ephesians, helps us to understand why infant Baptism established itself so self-evidently in the ancient church. From this perspective also the exclusiveness of the sequence, faith-Baptism, that is, the first of the three above-mentioned connections between faith and Baptism, falls by the wayside. Now the connection between faith and Baptism must in every case be decisively maintained, but here faith is expected also as a fruit of Baptism and the further activity of God through the church. Thereby the faith and intercession of the church are given great significance. Thus Augustine taught that the Sacrament of Baptism, as something administered by the believing church, takes the place of the child's faith. Thomas pointed emphatically to the vicarious faith of the parents and sponsors and, beyond that, to the faith of the church which could replace even the missing faith of the parents. Luther rejected the idea of a "vicarious faith," but in his "The Order of Baptism" he earnestly

151

exhorted the parents and sponsors to make intercession for the child to be baptized and to believe that this prayer would be heard. In the fellowship of the Holy Spirit the prayer for the Spirit's activity in the baptized may be uttered with confidence.

2. If Baptism is understood as an act of obligation on the part of the baptized, the church does not confront the person to be baptized as the vehicle through whose baptizing God justifies, sanctifies, and renews him. On the contrary, the candidate for Baptism approaches as one who is already justified, sanctified, and reborn and joins himself to those who by means of Baptism have confessed their faith and obligated themselves to the life of the justified, sanctified, and reborn. The passive incorporation into the body of Christ through Baptism is replaced by the active event of coming to Baptism and the church. The act of being gathered and united by means of God's saving activity in Baptism is replaced by the subjective act of gathering and uniting by means of the act of confession in Baptism. Now the church does not confront the sinner as the mother who through Baptism gives him birth, but rather the believers form themselves into a church by means of the baptismal obligation. Here too faith has indeed come into being through the church's proclamation, and to that extent the church exists before the individual and meets him as the instrument of God's activity. However, since not only Baptism but also the Lord's Supper are viewed as acts of confession, and since, furthermore, the faith-creating significance of the proclaimed Word often recedes behind experiences of Spirit Baptism, regeneration, and sanctification which then lead to Baptism, the understanding of the church as the organ of God's saving activity is at least weakened. The more the immediacy of individual spiritual experience is stressed as precondition for Baptism, the more the church is seen as an association of those individuals who have had similar experiences.

Over against the instrumental activity of the church another function now comes to the fore: The church tests the faith, repentance, and regeneration of those who desire Baptism, and demands of them the obligation to submit to her discipline. The church does not stop confronting the baptized but she does it in a different way. One of the most important writings of Balthasar Hubmaier bears the title, "Concerning Brotherly Punishment" (1527). In it the author states that "our water Baptism and our breaking of bread are also merely show and sham, yes, no better than the foolish infant Baptism and giving the Eucharist to

152

little children [*das Kinderleinfuttern*] have been in the past, if brotherly punishment and the Christian ban are not always present."[80] The Schleitheim Confession of the same year called for the ban in very close connection with believers' Baptism. "The ban shall be employed with all those who have given themselves to the Lord, to walk in His commandments, and with all those who are baptized into the one body of Christ and who are called brethren or sisters, and yet who slip sometimes and fall into error and sin, being inadvertently overtaken."[81] Admonition and church discipline indeed belong to the church's task, but this task assumes an altered significance when the church is no longer understood in the first instance as the instrument of God's saving activity. The imperative of admonition and threat which the church must proclaim is no longer the same when it is separated from its indicative basis in Baptism. This results in shifts of focus in the direction of legalism which not infrequently in the history of the Baptist movement have led to schisms.

If the congregation comes into being as a result of the believers' act of obligation, and if with the rejection of a sacramental function on the part of the church the function of church discipline comes to the fore, the understanding of the church will be concentrated, at the expense of the universal church, on the act of uniting locally under the obligation assumed in Baptism. "Every living congregation claims the full sovereignty of the church for itself." (Fritz Heyer)[82] It was not only differences in doctrine and spiritual experience which hindered the union of Baptists already in the 16th century and repeatedly thereafter. As a matter of principle the concern was directed so much to the individual congregation that in the history of the Baptist movement there has been very little interest in common confessional formulations and orders of Baptism, and, except for loose federative relationships among Baptist congregations, any kind of church union; and especially the establishment of administrative offices beyond the local level have generally been rejected.[83] Correspondingly, a part of the Baptist movement has been reluctant about participation in the ecumenical movement. However, it is not only the universality of the church in any one age, but also that which encompasses the centuries that is crowded into the background in a peculiar way over against the current mutuality of sanctification for which people have joined together in local congregations through Baptism. While the reformers acknowledged the Baptism

153

within the papal church even during the severest conflicts, conceded the presence of believers and regenerate in the midst of the papal church, and thus affirmed the continuity of the church throughout the centuries, judgments were soon voiced within Baptist circles that the primitive Christian church was continued neither in the Roman Church nor in the churches of the Reformation. On the contrary, they declared that with the introduction of infant Baptism the continuity of the church had been disrupted, and in any case they attempted to rediscover the church in the history of the heretics. The more the saving activity of God by means of Word and Sacrament recedes into the background or is even denied, the more the certainty concerning the one universal church, which bears the individual and which manifests herself in the local congregation as the fellowship of the brothers and fathers of *all* places and times, fades away.

The difference between the self-understanding of the churches which practice infant Baptism and that of the Baptist movement came to a point in that the latter rejected the combination of church and state which had consolidated itself since Justinian, both in Eastern as well as Western Christendom, and which also the reformers had retained. It is true that the attitude of the Baptists toward the state was not uniform. Hubmaier in 1525 was able to induce the political community of the city of Waldshut as a whole to become Baptist. In 1534—35 the Anabaptists took over the civil power to establish the millennium. But in general it was characteristic of the Anabaptists from the beginning to adopt a critical stance over against civil offices—in part even to the rejection of oaths and military service—and they declined the identity of citizenship and church membership which was implied in the idea of a *corpus christianum*. This led to a departure into voluntarist churches which was extremely significant for church history. These churches were forcibly suppressed by the state. This bloody persecution has shaped the self-understanding of Baptist churches to the present day. Yet it dare not be overlooked that even where other churches have subsequently separated themselves from the conception of the *corpus christianum* and have themselves become free churches, a difference remains between their understanding of the church and that of the Baptists.

It is possible to derive the Baptists understanding of the church from their understanding of Baptism. But more probably their rejection of infant Baptism is to be derived from their understanding of the church.[84] In the early writings of this movement the doctrine of Baptism indeed played an important role, and it is no accident that it received the "Baptist" label. Yet the concern was with a sanctification movement which embraced all functions of life, determined in part Biblicistically, in part more spiritualistically. It was a movement which demanded a repudiation of accustomed churchly and civil orders and thus a radical decision on the part of the individual. On the basis of this understanding of the church the first of the three above-mentioned definitions of the relationship between faith and Baptism, namely the temporal sequence of faith and Baptism, must receive no less than a constitutive significance, and every Baptism received without the decision of faith must seem null and void.

3. The understanding of the church may now also help us to understand the peculiar inconsistencies which struck us in the attitude of Zwingli, Calvin, and K. Barth toward infant Baptism.

Although Zwingli and the Anabaptists agree in the perspective of their understanding of Baptism, their opposite attitude toward infant Baptism follows from their divergent understanding of the church. Merely to demonstrate that Zwingli maintained the unity of membership in state and church, as it had become customary since the consolidation of the church of the empire, does not yet do justice to his concept of the church.[85] This is true enough, but behind it is the theological conception of the unity of the Old and New Testament covenant people. As all children born within the Old Testament covenant people are partakers in the promise which God gave this people, so also the children of Christian parents are members of the New Testament people of God. As circumcision assures the children of the Israelites of what they are by physical descent, so Baptism is the sign by means of which the church acknowledges and designates as her members the children born in her midst. As in the Old Covenant the legal order of the people had the character of sacral law, so the orders of church and state belong together (though, of course, distinctions must be made between the civil and the ecclesiastical office and their specific functions), and the community of Christians and of citizens must not be separated. In this view the differences between Old and New Covenant as well as between John's Baptism and Christian Baptism, and the New Testament dialectic of unity and differentiation of the Old and New Testament people of God have been peculiarly diminished or ignored altogether. In spite of rejecting a gracious activity of God through Baptism, Zwingli insisted on infant Baptism because the children of Christian parents are already members of the New Testament people of God. In spite of the fact that it was impossible for the children to obligate themselves through Baptism, Zwingli demanded their Baptism as a sign by which the church acknowledges the child as her member and assumes responsibility for its Christian training.[86]

Quite obviously also Calvin bases infant Baptism primarily on his ecclesiological arguments. Regeneration of the children and their incorporation into the people of God are not expected of Baptism. On the contrary, infant Baptism is supported by the argument that the children of Christian parents are already members of the people of God, reborn and sanctified. If "the children of believers are partakers in the covenant without the help of understanding, there is no reason why they should be barred from the sign. . . ." Those "infants who derive their origin from Christians, as they have been born directly into the inheritance of the covenant, are thus to be received into Baptism." [87] In this context we must also understand Calvin's reference to the possibility of the Spirit's activity in infants, yes, even in the fetus in the womb.[88] Calvin does not expect this activity of the Spirit through Baptism, and yet he refers to it in support of infant Baptism. For him as for Zwingli the unity of Old and New Covenant, the unity of Old and New Testament covenant people, and the substantive identity of circumcision, John's Baptism, and Christian Baptism constitute the principal arguments, although, in distinction from Zwingli, Calvin regards them as promise and signs of *God.* In addition there were pastoral concerns, such as consolation for parents, the congregation's assumption of responsibility, etc. As dubious as Calvin's doctrine of the unity of Old and New Covenants may be, it does not invalidate his ecclesiological arguments. For at the same time there is a strong and active conviction regarding the church as fellowship of believers, as the body of Christ, as temple of the Holy Spirit, as mother who bears and sustains the believers. While in Book IV of his *Institutes* Calvin discussed the church primarily as the "external means" by which God invites people to fellowship with Christ, he went beyond this in his commentaries on New Testament epistles and unfolded the church's reality as the body of Christ.

The fact that K. Barth in spite of all criticism maintains the validity of infant Baptism and is thereby distinguished from the Baptists appears in the last analysis also to have ecclesiological grounds. This reserve cannot be explained by his understanding of Baptism alone. It is true that his understanding of the church starts with the individual congregation, is consistently critical of supracongregational offices, and stands, as he himself says, close to congregationalism. Yet in his *Church Dogmatics* he taught in an impressive way that in the local congregation the reality of the "one, holy, catholic, and apostolic church" is present and transcends the boundaries of the denominations. This recognition of the ecumenical dimension of the church makes Barth's acceptance of infant Baptism intelligible.

e. The dogmatic justification of infant Baptism

As we draw conclusions from the preceding reflections, we must distinguish between the dogmatic and the practical problem of infant Baptism.

It is clear, on the one hand, that the entire doctrine of Baptism is involved in the discussions about infant Baptism. It involves not only the relationship of faith and Baptism but also the relationship of Baptism and God's deed, as well as Baptism and church, and thus the relationship of divine and human action in general, that is, the understanding of man's possibilities in the presence of God.

On the other hand, the answer to the dogmatic questions does not yet solve the practical problem of infant Baptism. The latter involves the ever-recurring concrete question concerning admission to Baptism and therewith the question concerning the proper structure of the order of Baptism. This responsibility, which is constantly imposed anew, demands not only the examination of those who desire Baptism but also the examination of the condition of the church that baptizes and by means of Baptism gives man into the body of Christ. The church must beware lest her baptismal practice promote a false understanding of Baptism and obscure God's saving activity through Baptism.

Since treatment of the practical problem of infant Baptism depends on a clarification of the dogmatic problem, we shall start with the latter and provide support for the justification of infant Baptism by means of the following 12 theses:

1. Although there is no explicit word of the Lord or of an apostle

which commands or forbids infant Baptism, the question of infant Baptism is by no means left up to the arbitrary decision of the church. On the contrary, the church may baptize children only if she is certain that in this way she is acting in the obedience of faith to the divine task assigned to her.

2. In baptizing the children that will grow up in her midst — whether they were born to members of the church or whether they are brought along at the Baptism of their parents — the church acknowledges that all men are born under the dominion of sin and of death. Even though the infants have not rebelled against God by their own decision and are different from adult sinners in this respect, they cannot by their own decision rid themselves of the dominion of sin as they grow up. "That which is born of the flesh is flesh, and that which is born of the Spirit is spirit" (John 3:6; cf. vv. 3 ff.). It is not by physical birth but only through rebirth that man comes to the kingdom of God.

3. In baptizing children the church acknowledges the revealed saving will of God that all men are saved by Jesus Christ and the power of the Holy Spirit. From the children's Gospel (Mark 10:13-16 and parallels) the church knows that this saving will extends also to the children. Although that text says nothing about a Baptism of the children, it does nevertheless say that Jesus by His blessing gave the children brought to Him participation in the selfsame kingdom of God in which since Jesus' exaltation He grants participation through Baptism.

4. The church baptizes children in the conviction that through Baptism God assigns them to Jesus Christ, crucified and risen for all the world, as the Lord. The church believes that through Baptism God embraces the entire subsequent life of the child in a saving way by giving it into Christ's death in order that it might participate in His resurrection life.

5. The church baptizes children in the conviction that through Baptism God gives them the Holy Spirit who leads into all truth — the first fruit of the Holy Spirit which is the guarantee of further activity by the Spirit. The beginning of the Spirit's activity in man is not bound to the precondition of human recognition and confession, but the Holy Spirit is the gift by means of which alone man can be awakened to the knowledge of faith.

6. The church baptizes her children in the conviction that through Baptism God makes them members of the church, of the body of Christ,

and of the prophetic, priestly, and royal people of God. Although the little children cannot yet fight the fight of faith, bear witness to Christ before the world, and intercede for the world, they are nevertheless witnesses in a different manner, namely in their unconcealed need and their undisguised dependence on Him from whom they received life. In this sense Jesus held the children up to His disciples as examples. "Unless you turn and become like children, you will never enter the kingdom of heaven." (Matt. 18:3)

7. In baptizing children the church is confident that God will hear the prayers with which the children are bought to Baptism and by which their growing up is surrounded. There are petitions for earthly gifts which can only be prayed with the qualification, "Not my will, but Thine be done." It is beyond doubt God's will to give His Holy Spirit wherever He is prayed for. Therefore the baptizer, the parents and sponsors, together with the congregation may pray without ceasing that God would awaken the baptized to repentance and faith — confident that God will hear their prayers.

8. In baptizing children the church is confident that God will prove Himself powerful by means of the Gospel with which the church will accompany the life of the baptized children. The Gospel is a divine word of action, a power of God, and the Lord's Supper is the Communion of the body and blood of Jesus Christ. With a view to the children growing up in her midst the church may have the confidence that through assurance, admonition, and instruction, as well as through absolution, Lord's Supper, and blessing Christ will prove to be their Lord and Savior and that the Holy Spirit will enrich them with His gifts and guide them.

9. In baptizing children the church acknowledges that not only the salvation of the believers but also the origin and preservation of their faith are God's deed which He accomplishes through the Gospel and the sacraments in the power of the Holy Spirit. All of man's striving for faith and all deciding for faith is encompassed by the saving activity of God through the Holy Spirit without any human basis whatsoever. Not only the salvation received by faith is a gift of grace, but also the believing reception itself.

10. In baptizing children the church acknowledges that faith and Baptism belong together. The church baptizes the children that will grow up in her midst, and she does so by faith in the saving activity of God who by means of Baptism assigns them to Jesus Christ, the ground

159

of faith, and to the Holy Spirit, the power of faith; and through the Gospel God continues to call to faith and strengthen in faith. Thus the church baptizes from faith to faith.

11. In baptizing children the church knows that the temporal sequence of faith and Baptism has been relativized by God's eschatological activity. For in Baptism God encloses the entire past life of the baptized as well as that which is still in the future. The temporal sequence of events in the course of life has been eschatologically nullified in Baptism: The baptized has in Christ already experienced his future death, and the life of the one risen from the dead has already been opened for him. In this eschatological bracketing the question whether the faith of the person to be baptized must necessarily precede Baptism fades away, and the temporal sequence of faith and Baptism cannot be made the norm of validity. But the connection between faith and Baptism which encompasses the course of life is decisive: Whoever does not believe will not participate in salvation in spite of the Baptism which he received. Since faith and Baptism belong together, the church will baptize only those children who will grow up under the witness of faith.

12. Thus the church, in baptizing the children born and growing up in her midst, is certain that she is acting in the obedience of faith toward the commission of her Lord, who has sent her to make disciples of all nations, by baptizing and teaching them (Matt. 28:19 ff.). In baptizing children before they can know and confess Christ themselves, the church is not neglecting their decision of faith but is rather helping them to come to the Yea of faith. The church is not violating their freedom but helping them to attain to the freedom of faith. Thus the church acts as the mother of the believers and by means of no other act confesses so unmistakably that it is God alone who saves man. For by means of infant Baptism the person is received into the kingdom of God without any contribution of his own. Just as the resurrection of the dead occurs without the assistance of the dead, so also the new-creation of man whose life is forfeit to sin and death is accomplished through Baptism. In no other act does the church confess so clearly that she lives by the promises which God has attached to the proclamation, the sacraments, and prayer. For without knowing in advance what kind of decision the baptized will one day make, the church is confident that God will not permit her witness and her prayer to remain without fruit with regard to this child.

f. The practical problems of infant Baptism

The dogmatic justification of infant Baptism has, of course, not yet answered the question regarding the justification of the practice of infant Baptism as it is currently in vogue in the state and people's churches which still exist but are to a large extent inwardly undermined. Both in areas of the Reformation churches as well as in areas of the Roman and Orthodox churches there are great masses of baptized people who do not go to church, do not pray, and refuse to be dealt with on the basis of the fact that through Baptism they have been given into Christ's death in order to walk in newness of life. Yet they want Baptism for their children. They are not willing to pray with their children, to introduce them to the Bible, and to accompany them to worship. Nor do they select sponsors from the perspective that they should serve as intercessory witnesses for the children. They want their children to be baptized because infant Baptism is customary, and with the observance of this custom they combine a variety of depraved ideas about Baptism. In part they see Baptism as a kind of act of initiation, that is, as an act of reception into society. In part they view Baptism as admission to a moral training aid which the church provides by means of her instruction. In part they understand Baptism as an offer of divine help without any obligations, and in part they bring the children to Baptism in the vague and magical expectation of some effective protection which they would not like to deny their children. Hence the promise to bring up the children in a Christian way is given without serious intent. The promise is reduced in practice to sending the children to the church's instruction. But the children grow up in the family in an intellectual environment which the word of the church confronts as a stranger.

What is the church to do in this situation?

As a rule the churches mentioned administer Baptism also in these numerous cases. They do it even when among the vast numbers of the baptized the number of the believers who attend worship and are enriched and guided by Word and Sacrament has become so small that this group is not able to embrace and bear spiritually all the baptized as they grow up. At the same time, the number of pastors in relation to the number of the baptized is often so small that it is impossible to give the necessary care and attention to each baptized person and his family. Thus the pastors and their congregations are not able to have the masses

161

of the baptized recognize the church as the sphere of life which encompasses them all. There are various reasons why the church has nevertheless continued the practice of infant Baptism. In part men close their eyes to churchly reality and seek to maintain the idea of a people's church by the number of baptized. Others see Baptism as a link which still establishes a contact with the church for those who have drifted away. Above all it is hoped that God will act on the person through Baptism, even though the motives behind the desire for Baptism are foreign to the essence of Baptism, and that later on in spite of all obstacles the church's instruction will make the baptized aware of what was begun in them in Baptism and lead them to affirm it.

In this widespread situation of our time, Baptism and faith fall apart in a terrifying manner. Even though Baptism is administered in faith, it is not desired in faith and not received in faith. The fellowship of believers, which is to be the immediate circle which surrounds the child at his Baptism and as he grows up with intercession and witness, in reality largely disappears. The child's home thwarts his growth into faith and the worship life. The church's instruction can undo the damage only with great difficulty, or not at all in most cases, and instances of children from unchurched homes who have become living witnesses of the Christian faith must not distract us from seeing the general rule, nor can such instances be adduced as proof that infant Baptism is the correct practice. By this practice countless people are in fact made dead members of the church. For here Baptism is separated not only from the faith of those who desire it but also from the divine saving activity which aims at accompanying and embracing the whole of human life through Word and Sacrament. But how can one perceive from a baptismal act so torn out of its context and from the masses of the baptized for whom their Baptism has become meaningless that Baptism is "the washing of regeneration and renewal in the Holy Spirit"? (Titus 3:5)

This problem cannot be solved if the churches continue to insist on granting the request of all who for whatever reason and intention bring their children to be baptized. Such motives and aims must be taken far more seriously than is generally the case. If the church tolerates or even welcomes the manifold depraved expectations of the parents in bringing their children to Baptism; if, for example, the church interprets magical expectations of protection as expectation of God's saving activity, then the church makes herself an ally of such depraved notions. If the church in her baptismal proclamation even adapts herself to such depraved expectations and proclaims Baptism as being only an offer or only gratitude, but not as a giving into Christ's death and as assignment to His rule, the church betrays the Baptism which she has been commissioned to administer. It cannot be the church's task to baptize every child of baptized people.

Nor, on the other hand, can this problem be solved by the church's renunciation of infant Baptism in principle. We may pass over the practical difficulties involved in such a break with tradition. Amid the radically changing situation of the church in the modern world such difficulties cannot be decisive. What is decisive, however, is the objection that by a rejection of infant Baptism in principle the understanding of Baptism as God's saving deed and the relationship of Baptism, faith, and church would be obscured. Wherever infant Baptism has been abolished as a matter of principle, or where groups have established themselves which regard infant Baptism as invalid and therefore rebaptize, more or less profound dilutions or even perversions of the New Testament understanding of Baptism have resulted, which need not be detailed here again. Since infant Baptism is justified in principle, the abuse of infant Baptism cannot be removed if the church denies the request of parents who believe in Christ and thus deprives their children of the saving deed of God which occurs in Baptism. So also it is no witness to this saving deed if Christians refuse to have their children baptized as a sign of protest against the abuse of infant Baptism.

The two preceding negations indicate the boundaries within which the solution to the problem raised by the practice of infant Baptism must be sought. But this in itself does not yet solve the problem. Rather, this now appears to point out the way to a case-by-case examination of the parents and sponsors who want a child baptized — an examination of their faith, their participation in worship, their understanding of Baptism, etc. On the basis of this examination the desire for Baptism should then be affirmed or rejected. It is clear that this procedure will conjure up other dangers that are extremely great. How can the faith of the applicants for Baptism be determined with certainty? Is there not unbelief also with those who regularly attend church, join in the confession of the Creed, and are able to give correct information about the church's teaching on Baptism? On the other hand, is it not true that also outside the ranks of those who regard themselves as good Christians there is faith, that is,

163

the plea, "Lord, I believe; help my unbelief"? Such questions must be addressed to the advocates and the opponents of infant Baptism in the same way. Nor can the Baptist groups evade them. There too the problems of "believers' Baptism" are becoming manifest in connection with the growing children of later generations. Dare the church ever forget that in the Gospel tradition Jesus on the cross was deserted by all of His disciples and that the one malefactor on the cross and the pagan captain were the first to confess the majesty of the Crucified One? If the church were to undertake to establish the borderline between faith and unfaith in a judicial way and make the administration of Baptism depend on this judgment, the church would confront man with her baptismal practice not as church of the Gospel but as advocate of the Law. Indeed, the church would anticipate the judgment which God has reserved to Himself.

The abolition of the abuses which are widely associated with the practice of infant Baptism must begin with the Gospel, that is, by reminding those who desire Baptism for their child through proclamation and instruction of the saving deed which God accomplished for them in Baptism. This saving deed must be presented to them, without diminution and without concession to their depraved preconception in all its offensiveness, as a giving into Jesus' death, as subjection to Christ's rule, and as a giving into the sphere of the Holy Spirit's power. They must be addressed on the basis of the fact that through Baptism God has opened a new possibility of human existence. The custom of infant Baptism which has become questionable must be breached by means of the offensive and liberating message of God's saving deed, and those who desire Baptism must by this message be placed squarely before the decision whether they want this Baptism for their children, that is, whether they wish the child to be given into Christ's death and thus be removed from their own control, in order that the child may live under the rule of Him who makes the claim of being acknowledged as Lord by parents, sponsors, and children together. The church may hope to reduce the abuse that has widely invaded the practice of Baptism, not by sorting out those who have become estranged from the church, but by preaching the Gospel to them. The proclamation of God's saving deed through Baptism must be made so unequivocally and clearly that the baptized will themselves raise the question whether they want to bring their child to Baptism. If infant Baptism has become a mere custom devoid of

164

content, it must be placed in question by the clarity of the message and by the challenge to responsible decision over against this message and over against the salvation which the adults have once received and which is now offered to their children.

In practice this means that the discussion on Baptism with parents and sponsors must be given incomparably more weight than is generally the case. The conversation cannot limit itself to determining denominational membership and making arrangements about place and time of Baptism, or only the conduct of the ceremony. On the contrary, the conversation must deal with the saving activity of God which has taken place for the parents and sponsors and is now to take place for the child. Parents and sponsors must be examined as to the motives and conceptions of their desire and on the basis of this conversation be again faced with the decision whether they wish their child to receive Christian Baptism.

The church should not impose Baptism on those parents who make no arrangements to have their children baptized or who decide against it after their conversation on Baptism. The church should go after such parents and their children in other ways and wait until they request Baptism in faith. The church should refuse to baptize the children of those parents and sponsors who, even after clear instructions on the implications of Baptism, insist on the children's Baptism notwithstanding their explicit rejection of the Christian faith and their refusal to promise a Christian training of their children. Nor should the possibility be excluded of suspending infant Baptism temporarily in a dead congregation, where the worship service is no longer attended, until a new desire for the Gospel manifests itself.

The churches must be consciously prepared for the eventuality that alongside the Baptism of children the Baptism of adults will become more and more frequent and that the custom of the ancient church will be revived; it will again become self-evident practice side-by-side to baptize the adults who desire Baptism as a result of their own decision of faith, and to baptize the children who are brought to Baptism as a result of their parents' decision of faith.

Thus in the last analysis the problem of administering infant Baptism is not a dogmatic problem but one having to do with the condition of the church. It involves the quest for Christian families and living congregations which in faith embrace the children born in their midst and guide and carry them through prayer and witness. It involves the courage of church authorities and pastors to be uncompromisingly radical in their proclamation of the divine saving deed and of the new life opened and demanded by this saving deed and thereby to confront the people with the decision and straightway call them to faith, without which the benefit of Baptism is not imparted.

5. The Most Profound Difference
in the Understanding of Baptism

It was not our task to present the history of the doctrine of Baptism. In the compass of this dogmatic treatment we had to limit ourselves to the most important historical points and the most important types of baptismal teaching, especially those which have established themselves as permanent basic types to the present day. As we look back on the references to the history of theology in chapters two and three and ask about the difference which is systematically most profound, we are faced with the far from simple and basic problem of making comparisons among dogmatic statements. It cannot be sufficient to make an *immediate* comparison of the wording of dogmatic statements that were formulated in completely different times. Translations are required here to enable us to recognize to what extent we are dealing in the differences with diversity in unity or with mutually exclusive antitheses.

Hence the historical setting in which the statements were formulated must be considered. It makes a difference whether the doctrine of Baptism had to be presented in opposition to a spiritualistic disparagement or a magical abuse. Thus in the first instance the major accent had to be on the grace which is effective in Baptism, while in the latter case the sign which promises grace needed to be stressed. In consideration of the various battlefronts quite different dogmatic statements can be understood as true teaching on the same Baptism or as a necessary complementary corrective.

The same is true of the *concepts* used by the various teachings on Baptism. It would be a deficiency in dogma and dogmatics if these were to limit themselves to the use of Biblical concepts. Just as many concepts of the New Testament baptismal statements were taken over from the Hellenistic environment and transformed, so also the subsequent teaching on Baptism rightly borrowed other terms from the environment and placed them into the service of the church's teaching. It is in this way that the message concerning Christ advances into the world. The fact that the East employed the idea of mystery while the West used that of sacrament and that the common distinction between visible and invisible was differently defined in detail in the East and the West need in itself imply an antithesis as little as the fact that this distinction, taken over from Platonism and Neoplatonism, is less congenial to current historical thinking than statements about God's activity through Baptism. Agreements and differences do not yet result from a verbal comparison of the statements but only as we attempt to translate from one conceptual context to another.

No less important is concern for the *structure* in which the dogmatic statements are made, and therewith the existential stance from which they are made. Thus statements about Baptism sound differently when they are made in the elementary structures of invitation to a believing reception of Baptism, of the promise of grace when Baptism is administered, and of hortatory recall of Baptism, or when such statements are made in the form of a reflecting definition of the relationships between Word, water, and grace. They sound differently when they summon to a believing reception and warn against an unbelieving reception, or when, in the course of reflection, concepts are developed by means of which the relationship is clarified between a believing reception of Baptism and its effects and an unbelieving reception. As in the New Testament the elementary statements about Baptism are determined by the act of believing reception; they summon to this kind of reception and recall it to mind. But the perspective from which reflective statements are made concerning the relationship of Word, water, and grace, as well as of believing and unbelieving reception, is removed from this concrete event which the believer experiences — a perspective from which the believing and unbelieving reception are theoretically surveyed and both are assigned their place by means of conceptual distinctions in a comprehensive formula. Over against statements that are determined by the concrete reception of Baptism in faith, such reflective statements have a secondary character.

This is not the place to consider the question whether and to what extent such a perspective apart from the baptismal event is justified, since theological thinking can ultimately adopt no perspective that is separated from God's concrete activity on behalf of man. It should, however, be said in principle that difference or identity in baptismal teachings can only be established if we do not stop with the differences in formulation but seek to translate reflective statements back into elementary ones that are determined by the act of a believing reception of Baptism. In the case of Augustine's baptismal theology his distinction between sacrament and grace will, in translation to statements concerning the believing reception, lead to a conjunction of Baptism and grace which is in practice no different from the ancient church's customary understanding of Baptism. But we must also ask what would result from a translation of Calvin's highly reflective teaching on Baptism into the elementary structures of the baptismal proclamation — that is, if we do not stop with the theoretical statements which are valid for believers and nonbelievers, but if we ask what can be gathered from these statements for faith and for proclamation. By faith in the promise offered in Baptism, in spite of Calvin's one-sided emphasis on the cognitive reference, not only the sign but also the signified grace, regeneration, dying, and rising with Christ are present. Translated into elementary statements of faith, Calvin's teaching on the parallelism of baptismal event and the operation of grace is not as far removed from the statements concerning God's activity through Baptism as may at first seem to be the case. In any case, the church of the Lutheran Confessions did not regard Calvin's teaching on Baptism church divisive as it did with respect to his teaching on the Eucharist. Following Calvin, Karl Barth in his earlier work on Baptism rightly spoke not only of Baptism as sign and picture but also of its "power" and "effect." "The efficacy of baptism consists in this, that the baptized person is placed once and for all under the sign of hope, in consequence of which he has death already behind him, and only life in front of him . . . ." [89] So reads the promise for faith. Naturally a structural translation will not be able to resolve all differences — not between Luther and Calvin either — but it can uncover surprising proximities or even agreements which were concealed under variously structured layers of statements.

Yet even after such necessary attempts at translation one difference remains, whose far-reaching significance must not be overlooked, and which must be termed an antithesis within the variety of baptismal theologies that have arisen in church history. That antithesis is the understanding of Baptism as God's deed or as man's deed, as the sign given men by God or as the sign of human self-obligation before God. Baptism is indeed administered by men, but God acts through this administration. Baptismal grace is grasped by faith, but this faith is the being grasped by God's activity; it is the reception of baptismal grace. As a sign of promise Baptism makes faith sure of salvation; yet the believer does not erect this sign, but he receives it. The most profound difference runs its course not between the Eastern Church and Augustine, nor between Thomas and Luther,[90] nor even between Luther and Calvin, but between all of these on one side and Zwingli and the Baptists on the other. The most profound difference is not the acknowledgment or nonacknowledgment of infant Baptism, but the understanding of Baptism either as God's deed or as the deed of human obedience.

Now, this antithesis between the two exists within the following things they have in common: Even where Baptism is understood as man's deed, this by no means signifies that Baptism had been originated by man. On the contrary, it is demanded as obedience to God's institution. Both sides teach the necessity of Baptism. Even where Baptism is not viewed as a means of salvation, the concern is with salvation here too, which, while not received through Baptism, is nevertheless confessed in connection with it. Both sides affirm salvation through Christ alone and the necessity of regeneration. Even where regeneration is seen as precondition but not as effect of Baptism, a connection between regeneration and Baptism is maintained. On the other hand, the churches that baptize infants have by no means given up the connection between Baptism and faith. Even though the infant cannot yet receive Baptism in faith, the Baptism is performed in view of the faith which God will create in the person through Baptism, proclamation, and in answer to intercession. On both sides the connection between faith and salvation is expressly emphasized, even though the temporal coordination is different. Furthermore, both sides acknowledge grace as the source of the new life, whether this grace is conceived as precondition or as effect of Baptism.

One should not immediately focus on the differences in the understanding of faith, of grace, of regeneration, and of the necessity of Baptism, but have an eye for what all have in common in spite of differences. But this common possession does not nullify that antithesis. If in spite of this common possession the mutual recognition of Baptism is denied — namely infant Baptism by the Baptists and their rebaptism by other churches—it becomes evident how deeply and divisively this antithesis reaches into the life of Christendom.

Now as a matter of course we cannot be content with merely comparing each other's *principles* of the doctrine and practice of Baptism. We must consider also the *reality* of the church's life, a reality which by no means always coincides with those principles.

In the preceding we placed the self-understanding of the churches that administer infant Baptism and the fellowships that reject it opposite each other in a kind of typifying way. But each of the two understandings contains elements of the other and beyond that there are considerable ecclesiological differences on each of the two sides—not only between the Roman Church and the churches of the Reformation. Already for this reason we cannot be satisfied with simply placing these two basic types in opposition to each other. Beyond this we must distinguish between the *understanding* of the church and the *reality* of the church.

There is an understanding of the church as the vehicle of the divine saving activity, as "mother of the believers," as the body of Christ that permeates everything, to which the reality of the church holding this ecclesiology does not correspond. There are churches whose self-understanding is determined by the statements of Paul and especially by Ephesians, but in whose reality neither the communion of charismatic gifts nor the spiritual dynamism of a witnessing advance into the world can be recognized. Furthermore, these churches do not surround the children baptized and growing up in their midst with prayer and witness in a manner that would seem to be self-evident on the basis of their understanding of the church.

On the other side there are communions in which the individual knows himself safe and borne by admonition and intercession, even though the church is here not understood as the "mother" that gives birth to the believers, but as the assembly which is constituted by the union of individuals through the confessional act of their Baptism. Although these groups do not start theologically with the concept of the church as the given reality which in her continuity and universality pervades and fills the ages and the cosmos, such communions, and especially the radicalness of their demand to renounce the world, in fact often manifested a dynamic of advance into the world which has outstripped many a church that understands herself as the sphere of Christ's universal rule but confines herself to preserving her own status.

170

In spite of the fact that we cannot avoid rejecting the Zwinglian and Baptist understanding of Baptism, we are obligated to point up the dangers connected with our own understanding of Baptism and the church and the positive possibilities that are not lacking in the Baptist understanding of Baptism.

CHAPTER FOUR

The Form of the Baptismal Act

1. The Administration of Baptism in the New Testament

It was already pointed out above that the New Testament gives no instruction on how to baptize — and certainly it does not offer a formula for Baptism. From the reports of Baptism in the Acts and to a lesser degree from the epistles we may draw some *a posteriori* conclusions concerning the manner in which Baptism was administered in the earliest period of the Christian church. But in many rather important details these sources do not present a clear picture. It is no accident that various attempts at historical reconstruction, for example, of the Baptism formula and the Baptism confession, diverge. The authors of the New Testament letters were not interested in the way, how, and by whom Baptism was administered, but they addressed the congregations on the basis of God's deed done to them in their Baptism. Nor are the accounts in Acts interested in a description of the baptismal act as such, but rather in reporting how certain persons and "houses" came to be baptized and what effects were linked with Baptism. The New Testament statements rarely address themselves to a Baptism that is still to be performed. Their main theme is the new-creating activity of God which took place in Baptism that had been performed. This activity is witnessed in a variety of concepts. An added item, in answer to the question concerning the form of primitive Christian Baptism, is the fact that also the history of the baptismal liturgy in the ancient church opposes the idea that the same rite of Baptism was used in the primitive Christian churches. Only the following can be said with certainty:

a. Baptism was preceded by the message concerning Christ, a desire for Baptism, and admittance to Baptism. The New Testament nowhere presupposes a temporal interval between the creation of faith and admission to Baptism, even though approaches to a fixed form of bap-

172

tismal instruction are discernible (for example, Rom. 6:17; Heb. 6:1 f.). Nor are there any indications regarding definite times for Baptism. Since several reports in Acts mention that there was no hindrance to admission to Baptism (8:36; 10:47; 11:17), it is possible that in the circle of Luke a corresponding formula of admission was already in use.[1]

b. Christian Baptism requires the use of water. The word "baptize" is used metaphorically in the New Testament very seldom (it is certainly so used in the logion of Jesus concerning the baptism of death, Luke 12:50). Rather, "Baptism" and "baptize" are technical terms for water Baptism. Thus Luke did not call the outpouring of the Spirit at Pentecost a Baptism. While Christian Baptism in the New Testament was administered with water (whether this is especially mentioned or not), this does not say how the water was applied. The secular Greek word "baptize" means dip, sink, and points to the total submersion of the baptized. But it is doubtful whether this meaning of the word justifies the conclusion that immersion was the only form of Baptism. The water situation in Palestine and neighboring countries makes this unlikely, as well as the fact that Jewish Baptisms were by no means performed only by immersion. Nor can immersion be derived without question from Romans 6, since Paul probably did not arrive at his statements about dying and rising with Christ from a symbolical interpretation of the baptismal act but rather from the interpretation of being "baptized into Christ." Also the numerous New Testament references to Baptism as a "washing" could be understood to indicate that Baptism was not administered exclusively by a complete immersion of the baptized. We cannot exclude the possibility that the baptizer stood in the water with the person to be baptized and poured water over him — a form of the act that is admittedly represented in Christian art only at a later date. Whether Philip, who went down into the water with the eunuch (Acts 8:38), immersed or poured water on the latter cannot be discovered from the text. While the New Testament has no direct reference to the manner of applying the water, the Didache states unequivocally that Baptism may be administered in various ways: ". . . baptize in running water. . . . If you have no running water, baptize in other water, and if you cannot use cold water, use warm. If you have neither, pour water on the head three times, 'in the name of the Father and Son and Holy Spirit.'" (7, 1-3)

c. When the New Testament speaks of Baptism upon (in) the name

173

of Jesus Christ, this indicates, first of all, the uniqueness of this Baptism in distinction from other Baptisms. But undoubtedly the reference to Christ found expression in the act of Baptism itself. We cannot, however, simply equate these designations with a baptismal formula. Neither the accounts of Baptism in the Acts nor the references in the epistles provide definite information on the way the name of Christ was given expression in primitive Christian Baptisms.

The phrase "baptize upon the name . . ." supports the assumption that the baptizer pronounced the name of Christ over the person to be baptized. This may have been done in various ways: by proclamation of the name of Christ or by invocation of God in Christ's name or also by direct invocation of Christ. Already the change in prepositions and the more precise formulations of the name of Christ in the New Testament baptismal texts would seem to oppose the assumption that a fixed formula was generally in use in the first congregations. The history of the liturgy in the ancient church shows that the usual formula current in Western Christendom, "I baptize you in the name . . . ," was not generally used in primitive Christendom.

It is also possible that the name of Christ was not uttered by the baptizer but by the baptized, either in the confession of Christ or in the invocation of Christ. The Baptism accounts in Acts mention a confession on the part of the baptized only once, and that not in the original text but in the later Western reading, "I believe that Jesus Christ is the Son of God" (8:37). Yet it is beyond question that the Christological confessions reported in the New Testament have their *Sitz im Leben* not only in the congregational assembly and the missionary proclamation, but especially in Baptism. In favor of this view is also the repeatedly mentioned close connection between faith and Baptism, and because of this connection the confession especially of those who had just come to faith became particularly urgent. However, a uniform baptismal confession in the primitive Christian congregations cannot be assumed.[2] Beyond the use of a variety of confessional formulas, it is also conceivable that the person to be baptized responded to the message concerning Christ in his own words of confession and invocation. If the name of Christ is spoken in Baptism by the person to be baptized, then a request or question by the baptizer may have preceded (cf. Acts 8:37). But this is attested as a fixed order only in later baptismal liturgies. It is also possible that the name of Christ was uttered both by the baptizer

174

and the baptized, for example, in the confession of the baptized and in the proclamation or invocation of the baptizer.

The New Testament speaks in only one place of Baptism "into the name of the Father and of the Son and of the Holy Spirit." Since this occurs in the institution of Baptism (Matt. 28:19), the idea of a formula in the mouth of the baptizer suggests itself. Here too we must not project later formulas back into early baptismal practice. In any event the history of the liturgy in the ancient church shows that Baptism upon the three-fold name could also be performed in that not the baptizer but the baptized confessed this name in reply to the questions of the baptizer.

d. Only two accounts of Baptism in the Acts mention a laying on of hands. At Paul's Baptism it precedes (9:17), while in the case of John's disciples in Ephesus it follows Baptism (19:5-6). In both cases there are special preconditions which by no means apply to all Baptisms. Paul approached his Baptism as a blind man and by the laying on of hands received healing and the Holy Spirit. The disciples of John in Ephesus had already received John's Baptism without the Holy Spirit before the Holy Spirit was imparted to them by the laying on of hands immediately after Christian Baptism. It would seem that these two instances of the laying on of hands should be understood in connection with the healings, blessings, and intercessions which also otherwise were accomplished in primitive Christianity by the laying on of hands, rather than leading to the conclusion that the laying on of hands was a fixed practice in connection with Baptism. The Samaritans in any case received the Holy Spirit through prayer and the laying on of hands, not at the time of their Baptism but later (Acts 8:14-24). Here, too, there is a special precondition, namely, the centuries-old cultic separation between Samaria and Jerusalem, which was now brought to an end by the laying on of hands on the part of the apostles, and by the reception of the same Spirit who had been imparted to the primitive church in Jerusalem. The rest of the baptismal accounts in Acts are silent about the laying on of hands. It has indeed frequently been assumed [3] that a laying on of hands must be presupposed as self-evident in every case, and this could be supported by the fact that in the parallel account of Paul's Baptism (Acts 22:12-16) the laying on of hands is not mentioned as it is in 9:17. Nevertheless, the general assumption that Baptism and laying on of hands belong together, even only in the circle of churches known to Luke, is unlikely, since the few accounts deal with special situations. It

175

is altogether impossible to presuppose a laying on of hands in the primitive Christian practice of Baptism as a general thing. Against this is already the fact that the baptismal statements in the epistles do not mention the laying on of hands. A single exception is Heb. 6:2, but from this listing of the foundational themes of instruction we cannot be sure whether this text is speaking of a laying on of hands in connection with Baptism. It could refer to a different kind of laying on of hands. As a fixed element in the Christian baptismal rite the laying on of hands cannot be attested until later — particularly the idea that only the forgiveness of sins is imparted through Baptism, while the Holy Spirit is not given except through the laying on of hands. In any case the account in Acts 8:14-24 does not warrant such a dogmatic generalization.

e. From the beginning Baptism was brought into relationship with the church. It was performed by a member of the church, and it made the baptized a member of the church. The baptized is added to the fellowship of prayer and the meal. It is all the more remarkable that according to Acts only the Baptism at Pentecost took place in the presence of the congregation — but otherwise in an encounter between individual members of the church and the person to be baptized. This is obviously based on the particular orientation of the Acts toward the missionary advance. References to parts of the baptismal liturgy which may be assumed in various New Testament letters point, on the other hand, to the "we" of the assembled congregations. (Cf. e. g., 1 Peter 1:3-5; Eph. 5:14 [?]; Rom. 13:11-14)

What we can gather with certainty from the New Testament regarding the administration of Baptism does not permit us to reconstruct a consistent form of the early Christian act of Baptism. We must reckon with a variety of ways of administration. But all of these Baptisms are one in their reference to Christ, whose name was subsequently not superseded by the name of the Father and the Son and the Holy Spirit, but was confessed again in another way.

2. The Problem of the Form of the Baptismal Act

It is clear that the New Testament statements on Baptism do not yet provide us with the form of its administration. There are indeed several indispensable qualifications which distinguish Christian Baptism from other baptisms, washings, and sprinklings, especially the reference to the name of Christ. These qualifications posit a series of personal re-

176

lations which cannot be given up and which must also reappear in every Christian Baptism, especially the submission to Christ as Lord and reception into the sphere of His spiritual rule, as well as the irreversible confrontation of baptizer and baptized, which excludes self-baptism, and finally the relationship between the baptized and the church. Thus basic structures of the form may be derived from the New Testament, but not the concrete form of the baptismal act itself.

The object of this dogmatic treatise is not the history of the baptismal liturgy. Nor does this chapter aim at providing the dogmatic foundation and interpretation of the baptismal liturgies which today are current in the churches of the Reformation. For the recognition of the validity of Baptism in other churches at the same time acknowledges that other forms of the baptismal liturgy are also dogmatically defensible. Nor is it my intention to sketch my own formula of Baptism on the basis of the preceding reflections. The intention is rather to attempt a systematic clarification of the possibilities for the form of the act of Baptism which follow from the New Testament material. It is not enough to be satisfied with the fact that the different churches in the main acknowledge each other's Baptisms. The attempt must be made to demonstrate by means of a systematic exhibit of the basically existing liturgical possibilities why the unity of Baptism can be acknowledged even where the forms of the baptismal act differ extensively among the churches.

Since the New Testament has not transmitted a definite order of Baptism, the concrete form of the administration of Baptism is entrusted to the church's freedom in much the same way as the form of worship of the congregation assembled in the name of Jesus generally.[4] This freedom of the church is the spiritual freedom of the believers who have been liberated by Jesus Christ from the ethical and ritual law of the Jewish cultic assembly as well as that of other religions. Just as Paul directs the church to allow for the manifold spiritual gifts in the worshiping assembly, in order that these gifts may find expression in manifold words of knowledge and wisdom, of prophecy and doctrine, as well as in a variety of prayers and hymns, so also a variety of forms of the baptismal act must be provided for. This variety dare not be curtailed. Here, too, the warning applies, not to "quench" the Spirit (1 Thess. 5:19) and not to resist Him. The spiritual freedom of the church must be safeguarded in the dogmatic and liturgical treatment of the problem of form.

But this freedom must be more closely defined and distinguished from arbitrariness. This has to do with the freedom which is granted through being bound to Jesus Christ—the freedom of the "slaves of Christ." For that reason the following limits must be observed which apply to every form of the administration and reception of Baptism in spite of all possible variety:

a. The basis for Baptism is in every case determinative. The baptismal command must not be separated from Jesus' death and resurrection, nor from the outpouring of the Holy Spirit, and these foundational saving deeds of God in turn must not be isolated from the promises of the Old Covenant and from John's Baptism, especially the Baptism which Jesus Himself received from John. These events in the totality of their historical relationship are the basis for Christian Baptism. Because the One promised in the Old Covenant has come and the Spirit of God has been poured out, Christian Baptism is eschatological fulfillment, and the form of Baptism must be determined from this basis. Even with all freedom in the form of the baptismal act the church dare never act as if she had originated Baptism. The church is bound by the commission of her Lord. She is not free to omit or to repeat Baptism, or to administer or acknowledge Baptism in a form which contradicts or obscures its origin. Especially does the church not have the liberty in her baptizing to omit the name of Christ or its triadic-trinitarian explication.

b. The form of Baptism must serve to bear witness to the saving deed which God accomplished in Jesus Christ and in the outpouring of the Holy Spirit, and which He desires to accomplish and does accomplish in the baptized. The form of Baptism must make clear to the baptized what God is doing to him in Baptism and what He demands of him on the basis of Baptism, and at the same time must demonstrate to the congregation what a gift is given her in each newly baptized person and what an obligation she assumes for the newly baptized. For God's saving deed in Baptism embraces eschatologically the entire subsequent life of the baptized, including his prospective death and his future resurrection from the dead. In view of the overwhelming greatness of this event and the great variety of the New Testament statements which witness to this event, the liturgical attestation to the soteriological significance of Baptism in its Christological, pneumatological, and ecclesiological contexts and its anthropological consequences is an unending task. The form of the order of Baptism cannot be determined only by this or that individual New Testament statement but must allow for the riches of the baptismal statements. Above all, the church is not free to obscure the divine saving activity by emphasizing one-sidedly the activity of the person to be baptized or even by reducing the significance of Baptism to the decision of the baptized.

c. The form of Baptism must be further determined by the universality of the command by which the Lord sent and sends His own to all nations for the service of proclamation and baptizing. The baptizing occurs in combination with the progress of the Gospel into ever new areas of the human race and into encounter with very different expectations, conceptions, and rites. These are breached by Baptism. Baptism involves a change in rulers, a renunciation of the former powers, and a submission to Jesus Christ. At the same time these conceptions are enlisted to bear witness to the new that breaks in through the Gospel and Baptism. This process of breakthrough, enlistment, and reshaping occurs whenever the Gospel is preached in another language. Such an enlistment of alien words and concepts is a critical and transforming act whose peculiarity cannot be adequately encompassed by the term syncretism. It is not a matter of adulterating the Gospel but of its dynamic advance toward concrete man in his historical sphere. The process of a critical use of alien conceptions is discernible already in the baptismal statements of the New Testament, especially in the transforming application of concepts used in the piety of the Hellenistic mysteries. This advance must in principle and in fact continue if the saving significance of Baptism is to be concretely witnessed on new historic fronts. This process is not confined to words but may also take place in the critical enlistment of signs and rites. In this respect the New Testament permits nothing more than surmises. Yet the history of the baptismal liturgy in the ancient church shows clearly that the church did not stop with a critical enlistment of extra-Christian words and conceptions. Nor can the unfolding of the import of Baptism by means of symbolic actions be rejected in principle. The Second Vatican Council rightly called attention to this possibility. In this freedom the church is indeed obligated to beware lest the critical and enlisting advance becomes an adaptation, and hence an adulteration, which obscures the baptismal event or even makes it unrecognizable.

d. The form of Baptism must demonstrate the connection that exists between Baptism, faith, and church. The baptismal act can be separated neither from the faith of the baptized nor from the faith of

179

the church. The preservation of this connection is, on the one hand, the responsibility of the instruction and examination of the catechumens before their admission to Baptism and, on the other hand, the instruction of the children after Baptism. In every case the instruction is concerned with the confession of faith, whether in connection with a desire for Baptism or as a result of having already received it. In view of the problems of infant Baptism discussed above, the connection between Baptism, faith, and church must be newly emphasized and given expression in the form of the baptismal act. This includes that Baptism be administered in a larger sphere than is usually done — the midst of the assembled congregation. In this way it would become more evident that the *Credo* of the baptized and of his parents and sponsors means joining in the *Credo* of the church which encompasses child, parents, and sponsors and further accompanies them with her intercession and witness.

e. The church's freedom in shaping the act of Baptism is further limited by the unity of Baptism. "There is one body and one Spirit, just as you were called to the one hope that belongs to your call, one Lord, one faith, one Baptism, one God and Father of us all . . ." (Eph. 4:4-6). In all the variety of possible forms every Baptism must clearly demonstrate that here the same Baptism is being administered by means of which God at all times and in all places has given and continues to give men into Christ's death and into the sphere of His spiritual rule — that therefore the one Baptism is administered whereby God makes men members of the one body of Christ. This does not mean that uniformity in the baptismal liturgy is called for. Quite properly the attempts to impose such a uniform liturgy on Christendom have failed. At the same time it was right that in the individual congregations definite forms of the baptismal act soon arose — forms which received the character of an order to which every one felt himself bound. Such orders were then quite properly taken over by daughter churches that resulted from the missionary enterprise, so that in any one area of the church Baptism was administered in the same form. The fact that Baptism was administered in different ways in different areas of Christendom need not make the unity of Baptism questionable. For the basic structure of the church is fellowship and hence unity in diversity. To that extent the uniformity in the baptismal act conforms neither to the essence of Baptism nor to the essence of the church. Yet there must be a con-

180

sensus among the churches about what constitutes the center and essence of every Christian Baptism, and this consensus must be given expression also in the form of the baptismal act. Also Christians who are not trained in liturgical science as well as non-Christians must be made to see the unity of Baptism, and any obscuring of this unity by an abuse of freedom must be resisted.

f. There is a tension between the points of view expressed in the two preceding paragraphs. On the one hand, the unity of Baptism is as a rule given expression by the preservation and spread of a definite, historically established baptismal liturgy. On the other hand, the advance into new areas of the world demands changes. Thus also the question concerning the form of Baptism involves the problem of the relationship between tradition and renewal. Undoubtedly there are forms of Baptism which arose at one time in the missionary advance into new religious and cultural areas, but these forms have now become strange and unintelligible. Extra-Christian conceptions and rites which were then breached and taken over today confront us as a preservation of past religions and cultures within the church. For missionary work this raises problems similar to those connected with the transmission of dogma. For example, is the Hindu required to study Plato, Aristotle, and Neoplatonism before he can understand the Christian dogma? Must he study Hellenistic piety and Hellenistic mystery religions before he can understand the baptismal liturgy? Without a doubt the liturgical tradition has often become an obstacle to the understanding of the baptismal event. It is an important undertaking to proceed from the Lord's baptismal command and the New Testament witness and make ever new advances, and also to change venerable liturgical traditions in the process of breaking through conceptions and rites of the respective environment and making use of them. In such transformations the center of the baptismal event, its unity and wholeness, its uniqueness and nonrepeatableness, must be unconditionally maintained. At the same time the form of Baptism must show clearly what God desires to do with people today. The difficulties and dangers of such changes in the tradition are obvious. The danger of raising questions about the unity by means of a multiplicity of constantly changing forms is no less than the danger of a traditionalism which clings to a form of Baptism that has become unintelligible. These dangers can be mitigated if not all the parts of the baptismal formulas are fixed verbatim

181

and if from the start provision is made for free witness and free prayer. Tradition and new actualization will then result in relation to each other rather than in opposition, and the new form then becomes not a break with tradition but rather its unfolding and corrective. Like the church, so also the form of the baptismal act must be "constantly reformed."

The preceding reflections on the limitations of the church's freedom in her exercise of it do not imply a challenge to this freedom. On the contrary, this freedom rests precisely in the commission of her Lord and in the saving deed which God accomplishes through Baptism. Therefore the church's obedience to the Lord's directive is not demanded as obedience to the Law but to the Gospel. But this obedience is joy in the Holy Spirit. Since therefore the form of Baptism is the practical application of the spiritual spontaneity of the community of believers, no order of Baptism may be understood as a law and the validity of Baptism cannot be made to depend on the observance of a single order. As in canon law, so also here a distinction must be made between "divine right" and "human right," more exactly, between the divine command and the historical realization. However, this realization cannot be separated from the love which maintains the unity of all the baptized and to which it gives expression in the form of Baptism. In principle the freedom of form dare not be curtailed, and the form dare not be misconstrued as dogma. Yet the observance of specific orders of Baptism is not a repeal of this freedom but rather obedience to the law of love, according to which the individual baptizer and the individual congregation renounces the exercise of the given freedom in order that the unity of Baptism may be manifest to all Christians and to non-Christians as well.

In what follows we shall confine ourselves to the form of the baptismal act itself. At this place we shall not enter upon the form of preparation and of admission of the person to be baptized, nor upon the church's instruction after Baptism. This belongs in part to catechetics, in part to the doctrine of confirmation. The basic questions concerning the connection between faith, desire for Baptism, and the administration of Baptism have already been treated, especially in discussing the problem of infant Baptism. In what follows we presuppose agreement in the Christian faith, and hence in the *Credo* of the church, between those who desire Baptism for themselves or their children and the one who administers Baptism. Since the history of the baptismal liturgy has just been presented in the new and thorough researches of George Kretschmar and Bruno Jordahn,[5] we can be brief in what follows.

3. The Constitutive Center of Baptism

According to the various orders of the churches the act of Baptism as a rule includes words of proclamation, of confession, of prayer, of blessing, and largely also acts like the laying on of hands, signing with the cross, etc. Here we desire, first of all, to ask concerning the center of the baptismal act, that is, what must be maintained as the indispensable condition for the recognition of a validly administered Christian Baptism, when all further words and actions have been stripped away. This is both a dogmatic and a canonical, as well as a liturgical question. This constitutive center is the baptismal act itself. In the baptismal practice of the churches this fact becomes evident again and again, wherever emergency Baptism is administered in the face of death, and the form of this act must be limited to what is indispensably necessary. In the two following sections the liturgical developments of the act of Baptism will be treated from the perspective of this center—first of all those developments which stem from the Word and then those expressed by further actions.

In the administration of Baptism the center is the application of water to the baptized by immersion or pouring, together with the invocation of the name of the Father and of the Son and of the Holy Spirit. The name is decisive in so far as through it the water becomes a Baptism. By means of the name invoked Christian Baptism is distinguished from all other religious baptisms, washings, and sprinklings.

a. It cannot particularly be deduced with certainty from the New Testament statements about Baptism: "upon [in] the name of Jesus Christ," "of the Lord Jesus," "of the Lord Jesus Christ," as well as "into the name of the Father and of the Son and of the Holy Spirit," whether these expressions refer to designations of Baptism or to formulas used in Baptism. It is certain, however, that the name was spoken in connection with the act of Baptism and that this was not done everywhere in one and the same formulation. From this it follows that in principle various formulations of the name in Christian Baptism are possible. In the ancient church the invocation of the name of the Father and of the Son and of the Holy Spirit soon became general practice and the

183

trinitarian understanding of this triadic formula established itself. Later on Baptisms in the name of Christ alone were even regarded by some as invalid. Even if we do not concur, we must nevertheless insist that in her Baptism the church can no longer go back behind the trinitarian name. This name is not a surrender of the name of Christ but its interpretation. The activity of Jesus Christ cannot be separated from the Father and the Holy Spirit. It is at the same time the activity of the Father and the Holy Spirit. As the advance of the Gospel beyond the borders of Jewish monotheism into the pagan world necessitated supplementing the confession of Christ by the confession of God the Creator, so also the baptismal formula had to be expanded. Also today the trinitarian name is of the greatest significance in the midst of the post-Christian secularized world in which many lay claim to the name of Jesus while denying the name of God. Moreover, all of Christendom should in Baptism invoke the one "name of the Father and of the Son and of the Holy Spirit" for the sake of a universally recognizable identity of Baptism.

On the basis of the New Testament accounts the possibility must be conceded that the name used in Baptism was uttered by the baptizer or the baptized or both. Therefore the way, namely by whose mouth the name is spoken in Baptism admits in principle of several possibilities. Such possibilities were actually realized in the baptismal liturgies of the ancient church. In an increasing measure, however, both in the East and in the West, the custom established itself of having the baptizer speak the trinitarian name at the immersion or pouring. This order did not come only with the increase of infant Baptism where the child could not itself say the name. The fact that the baptizer, and not the baptized, invokes the name of the triune God in the midst of the baptismal act is appropriate to the nature of Baptism in that Baptism is something done to the baptized: God is the one acting through Baptism, while the baptized is simply the receiver, indeed the one dying and awakened to life in Baptism. The name and the new-creating power of the triune God comes to the person in Baptism, grasps him, and liberates and renews him. Although in principle there are various possibilities for the utterance of the name, for the sake of the visible unity of the church Christendom should also insist that the baptizer speak the name over the baptized.

The formula by which this is done is different in the East and the

184

West. The Orthodox Church uses the words: "N.N. is baptized in the name of the Father and of the Son and of the Holy Spirit." The Roman Church and the Reformation churches say: "N.N., I baptize you in the name of the Father and of the Son and of the Holy Spirit." The Orthodox passive form, in which the baptizer is not explicitly included, gives especially pointed expression to the exclusive activity of God. But the Western form would be misunderstood if it were seen as giving prominence to the person of the baptizer. Also in the Western understanding the baptizer is only the instrument, while God is the one who is acting. In this respect there is no essential difference between the two formulas. In any case the person and the name of the baptizer is of no significance for the baptismal event. Yet the person of the baptized, in whom God is acting through Word and water, is important. In this respect it is appropriate that the baptized be mentioned or addressed by name in connection with the baptismal formula.

In the New Testament texts the most common preposition before the invoked name is *eis* (εἰς "upon the name," or more accurately "into the name"), while *en* (ἐν) and *epi* ἐπί) are also used. Also in Matt. 28:19 Baptism is commanded "into the name of the Father and of the Son and of the Holy Spirit." This *eis* expresses not only a relationship to this name but assignment to the divine reality designated by the name. In the later form of baptizing "in the name of the Father and of the Son and of the Holy Spirit," the accent now lies on the fact that the Baptism is being performed by the command and authority of the triune God, and therefore God is the one acting. This indeed corresponds to New Testament baptismal statements, but the special aspect of assignment no longer finds expression in this formula itself. For that reason thought should be given to whether the formula ought not incorporate the New Testament language of assignment and read "into the name of the Father and of the Son and of the Holy Spirit," especially since the Latin *"in nomine"* and the German *"im Namen"* [as well as the English "in the name"] have a more limited meaning of authorization than the *en* and *epi* of the Greek *Koine*. In any event it is the task of instruction for Baptism to give clear expression to the aspect of assignment linked with the speaking of the name.

b. The manner in which the water was applied in early Christian Baptisms cannot be determined with certainty from the New Testament. Complete immersion of the baptized was possibly the rule. So it was in the ancient church and remained the custom in the West until the Middle Ages. The Eastern Church observes this custom to the present day and the Baptist movement revived it in the West. However, there are indications that already the early Christian Baptisms were not administered exclusively by complete submersion but also by pouring. This possibility is in any case explicitly mentioned in the *Didache* and further attested especially in connection with the Baptism of the sick. After the Western Church in the 14th century had universally granted pouring alongside immersion, pouring established itself more and more and was also adopted by the Reformation churches. But while Luther still baptized by holding the naked child over the font and pouring water over the entire child, the application of water [affusion] was later confined more and more to the breast, the head, or the forehead. Beyond this, in modern Protestant circles, Baptism is frequently "reduced from a real wetting to a sprinkling and eventually in practice to a mere moistening with as little water as possible." To this ironic observation Karl Barth rightly added the question, "Who would think that Paul according to 1 Cor. 10:1-4, saw the prefiguration of baptism in so critical an experience as the passage of the Israelites through the Red Sea?" [6]

Since the New Testament tradition prescribes no specific form of applying the water and since the statements concerning the saving significance of Baptism make remarkably little use of a symbolical interpretation of the water, the validity of Baptism cannot be made to depend on the way in which the water is applied in Baptism. Yet it should be made clear by the use of the water that in Baptism the life of the baptized is taken hold of in a way that involves the whole person. For that reason the appropriate forms of application are immersion or pouring with as much water as possible. Apart from the Baptism of the sick, sprinkling and certainly a mere moistening are to be rejected. Whether the immersion or pouring is done once or three times is a matter of indifference. If this question is brought into relation with the trinitarian name, reasons may be cited in favor of both a single or a triple application, as this was in fact done in the history of the baptismal liturgy.

4. Developing the Baptismal Act Through the Word

The invocation of the triune God contains acknowledgment of the saving deed which God accomplished once for all in the sending of Jesus Christ and the Holy Spirit and which God desires to accomplish

186

through Baptism. Just as the Christological titles of majesty by means of which the post-Easter church confessed Jesus presuppose the history of Jesus and acknowledge it as the historical way of the Christ, so the triune name of God contains the acknowledgment of all the deeds which God has performed and which He has promised to accomplish. This concentration contained in the name is to be developed in the baptismal liturgy. Because of the decisive significance of the name, and hence the Word, in the center of Baptism, this expansion must take place above all through the Word.

Here all basic forms in which faith responds to the proclaimed Gospel must be considered: In the invocation of God and in the address to men, that is, in *prayer* and *adoration* on the one hand, and in *witness* and *teaching* on the other hand. But these different forms of expression are concentrated in the confession which the believer makes in the presence of God and to the public. The *blessing,* in turn, combines the invocation of God with the assurance given to men.

In the liturgical development of the baptismal act consideration must be given furthermore to the fact that (apart from infant Baptism) the faith and request of the person to be baptized precede the administration of Baptism. Hence the developing of the baptismal act must allow the *person to be baptized* to express himself, as he utters his desire for Baptism and confesses his faith. Furthermore it must be borne in mind that through Baptism God is acting toward the *church.* He not only enlists the church as the instrument of His baptizing but He makes the baptized a member of the church, causes the church to grow through Baptism, and entrusts the baptized to her for the rest of his life. Therefore also the church must be allowed to express herself in the liturgical development of the baptismal act. It is true that the connection between Baptism and church has always been consciously maintained dogmatically and in canon law, but in the practice of Baptism this has often been neglected.

Thus the developing of the baptismal act must be achieved not only in the variety of basic forms of expression by means of which faith calls upon the triune God, bears witness to Him, and confesses Him, but also in the variety of the voices of the persons which as baptizer, baptized, and congregation are united in the same faith and are at Baptism associated with each other in irreversible personal relations: the baptizer as the instrument through which God performs the Baptism and proclaims this event to the baptized and the congregation; the person who desires Baptism and receives it upon the confession of his faith; and the congregation which surrounds the baptized with her intercession, receives him from God as a gift, and adopts him for all time as her own. In all these relations the significance of the trinitarian name must be unfolded and the historical saving deed of God extolled as His present activity.

Finally it must be remembered that, as the variety of the New Testament assertions demonstrates, the gift of Baptism is too great to be adequately expressed by means of only one category of concepts. No single dogmatic or liturgical formulation is sufficient to bear full witness to these riches. Therefore alongside the fixed portions in the baptismal liturgy space must be given for alternate formulations, and specifically also for the *free* word of witness and prayer, so that the fullness of the New Testament understanding of Baptism may be given expression. Consideration of the church year can also be helpful in the liturgical development of the various Christological and pneumatological implications of Baptism. If, as in the ancient church, preference is given to the seasons of Easter, Pentecost, and Epiphany for the administration of Baptism, definite meaningful combinations will almost automatically suggest themselves.

It is not the task of the dogmatic presentation of Baptism to develop a baptismal liturgy but to clarify its basic principles in a systematic way. In this sense we shall confine ourselves in what follows to a few basic observations. The details regarding the components of the liturgy of Baptism (the number of elements, their wording, and their sequence) as well as regarding the persons speaking (baptizer, person to be baptized, sponsors, congregation) are left to the area of liturgics.

a. Although the Biblical statements in support of Baptism belong in catechetical instruction, it is natural to read the most important *Biblical texts* again at the beginning of the baptismal service. This applies especially to the baptismal command of Matt. 28:18-20, since it provides the authorization for what follows. Mark 16:16 is often added. But it should be considered whether instead of this text it would not be better to read the account of Jesus' Baptism by John before the baptismal command. The Baptism of Jesus does not play a role in the history of the baptismal liturgy, but it is basic, and rightly so, in the church's teaching on the institution of Baptism.

188

Because of the current crisis in Baptism no Baptism (except in cases of emergency) should be administered without a *Baptism address,* however brief, preceding it. This address should always be based on one of the New Testament baptismal texts, and its specific baptismal witness must be applied to the baptized in his concrete situation. At the same time the specific witness of this text is to be used to remind the congregation of the benefit of Baptism already received. By the alternation of baptismal texts in succeeding baptismal services and by the proclamation linked to the specific content of each text the congregation would become aware of the riches of the baptismal event. This address to the concrete situation of the baptized and the congregation cannot be replaced by fixed formulas in the ritual. However, the purpose of the baptismal address is not realized by means of general remarks on God's love and grace. It is the gracious activity of God particularly in Baptism that must be emphasized.

As the epistles combine witness to Baptism as God's new-creating deed with the exhortation to walk in newness of life on the basis of this deed, so the baptismal address must combine promise and *exhortation.* But since the New Testament exhortations are based on Baptism already administered, it is worth considering whether the admonitions should be separated from the baptismal address and addressed to the baptized after his Baptism. The address preceding the baptismal act itself should primarily proclaim the saving deed which God desires to accomplish through Baptism.

While the baptismal address proclaims the deed which God desires to accomplish through Baptism, the "post-baptismal *votum*" presupposes Baptism. This *votum* in the form of blessing assures the baptized of what happened in the name of the Father and of the Son and of the Holy Spirit: "Almighty God, the Father of our Lord Jesus Christ, who has begotten you again by water and the Holy Spirit and has forgiven you all your sins, strengthen you with His grace to life everlasting."

As every exhortation in the divine service is surrounded and borne by the invocation of God, so it is also with the baptismal proclamation. The address to man and the address to God belong together in essence. Also the *baptismal prayers* give concrete expression to the significance of the triune name of God. In the prayer before the act of Baptism, intercession is made for the person to be baptized, namely the petition that God would grant him the gifts promised in Baptism. At this point the prayer for the Holy Spirit is to be especially emphasized. This prayer acknowledges at the same time that the church is not in control of the baptismal grace. On the contrary, it is granted by God in His sovereign freedom. In the prayer after the Baptism and the post-baptismal *votum* the praise and thanksgiving of the baptized and the congregation are offered to God for what He has accomplished through Baptism. Here the adoption as a child of God which has taken place in Christ should be stressed. Also the prayers should not be offered only in one and the same formulation but give expression to the trinitarian riches of the baptismal gift.

b. If the precondition for the reception of Baptism is faith and the desire for Baptism, then in the developed form of the baptismal act both must be expressed by the person to be baptized. This can be done in various ways, especially as far as the *confession of faith* is concerned, as is evident from the history of the liturgy. This confession can be made by means of the simple Yes to the respective baptismal questions ("Do you believe in . . . ?"), by means of repeating the assertions of faith contained in the questions, by means of the creed spoken jointly with the baptized or the sponsors or the entire congregation, or also by means of the confession spoken only by the baptized in response to the baptizer's request. The last mentioned form of confession is probably the most appropriate. As surely as the baptized with his *Credo* joins in with the church's *Credo,* so he is not yet a member of the church but desires to be received into the church through his Baptism. To that extent he must, in the presence of the congregation, clearly enunciate his confession as his own.

Neither the New Testament accounts of Baptism nor the history of the liturgy in the ancient church furnish a single formulation of the confession. Yet early in the history of the baptismal confession there was the same expansion of the Christological confession into a trinitarian one as was the case in supplanting the name of Christ with the name of the Father and of the Son and of the Holy Spirit in the act of Baptism. But even with this development of the confession to Christ a great variety of different territorial forms of confession were in use for a long time. These formulas were only gradually made uniform in the church of the empire. It follows that the validity of Baptism does not require the same formulation of the confession, but it does require the same content of confession. For the sake of the unity of faith which

190

should be evident to every one the person to be baptized ought to confess his faith in the same words as the church from which he desires Baptism. For the same reason it makes good sense for as many churches as possible to use the same text of the baptismal confession in their catechetical instruction and in the administration of their Baptisms. In Western Christendom this is the Apostles' Creed. In any case the churches cannot go back behind the trinitarian development of the Christological Creed any more than they can go back behind the trinitarian name of God upon which and in which they baptize — and for the same reasons.

In the confession of faith the believer gives glory to God, commits himself to Him as the Lord, and bears witness to Him before men. This turning to God at the same time includes the knowledge of sin and its renunciation, as well as the resolve to serve God alone henceforth. The act of confession includes various acts of turning to and turning away from — turning to God and the fellowship of believers and turning away from sin and former social ties to the extent that these were determined by the rule of sin. True, this is not expressed in the wording of the creed. With the same "objectivity" as that which characterizes doxology and adoration the affirmations of the creed mention the great deeds of God and extol the triune God. The ego of the confessor becomes explicit only in the word, "I believe," and there the believer is looking away from himself to God. The *Credo* is directed altogether to God. But in every confession of faith the confession of sins and the resolve to sin no more are implicitly contained.

These implicit aspects may become explicit in special statements. Indeed, they fairly cry for expression. In the history of the baptismal liturgy this was done especially in the *abrenuntiatio* (renunciation of Satan) and the *syntaxis* (pledge to Christ), as well as in the baptismal vow. In principle these liturgical pieces say nothing different from what in fact takes place in the confession of faith. They are liturgically fixed formulations of aspects which are present in the creed.

In the course of history the *abrenuntiatio* experienced various formulations. But always it concerned renunciation by the baptized of the devil's dominion, often in direct address to the devil. Confessions of sin, on the other hand, seldom become explicit in the baptismal liturgy. According to the New Testament the dominion of sin and of the devil belong together, and this connection has been retained in the

191

church's teaching on Baptism (cf., e. g., Luther's answer to the second question in the Fourth Chief Part of the Small Catechism: [in] Baptism [God] "forgives sin, delivers from death and the devil, and grants everlasting salvation to all who believe . . ."). Yet it cannot be overlooked that the customary form of the *abrenuntiatio* represents a shift over against the New Testament baptismal statements. These place deliverance from the rule of sin into the foreground — not liberation from the rule of demons. Therefore the more recent evangelical liturgics has properly subjected the *abrenuntiatio* to critical review. It would be more appropriate to give explicit expression in the order of Baptism to the aspect of the confession of sins contained in the confession of faith. While the place for the renunciation or the confession of sins in the order of Baptism is before the confession of faith, we need to ask whether the *baptismal pledge,* if this aspect is to be given special expression, should be spoken by the person to be baptized before or after the act of Baptism. Since the possibility to walk in newness of life is the result of Baptism, it would be appropriate to place the promise of obedience *after* Baptism as a response to the corresponding admonition.

c. The congregation participates in the Baptism in an active and receiving way. Not only the baptized person but the congregation is the instrument of God's activity, and in the baptized the congregation receives a new member. For this reason Baptism should be administered in the presence of the assembled congregation. Only the sick should be granted Baptism at home or on the sickbed.

Since the baptismal action is unfolded by the Word, the congregation must have something to say also, and her participation cannot be limited to silent prayer, listening to the sermon and the confession, and being eyewitnesses of the baptismal act. By means of her hymns the congregation should pray for the coming of the Holy Spirit and thank God for what He has accomplished for the baptized and the congregation through Baptism. With her Amen the congregation should receive the confession of the baptized. Together with the baptizer and the baptized the congregation should join in the Lord's Prayer which is often spoken only by the baptizer (or the baptizer and the sponsors). If an exhortation follows Baptism, it is worth considering whether the pledge of the congregation should not join the pledge of the baptized and thus receive him as her own in love and accompany him in the future — a custom that has been practiced at many places during the persecutions of this century.

d. The Baptism of adults and of children is one and the same Baptism. This identity is expressed in that in both cases Baptism in its constitutive center is administered in one and the same way. It is true that infant Baptism raises special problems for the further liturgical development of the baptismal act.

In the missionary situation of the early church the baptismal act came into practice exclusively with reference to adults who had come to faith and requested Baptism. The same liturgy was then also used for the Baptism of children. This practice was maintained even when subsequently infant Baptisms outnumbered adult Baptisms. Hence the questions concerning renunciation, desire for Baptism, and faith were addressed to the child but answered by the sponsors as guarantors. Thus the sponsors take the place of the infants and answer in their stead. The precondition for this—as shown in the previous chapter (three, 4,d)—is the understanding of the church as the sphere of Christ's power and as the fellowship of the Holy Spirit, in which one represents the other and God answers prayer and consummates what He begins in Baptism. The baptized is no longer an individual but a member of the spiritual body of Christ.

It should indeed be asked whether this ecclesiological connection remains too obscure and is inadequately demonstrated when the order for adult Baptism is also used for infant Baptism. There is some shift in the baptismal questions already in Augustine in that the questions are not addressed to the child but to the sponsors. They are to affirm that the child renounces the devil, believes, and desires Baptism. In this way, however, the problems associated with the questions at infant Baptism are not solved but merely pinpointed. It would seem appropriate then, in connection with infant Baptism, to reshape the questions in such a way that the parents and sponsors are asked concerning their faith and their desire to have the child baptized. According to this order the parents and sponsors make confession of their own faith in the presence of the congregation, and the statements about the faith of the children are turned into a prayer for the faith of the children. The statement about the child's renunciation then becomes a prayer for the child's deliverance from the dominion of sin and the devil. The pledge of the

193

person to be baptized becomes the pledge of the parents and sponsors to rear the child in the Christian faith. Since the assumption of this responsibility is the prerequisite for the administration of infant Baptism, its appropriate place (in distinction from the pledge of an adult) is before the baptismal act. Lutheran and Reformed churches in southwest Germany have moved in this direction by the development of special formulas for infant Baptism. These formulas have since been widely disseminated. In them the differences between adult and infant Baptism are confined in essence to the baptismal questions and the addition of the pericope of Jesus' blessing of the little children. This reshaping of the baptismal questions does raise the danger that the elementary significance of Baptism as an event between God and the baptized is itself not made clearly manifest, and that the impression might be created that God is doing something different in infant Baptism than in the Baptism of an adult.

5. Developing the Baptismal Act Through Further Acts

The Book of Acts reports isolated instances of the laying on of hands in connection with Baptism. But in the course of the history of the liturgy not only the laying on of hands but various additional acts soon became a fixed part of the baptismal liturgy. (Like the laying on of hands) in part they came from Judaism, in part they are transpositions of metaphorical terms for Baptism in the New Testament (like "anointing" and "seal") into acts which in turn have Old Testament antecedents, and in part they are taken over from the Gospel tradition (like exorcism, Ephphatha, or footwashing). The accompanying actions are shaped primarily by Old and New Testament traditions, but influences of the religio-historical, specifically Hellenistic environment likewise played a role — as was the case also in the development of the mystery theology of the ancient church. As a rule these actions surrounding Baptism were linked with a word which either promised the baptized a special effect of the baptismal event or interpreted the accompanying action.

The ancient church adopted such actions in a great variety of forms and meanings and placed them into the service of a liturgical development of Baptism. Even though certain actions from among this variety, especially the laying on of hands, the anointing with oil, and the sign of the cross, were widely spread and in a sense became constants of the

194

baptismal liturgy, their significance was not everywhere the same. One and the same action, performed before or after Baptism, could have a different meaning. The meanings of the various actions could coalesce. A number of different actions could also be combined. Thus the significance of these rites cannot always be determined exactly.

In spite of all variety these actions have this in common, however, that they were almost always performed on the baptized by the baptizer (or his assistant). From him the baptized receives the laying on of hands, the anointing, the sign of the cross, etc. Among the rites surrounding Baptism there are scarcely any that are to be performed by the baptized (e. g., turning from the West to the East). Even when the baptized participates (as with the putting on of the white baptismal robe or carrying the baptismal candle or the baptismal crown), this is in its decisive aspect not a matter of his activity but rather of the reception of this gift, of being robed and crowned, of being entrusted with the light of truth. This shaping of the baptismal ceremonies by that which is done to the person in his Baptism conforms to the tendency of the New Testament baptismal statements which primarily bear witness to God's activity upon the baptized. The riches of this divine activity are to be elucidated by means of the accompanying acts. These acts highlight individual aspects of God's action in Baptism.

This dogmatic treatise is not concerned with setting forth the history of the origin and spread of these ceremonies, nor their place, their frequency, and their specific meaning in the various liturgical traditions. That task was performed in the detailed analyses by George Kretschmar[7] and may be taken for granted here. Nor are we aiming at a complete listing of the ceremonies which have come into use anywhere in the history of Christendom. We shall confine ourselves to brief references to the most important ones in order to get at the basic problems raised by them for the form and the understanding of Baptism. From this perspective a distinction will be made between rites performed in connection with the baptized and those performed on baptismal elements. The latter are of course also related to the baptized — but not directly.

a. The *laying on of hands* immediately after the act of Baptism is widely attested[8] in the various baptismal liturgies of the ancient church and is still practiced in most churches in connection with the postbaptismal *votum.* This act places special emphasis on the significance of

195

Baptism as the impartation of the Spirit. However, it is found in the baptismal liturgies not only at this place and in this sense. It is also used in combination with other words and actions (for example, anointing, sign of the cross, and Lord's Prayer). This conforms to the fact that also the New Testament reports the laying on of hands in quite different contexts.

The act of *anointing*[9] soon became a fixed ritual also, and in part it complemented the laying on of hands or in part replaced it. It was performed at times before, at times after Baptism—sometimes applied to the whole body, sometimes only to the forehead. This act also stresses the imparting of the Spirit aspect—but to a large extent in the special connection of understanding anointing as consecration to the priesthood or also as inauguration to kingship. Where this is done consciously, the anointing testifies that the believer becomes a member of the priestly and royal people of God through Baptism and the Holy Spirit. In this way the Christological relationship of Baptism comes to the fore at the same time; for in confessing the name of Christ the church acknowledges Jesus as the anointed Messiah-King. In the Orthodox Church the chrism has received a special dogmatic weight which in a certain sense corresponds to the laying on of hands practiced by the Roman Church in connection with confirmation. But in distinction from the latter, the Orthodox chrism has remained a component of the baptismal act.

The act of *signing the baptized with the cross,* already well attested at the end of the 2d century, calls special attention to the aspect of sealing contained in Baptism.[10] While in the New Testament the act of sealing, as also the anointing, was a metaphorical designation of Baptism with a view to the impartation of the gift of the Spirit,[11] the sealing became a ritual in the ancient church whereby the Christological significance of Baptism, namely the subordination of the baptized under the rule of the Crucified, was emphasized. Thus the act of signing with the cross could also be interpreted as "obligation to the military service of Christ."[12] In some liturgies the sign of the cross is applied together with the anointing; in some it is connected with the laying on of hands. But also the anointing without the sign of the cross was occasionally interpreted as a sealing.

Exorcism[13] gives expression to the process contained in Baptism, that the believer is removed from the sphere of satanic-demonic power. It is the concrete development of the negation contained in being assigned to Christ, but it is now not spoken by the baptized in the form of renunciation but by the baptizer in the form of a command to Satan to come out of the baptized. The word of exorcism is not always connected with the same act in the various baptismal liturgies. Sometimes it is linked with blowing on the baptized, sometimes with touching the baptized with the baptizer's saliva. Occasionally also the laying on of hands, the sign of the cross, and other actions accompanying Baptism were understood in an exorcistic sense. The prominent role which exorcism plays in some baptismal liturgies and which is expressed in a multiplication of exorcisms represents an obvious shift away from the New Testament baptismal statements. While these clearly attest the change in rulers accomplished in Baptism, they speak less of deliverance from Satan than of deliverance from the rule of sin.

The *gift of salt,* which is of later origin, was widely interpreted in an exorcistic sense. Yet its significance cannot be limited to that. There is much in favor of the claim that this act gives expression to the aspect of establishing the covenant contained in Baptism. In any case the Old Testament speaks of a "covenant of salt" (Num. 18:19; 2 Chron. 13:5), and the joint eating of salt is mentioned also in the Oriental and Hellenistic environment to signify that the participants are entering upon a "relationship of friendship and trust." [14]

The food consisting of *milk* and *honey* [15] takes up the Old Testament promise of the land "flowing with milk and honey" (Ex. 3:8 et al.) and might be understood as pointing to the eschatological future of the people of God and, in combination with the Lord's Supper, as a sign of awaiting the banquet in the kingdom of God.

b. The ceremony of *consecrating the water* lays special stress on the aspect contained in the baptismal act of enlisting the water for God's activity through Baptism. The unity of this act with Baptism is preserved in that as a rule it is also performed in the name of the Father and of the Son and of the Holy Spirit. To the extent that the water is consecrated at a time other than the act of Baptism, so that the same consecrated water is used for many Baptisms, this ceremony gives expression to the aspect of ecclesiological unity contained in every Baptism. It cannot be overlooked, however, that the consecration of water suggests a change in perspective over against the New Testament statements, even though the ceremony highlights an aspect that is present in every baptismal act. While in the New Testament the water together with the Word is the vehicle of God's action in the baptismal act, the consecrated water is given an independent significance along-side the baptismal act. The focus is shifted from the *act* of immersion or pouring toward the *substance* of the water. Before long, questionable ideas of the consecrated water as bearer of the Holy Spirit were associated with this ritual.[16]

Similar observations may be made about the *consecration of oil*.[17] Here shifts of that nature are even more serious, because the anointing is not essential for the act of Baptism.

In surveying the various ceremonies mentioned, especially those in group a. [above], we are permitted to say that in spite of the variety of their meanings those elementary contexts of meaning recur in which the New Testament would have us understand Baptism: the Christological, the pneumatological, and the ecclesiological context. The pneumatological significance occupies the foreground. Each of these contexts also contains implicitly the separation which takes place through Baptism. This separation is made explicit especially in the exorcism and indeed — by means of repetition — given expression in a one-sided way.

The fact that in the course of the history of liturgy the baptismal act was developed not only by means of words but also by means of actions can by no means be condemned in principle. Such development is justified to the extent that by it aspects of Baptism itself are especially accented and clarified. Under those circumstances the addition of such ceremonies is an expression of the freedom which was granted the church with the commission to preach the Gospel. In this freedom the church may witness to God's saving activity also by means of visible signs. Nor can there be any objection to the fact that the ancient church also enlisted conceptions and customs from the religious environment. It is precisely in the advance into the world, in penetrating and transforming the world's conceptions and customs, that the rule of Christ is to be attested. Hence there can be no objection in principle if in its advance into areas of other cultures and religions Baptism is made meaningful by the use of different signs, and traditional ceremonies that are unintelligible in the new context are discarded.

If the acts accompanying Baptism are viewed as symbolical clarification of what God does through Baptism, their variety should not be surprising. The riches of the divine activity cannot be expressed by just one word either. Nor should there be any surprise in the fact that the meanings of these acts often coalesce in a peculiar way and are often difficult to delimit in detail. These acts bear witness to one and the same baptismal event. If the witnessing character of these acts is retained, one can also understand why the sequence in which they follow in the structure of the various liturgies is often so different. This applies least of all to exorcism, but more in the case of the laying on of hands and the anointing—acts which in some liturgies are performed before the act of Baptism, in some after it. If they are illustrative witnesses to the one baptismal event, they all point to the same center.

The awareness of all the churches that the accompanying ceremonies have no constitutive significance for the validity and effect of Baptism is shown by the fact that they may be omitted in emergency Baptism. Only the invocation of the triune name and the use of water are essential. The liturgical acts which surround the baptismal act itself do not have constitutive significance, but they illustrate the constitutive center. Everything that these ceremonies attest and symbolize is imparted fully and completely to the baptized through the simple act of immersion or pouring in the name of the Father and of the Son and of the Holy Spirit.

6. The Danger of Obscuring the Understanding of Baptism

First of all, we understand the actions which in many churches surround the baptismal act to be illustrative witnesses and symbolic clarifications. But theological interpretation and especially folk piety do not stop with this understanding. This is not true of all baptismal ceremonies in the same way. It is especially the exorcism, the imposition of hands, and the anointing that have been viewed as efficacious means of grace and hence not only in a significative but also in an effective sense. This is confirmed by the words connected with these acts. These words frequently have not only an allusive and witnessing character, but also a promissory and imparting character. But this raises the question as to what conclusions are to be drawn from such an effective understanding of these accompanying acts for the understanding of Baptism itself, that is, the constitutive center of the baptismal act.

This question can be attacked from various angles. Undoubtedly understanding of the times plays a special role here. For that reason the problem will be approached from this perspective.

If the actions which precede or follow the baptismal act itself are themselves understood as means of the divine saving activity, it is easy to reflect on their temporal sequence and to regard the ceremony either as precondition for Baptism or as its completion. But then we must ask what these ceremonies convey in distinction from Baptism. Now such questions need not necessarily follow, even if the accompanying ceremonies are viewed as effective. It is possible to ignore the temporal sequence in the liturgical interpretation and to see the various actions as circling around the center of the baptismal act. Such a conception is present particularly in Eastern thought. In contrast to the Roman Church the Orthodox Church refuses to fix the moment of the consecration of the elements in the Lord's Supper (is it by means of the epiclesis, the words of institution, or the totality of the eucharistic prayers?), and thus in the eucharistic celebration in the view of eternity time in a certain sense stands still. So also in Baptism the temporal sequence of the individual acts of the baptismal liturgy may become unimportant in the awareness of faith. In that case the preceding and following ceremonies are understood as a unity with the baptismal act itself. Then nothing else is imparted through these ceremonies than through Baptism itself. Even though they are regarded as efficacious means, they merely unfold the riches of Baptism itself. The Christological, pneumatological, and ecclesiological unity of the divine activity through Baptism can be preserved intact, along with an effective understanding of the accompanying ceremonies; indeed, these ceremonies may clarify that unity. Although these ceremonies occur in a temporal sequence, they need not be interpreted in the sense of conditions and supplements of Baptism. But this has in fact happened by no means rarely, more so in the Latin church than in the Greek church. Not only was the question raised whether deliverance from the dominion of the powers of perdition was achieved by exorcism or Baptism, or whether the Holy Spirit was imparted through Baptism or the laying on of hands, etc., but there were answers to these questions which reduced acknowledgment of God's activity in Baptism. Already Tertullian was of the opinion that Baptism imparted only the forgiveness of sins, but not the Holy Spirit; the latter he expected of the imposition of hands.[18] Wide currency was also given to the notion that exorcism was required before the renewal through the baptismal act could take place. Examples of such interpretations could be multiplied. In that case the ceremonies no longer serve to bear witness to Baptism itself, but they take their place beside Baptism as special means of salvation. They no longer develop specific aspects of Baptism, but they bring about these aspects in place of Baptism.

Corresponding questions arise when we consider the repetitions of one and the same ceremony in some baptismal liturgies. This applies especially to exorcism and anointing. Such repetitions make the question still more urgent as to what the baptized receives through the accompanying acts in distinction from Baptism itself. Do not the repetitions give these acts an additional importance of their own? Do they not by their very number lessen the importance of the onetime Baptism? Also these questions need not be unconditionally answered in the affirmative. If we ignore the temporal sequence and view these accompanying acts not as preceding condition or as subsequent supplement, but in spite of their temporal sequence as simultaneous development of the single act of Baptism, these repetitions can also be understood as a fullness of witness and an all the more impressive guarantee of what is imparted to the baptized and the congregation through Baptism. However, these repetitions were by no means understood only in this way. On the contrary, men reflected on their temporal sequence, and with an effective interpretation it was hardly possible to avoid getting into a quantitative way of thinking. So, for example, the exorcism was regarded as a precondition for the reception of baptismal grace, and this led to the idea that only one exorcism was not adequate but could be fully effective only if repeated. In that case multiplication and repetition of the same ceremonies no longer represent a fuller reference to the power of the one Baptism, but now anxious considerations suggest themselves as to whether the preconditions for receiving the baptismal grace have been adequately met and whether what is missing in the baptismal act itself is adequately supplied by further subsequent actions.

The problem of what belongs to the baptismal act itself is raised in yet another way when ceremonies are removed from the baptismal liturgy in point of time and are performed as independent acts, or when the same ceremonies appear both in the rite of Baptism and also at a different time. For example, if exorcism is performed already during the catechumenate before Baptism, or if the laying on of hands is performed in temporal isolation after Baptism as confirmation, then the question can arise in heightened measure whether the effect of Baptism must not be regarded as being reduced to the extent of those effects which are assigned to the ceremonies. Again, this reduction does not necessarily follow. Careful attention must be given to the interpretation of such actions that are separated in time from Baptism.

In this connection it must be remembered that while Baptism is to be administered only once, it determines the entire subsequent life and to that extent is done once for always. Hence there are aspects in Baptism which call for expression also in the later life of the baptized, even though Baptism itself is unrepeatable. This applies not only to the act of repentance and faith in which Baptism was received and in which the further Christian life consists; it also applies to the forgiveness which was granted in Baptism and on which the baptized must depend as long as he lives. This applies also to the reception of the Holy Spirit. Just as in distinction from the Incarnation the pentecostal outpouring of the Spirit was not a onetime event but occurred for the first time, so also the gift of the Spirit in Baptism is the beginning of further activity by the Spirit, the guarantee of further gifts of the Spirit. The coming of the Spirit is to be expected again and again and His gifts are to be prayed for. All of this is true — regardless of whether it involves the Baptism of an adult or of a child. Just as special acts of absolution need not cast doubt on the deliverance from the dominion of sin experienced in Baptism, so special acts of the imposition of hands, separate from Baptism, and in connection with the prayer for the gifts of the Holy Spirit, need not cast doubt on the gift of the Spirit in Baptism. Similarly, the repetition of the sign of the cross need cast no doubt on the sealing that took place in Baptism. On the contrary, as a reminder of the assignment to Christ which took place in Baptism, this assignment is to be made over and over again.

Similar points of view can be advanced also for many of the rites preceding Baptism. The power of God is at work not only through Baptism but also through the preaching of the Gospel that preceded. The history of theology shows, however, that baptismal ceremonies given temporal independence have in fact often led to notable shifts in the understanding of Baptism. It was no accident that in the early Middle Ages the number of sacraments became a serious problem which was only poorly solved by the distinction between sacraments and sacramentals. In fact by the large number of other sacramental acts the significance of Baptism was greatly reduced, at least in folk piety.

Nor did the churches of the Reformation escape these problems. If the gift of the Holy Spirit is expected of confirmation, what was imparted in Baptism? The discussions in the Anglican Church concerning the relationship between Baptism and confirmation have made the problem of the particularity of both acts especially clear. In all churches the saving activity of God through preaching, Baptism, and Lord's Supper has been developed in further acts (e. g., the blessing of children in the Baptist Churches), but the relationship of these acts to preaching and the two "chief sacraments" is frequently so little clarified that the saving significance of Baptism is obscured.

Also the temporal separation of the consecration of water and oil from Baptism need not cast doubt on its significance. Here water and oil are enlisted for Baptism in such a way that the consecration performed by the bishop or the priest at the same time bears witness to the unity of the many Baptisms administered with the same consecrated elements. Yet it cannot be overlooked that this separation has led to a serious shift from the act of Baptism to the substances of the consecrated elements and has turned eyes away from God's concrete action through Baptism. All too easily men could now ascribe to the consecrated elements an inherent power of grace and a salutary effect of their own even apart from the act of Baptism. This too did not remain merely a threatening possibility but actually took place — both in theological statements and in the piety of the people.

Thus the accompanying ceremonies can not only illustrate and confirm God's new-creating act through Baptism, but they can also obscure it. Their large number, their repetition, and their effective interpretation can conceal the uniqueness and power of Baptism. They bear in them the danger of devaluating the baptismal act itself and of emptying the understanding of Baptism. This danger becomes all the greater the more the ritual development takes place at the expense of the baptismal proclamation, as the words of the baptismal liturgy are frozen in formulas, and as Baptism is even performed in a language that is foreign to the congregation.

Throughout the history of the church these dangers have been recognized again and again and have been counteracted repeatedly by emphasizing the unity of the baptismal act theologically and by giving expression to this unity by means of tightening up the liturgy. In this context we must view also the two orders of Baptism which Luther presented in his Baptism booklet of 1523 and again in 1526.[19] For one thing, it is important that Luther proposes the use of the German language. Quite apart from the opening admonitions, the unfolding of the baptismal action by means of the Word in this way received special weight. The Word is here understood primarily not as an efficacious formula but as promise and assurance. Also significant is the reduction in the ceremonies accompanying Baptism. While the first edition of the Baptism booklet was still quite restrained in this respect, the second edition went farther. Only the exsufflation [being breathed upon], the signing with the cross, one exorcism, the laying on of hands, and finally, the putting on of the baptismal robe were retained. Lutheran orders of Baptism in southwest Germany made further reductions from the beginning. They dropped the exsufflation, the exorcism, and other ceremonies still retained by Luther.[20] In the baptismal orders of Zwingli and Calvin such accompanying actions are missing altogether.[21] In contrast the baptismal admonitions received increasingly more emphasis. But even in those Lutheran churches whose orders of Baptism were modeled after Luther's Baptism booklet of 1526, the exorcism soon began to become a problem [22] which the churches tried to overcome, at first by means of a theological reinterpretation of exorcism, later by making it optional, or finally by getting rid of it altogether. However the imposition of hands and the signing with the cross are still almost universally in use.

To fear the danger of an obscuration of the understanding of Baptism only from an increase in accompanying ritual actions would, of course, be wrong. The danger threatens no less from an increase of words surrounding the baptismal act without bearing clear witness to the baptismal event. There are addresses, prayers, and admonitions that devaluate and empty Baptism, since they do not deal with the center of the baptismal event, namely, God's new-creating activity, but lose themselves in general talk and in familiar sentimentalities. In such cases their content is, for example, the happy event of the birth but not the new birth—the enrichment of the family but not the fact of being added to the people of God. They perhaps point to the prospect of some sort of divine help for the earthly life, but they have nothing to say about the baptized being given into Christ's death for a new life.

Baptism can also be obscured if this act is developed neither in word nor in accompanying actions. There is a flatly mechanical way of baptizing which is satisfied with the barest essentials even when there is no emergency, and declines to make concrete application of the baptismal event. While the validity of such Baptisms cannot be questioned, the perfunctory manner of their administration permits neither the baptized nor the congregation to recognize the riches of what God is here doing for them.

Thus the danger of obscuring Baptism by its form can come from completely different sides. It is the church's task to recognize these dangers in her baptizing and in vigilance and love seek the way for a liturgical activity which will lead through these dangers. The possible forms of the baptismal liturgy are numerous. What is decisive is that God's saving action in Baptism, whether through words or through ceremonies, be prayed for and applied and that faith be thus strengthened.

Conclusion:
The Ecumenical Significance of Baptism

The different segments of Christendom have diverse formulations of dogma and diverse church orders. For example, they have no common doctrine of justification, of the Lord's Supper, and of orders. These differences are regarded as being so profound that most churches do not have altar fellowship with each other and do not acknowledge each other's ministries. In spite of various gradations in detail, they do not acknowledge each other as church in the full sense of the "one, holy, catholic, apostolic church." Thus Christendom is split to its foundations.

In the midst of these differences and antitheses Baptism occupies a special place. It is true that Christendom has no common doctrine of Baptism and no common order of the baptismal liturgy and baptismal practice. Yet, transcending the existing differences and antitheses, the churches acknowledge the validity of each other's Baptisms administered "in the name of the Father and of the Son and of the Holy Spirit." The Baptist Churches are the exception. They do not acknowledge infant Baptism and, in part, also the adult Baptism of others, whereas the rest of Christendom rejects the "rebaptisms" of these groups as invalid. However, the first attempts at overcoming this profound difference are appearing. Among the Baptists the New Testament witness to God's gracious activity through Baptism is being rediscovered, and the traditional churches are beginning to take seriously again the ethical obligation connected with Baptism.

It is by no means self-evident that Baptism would be acknowledged as valid in a way transcending most of the separations of churches. This acknowledgment came only after a long time and in part after serious conflicts within Christendom. When Pope Stephen I in the middle of the 3d century acknowledged the Baptism administered by heretics and schismatics and received such people into the Catholic fellowship by the mere laying on of hands, this position by no means conformed to the general practice of the contemporary church. In any

206

case there are several testimonies and synodical resolutions of that time which declined to acknowledge heretical Baptism and demanded rebaptism.[1] Thus Cyprian, in his controversy with Stephen, could appeal not only to the tradition of the African church, but he also found support among bishops of other areas of the church, especially Cappadocia and Cilicia. He argued against Stephen that there was no forgiveness of sins and no gift of the Holy Spirit outside the church. For that reason no one could effectively baptize outside the church. Stephen's reasons for acknowledging heretical Baptism are no longer clearly discernible. On the one hand he appealed to the tradition of the church in Rome, and it is possible that both the claim on the return of the heretics and the endeavor to make it easier for them to take this step may have played a role. On the other hand, Stephen stressed the efficacy of the trinitarian name in which also the heretics were baptized. Cyprian's position was subsequently undermined within the African church by the fact that the Donatist Tyconius opposed a rebaptism of converting Catholics and that also the Catholic church in Africa was not inclined to make the transfer of the Donatists difficult by a repetition of their Baptism. Augustine then carried Rome's practice through in Africa and provided the theological basis by adopting some of the thoughts of Tyconius. Consequently the worth of Baptism does not depend on the church which administers it, nor on the church's ministry, nor on the membership or sanctity of the baptizer, but on the triune name of God – on the Word which makes the water a sacrament. In its decisive aspect Baptism is God's deed, not the church's deed, even though grace is imparted exclusively within the Catholic Church.

Henceforth the Western Church generally acknowledged heretical Baptism if it was administered in the name of the triune God, while the Eastern Church continued for a long time to hold back. Thus in Alexandria Athanasius rejected the Baptism of the Arians as invalid, even though it was administered in the same way as in the Catholic Church.[2] To be sure, distinctions could be made in the Eastern Church between serious and less serious heresies. Thus the Council of Nicea acknowledged the Baptism of the Novatians but not of the followers of Paul of Samosata, while the Concilium Quinisextum acknowledged the Baptism of the Arians, the Novatians, and the Quartodecimans, but not of the Montanists and Sabellians. But viewed as a whole, the Eastern Church, on the basis of her understanding of the unity of the church, of the Holy Spirit, and of Baptism, for a long time continued to raise objections to the acknowledgment of heretical Baptism which the West maintained in principle.

The decision of the ancient church in the West was maintained also in the 16th century separation of the churches. The Roman Church acknowledged the Baptism of the Reformation churches and vice versa. Yes, in case of emergency the Lutheran Church even permitted the service of a Roman priest for the administration of Baptism. Also the Reformed theologian Peter Martyr affirmed this possibility.[3] It is true that in the case of conversions from Reformation churches the Roman Church frequently repeated Baptism and thus raised the suspicion of refusal to acknowledge Baptisms administered in the name of the Trinity. However, the Roman Church retained the principle of acknowledgment to the extent that such Baptisms were administered only "conditionally," that is, on the condition that the first Baptism may not have been correctly performed. Otherwise the Roman Church has today become much more sparing with such rebaptisms.[4] The Eastern Church, on the contrary, largely rejected the Baptisms of the Reformation churches. Thus in 1645 the marriage planned by the Russian Czar for his daughter with Count Woldemar, son of the Danish king, came to nothing because as a Lutheran the count refused to be rebaptized by the Orthodox Church. This demand had been made by the Patriarch of Moscow and confirmed by the Ecumenical Patriarch in Constantinople and by the decision of a synod convened there.[5] But when the Orthodox Church did acknowledge evangelical Baptisms, it did so less in the sense of an acknowledgment in principle as from "economy" [divine dispensation], that is, from an approach in love that transcends canonical order. Today the Baptisms of the Reformation churches are generally acknowledged by the Orthodox Church. At any rate the Orthodox representatives at the World Council of Churches convention in Edinburgh, 1937, raised no objections to the sentence: "When Baptism is administered in the name of the Father and of the Son and of the Holy Spirit, it is a sign and seal of Christian discipleship in obedience to the command of our Lord."[6]

Originally the acknowledgment of heretical Baptism did not yet mean much. At any rate, in the interpretation given by Augustine and held for a long time thereafter, heretical Baptism did not mean obtaining salvation. Outside the church "only the sacrament" was imparted, but not "the matter," only the "sign" or the "character," but not grace, forgiveness, and the Holy Spirit.[7] This "character," received by those baptized outside the Roman Church, was then interpreted by Thomas Aquinas primarily as an obligation and was likewise distinguished from the renewal through grace. The Roman Church took the same position over against the Baptisms of the Reformation churches and from their recognition derived her claim on the baptized.

This coupling of baptismal grace and membership in a specific church was shattered by Luther. He acknowledged that faith in the sole merit of Jesus Christ also in the Roman Church receives not only a valid Baptism but salvation. The Reformation churches did not confine the gracious activity of God through Baptism to the Baptisms administered in their midst. This greatly advanced recognition of the Baptisms of other segments of Christendom has been increasingly accepted with the rise of the ecumenical movement. The Eastern Church had in any case never distinguished between the validity and grace of Baptism as Western theology had done. The Eastern Church's present recognition of other Baptisms signifies at the same time an acknowledgment of the Holy Spirit's activity there. But also the Roman Church has spoken in Vatican Council II about God's gracious activity in those baptized outside her borders and has by no means still regarded these Baptisms only as signs without grace.[8] Hence the concept of the recognition of Baptism has experienced an extremely important expansion in our time. Beyond the borders of the individual churches Baptism is acknowledged as the vehicle of God's saving activity.[9]

In this way the boundaries between the different parts of Christendom have been breached at an important point. If it is acknowledged beyond these borders that Baptism grants assignment to Christ and the activity of the Spirit, then this means at the same time the incorporation into the one body of Christ. In this way the body of Christ is recognized as transcending the borders of the individual separated churches. Hence the mutual recognition of Baptism has great ecclesiological significance. It is all the more noteworthy since it comes about in spite of differing baptismal teachings and liturgies, also in spite of a difference in accompanying baptismal rituals and their interpretation, and beyond this, in spite of the diversity in the rest of the dogmatic and canonical obligations of the respective churches. The recognition of Baptism seems precisely to bring about in a paradigmatic way what has been proclaimed repeatedly by both the World Council of Churches and the Roman Church as a basic principle for ecumenical union: "Unity in diversity."

It should be asked whether this fellowship of the one Baptism does not lead to conclusions for eucharistic fellowship. There is no history of a recognition, increasing through the centuries, of the Lord's Supper in different segments of Christendom corresponding to the history of a growing mutual recognition of Baptism. In spite of the manifold approaches resulting from the ecumenical movement, the large church bodies, viewed as a whole, continue to confront each other without Communion fellowship. Yet the differences in the doctrine of Baptism are hardly any smaller than those in the doctrine of the Lord's Supper. Is it not possible also in the question of the Lord's Supper to advance through the dogmatic differences to the elementary act of a believing reception? Also the differences in the liturgical order are no smaller. Is it not possible, as in the case of the recognition of Baptism, where all the emphasis lies on the invocation of the trinitarian name, to direct the attention also in the position on the celebration of the Lord's Supper in the other churches to the use of the words of institution of Jesus Christ to which the distribution of bread and wine refers? If in the recognition of Baptism the baptizer is understood as the instrument of the divine activity without regard for his office and his membership in a specific church, would not something similar be possible also in the case of the one dispensing the Lord's Supper, if only he does what must be done in accordance with the words of institution? Self-evidently it cannot be overlooked that the structure of Baptism and of the Lord's Supper are not the same (for example, the baptismal command does not contain words of administration comparable to the institution of the Lord's Supper). At the same time it must not be forgotten that each of the two sacraments grants participation in the body of Jesus Christ. If it is acknowledged that through Baptism there is incorporation into the one body of Christ beyond the borders of the individual churches, should not also the fellowship of the one body of Christ in the Lord's Supper be realized?

Notes

Notes to Chapter One

1. Cf. Julius Schneewind, "Das Evangelium nach Matthäus," in *Das Neue Testament Deutsch (NTD)* 2 (Göttingen, 1964), 11th ed., p. 276; and Otto Michel, "Der Abschluss des Matthäusevangeliums," *Evangelische Theologie (Ev. Th.)* (1950), p. 22.

2. *Summa Theologica,* III, qu. 39, 1, tr. Fathers of the English Dominican Province. (London: Burns, Oates & Washbourne, Ltd., 1926), Vol. 16, 169 f.

3. *Comment. in Joan.,* 3, 19.

4. Hymn 401, 1, tr. Richard Massie. *Evangelical Lutheran Hymn-Book* (St. Louis: Concordia Publishing House, 1928).

5. Cf. Wilhelm Brandt, "Die jüdischen Baptismen," *Beihefte zur Zeitschrift für alttestamentliche Wissenschaft,* XVIII (Giessen, 1910), pp. 14 f.

6. The Talmudists then make the claim that already the Law had demanded cleansing by immersion of the body. But this is not correct. Cf. W. Brandt, p. 28.

7. Albrecht Oepke, in *Theological Dictionary of the New Testament (TDNT),* tr. Geoffrey W. Bromiley (Grand Rapids: Eerdmans, 1964), Vol. I, 536, and note 34. Cf. Johannes Leipold, *Die urchristliche Taufe im Lichte der Religionsgeschichte* (Leipzig, 1928), p. 1: These immersions "do not aim at washing away one sin, but at removing the cultic sequence of experiences or deeds which need not make any one guilty in the ethical sense."

8. Cf. J. Leipold, p. 2.

9. Cf. Joseph Thomas, *Le mouvement baptiste en Palestine et Syrie* (Gembloux, 1935).

10. Cf. the texts cited by G. Kretschmar in *Leiturgia,* V, 12 ff., as well as *The Manual of Discipline,* III, 6—9. *The Dead Sea Scriptures in English Translation,* 2d ed., tr. T. H. Gaster (Garden City: Anchor Books, 1964), p. 50.

11. *Manual of Discipline,* III, 8.

12. "Die Täufertaufe und die Qumranischen Waschungen." *Theologia Viatorum,* Vol. IX (1964), 3 f.

13. Cf. Emil Schürer, *Geschichte des jüdischen Volkes* (Leipzig, 1838), 3d ed., Vol. III, 130 ff. (fn. 78 contains a listing of the older literature); W. Brandt, pp. 57 ff.; Strack-Billerbeck, *Kommentar z. N. T. aus Judentum u. Midrasch,* 4th ed., I (Munich, 1965), 102 ff. and 924 ff.; J. Leipold, 2 ff.; Joachim Jeremias, *Infant Baptism in the First Four Centuries,* tr. David Cairns (Philadelphia: Westminster Press, 1960), pp. 24 ff.

14. Leipold, p. 19.

15. Bab Jebamoth, 48b, 62a (cited in Strack-Billerbeck, II, 4th ed. [1965], 423. Further passages at that place).

16. So Jeremias, p. 33.

17. Cf. Leipold, 22 f.

18. Oepke, *TDNT,* I, 536.

19. "Kerithoth II, 1" (cf. Schürer, III, 130).

20. "Die urchristliche Überlieferung von Johannes dem Täufer," in *Forschungen zur Religion und Literatur des Alten und Neuen Testaments,* ed. Wilhelm Bousset and Herman Gunkel (Göttingen, 1911), XV, 134.

21. So, for example, H. G. Marsh, *The Origin and Significance of the New Testament Baptism* (Manchester, 1941). Words of Adolf Schlatter already pointed in the same direction, but he adds: "Yet even when the assurance of forgiveness of sins was conceived as a promise which would be fulfilled with the beginning of God's rule, this promise completely transforms the relationship of the baptized to God. Even the promise of grace is a bestowal of grace" (*Markus, der Evangelist für die Griechen* [Stuttgart, 1935], 22 f.).

22. Most recently, again, Hartwig Thyen, "Baptisma Metanoias eis Aphesin Hamartion," in *Zeit und Geschichte, Dankgabe an Rudolf Bultmann zum 80. Geburtstag* (Tübingen, 1964), 98; cf. 100 and 106. This interpretation is here in the framework of a conception according to which this sacramental understanding of John's Baptism stood at the beginning of the tradition, but in the course of the debates between the Christian community and the disciples of John who "soon after his death messianized" John, this idea was more and more dissipated and finally removed in John's Gospel.

23. "The Origin of Baptism," in: *Interpretationes ad Vetus Testamentum pertinentes Sigmundo Mowinkel* (Oslo, 1955), pp. 36—52.

24. A listing of the reasons that permit John to appear as a pupil of the Essenes is found in W. H. Brownlee, "John the Baptist in the New Light of Ancient Scrolls," *Interpretation* 9, (1955), 71—90; and in Krister Stendahl, ed. *The Scrolls and the NT* (New York: Harper, 1957), pp. 33—53.

25. "*Taufe II. Im Urchristentum,*" *RGG,* 3d ed., Vol. VI, col. 628.

26. *Die jüdischen Baptismen,* p. 78.

27. "Das Evangelium des Markus," in: *Kritisch-exeget. Kommentar über das Neue Testament* (Göttingen, 1967), 17th ed., p. 23.

28. "Das Evangelium nach Matthäus," in *NTD,* 2 (1964), 11th ed., p. 27.

29. Cf. Ferdinand Hahn, *Christologische Hoheitstitel* (Göttingen, 1966), 3d ed., pp. 340 ff.

30. "Das johanneische Zeugnis vom Herrenmahl," *Ev. Th.* (1953), p. 346.

31. From 1 Cor. 12:13 we may conclude that Paul "presupposes . . . the Baptism of *all* Christians as self-evident" (E. Dinkler, *RGG,* VI, col. 629). This text, "understood biographically, leads us back to something like 33 A. D." (Oepke, *Theological Dictionary of the New Testament,* I, 539).

32. For a recent discussion of this question in Roman Catholic circles (De Puniet, Brinktrine, et al.) cf. A. Stenzel, *Die Taufe* (Innsbruck, 1958), pp. 24 ff. In Protestant circles Baptism in the name of Christ is generally regarded as the original.

33. There are several theories about the original wording. E. Lohmeyer, for example, regards the short form given by Eusebius ("In My name") as the original ("Das Evangelium des Matthäus," ed. Werner Schmauch [Göttingen, 1967], 2d ed., pp. 412 f., *Kritisch-exeget. Kommentar über das Neue Testament,* Sonderband).

34. Alfred Seeberg, *Die Taufe im Neuen Testament* (Berlin, 1913), 2d ed., pp. 14 ff., esp. p. 19 (*Biblische Zeit- und Streitfragen,* ed. Kropatschek, 1, 10).

35. R. K. Bultmann, *Theology of the New Testament,* tr. Kendrick Grobel (New York: Charles Scribner's Sons, 1951), I, 139.

36. *Theology of the New Testament,* I, 139.

37. Already in connection with his purely religio-historical analyses Richard Reitzenstein observes that he "knows of no passage which in sober exegesis permits a genuine conclusion in the direction of this alleged evolution of Christian Baptism" (*Die Vorgeschichte der christlichen Taufe* [Leipzig and Berlin, 1929], p. 161). But also in New Testament scholarship the original connection between forgiveness of sins and gift of the Spirit is today again affirmed more strongly. Cf. Oscar Cullmann: "The connection in Christian Baptism between forgiveness of sins and transmission of the Spirit is, however, more deeply rooted. It is not simply as if a new element, the imparting of the Holy Spirit, were added to the old immersion for the forgiveness of sins. The new element rather concerns the fulfillment of just this forgiveness of sins, and this in the closest connection with the transmission of the Holy Spirit." *Baptism in the New Testament,* tr. J. K. S. Reid (London: SCM Press, Ltd., 1958), p. 11. See also G. W. H. Lampe, *The Seal of the Spirit* (1956), pp. 46 f.

38. Cf. E. Schlink, "The Structure of Dogmatic Statements as an Ecumenical Problem," in *The Coming Christ and the Coming Church* (Philadelphia: Fortress Press, 1968), pp. 16 ff.

39. Cf. Wolfgang Nauck, "Eph. 2:19-22 — ein Tauflied?" *Ev. Th.,* 13 (1953), pp. 362 ff.; G. Schille, "Liturgisches Gut im Epheserbrief," diss. Göttingen, 1953.

40. Ernst Käsemann, "Eine urchristliche Taufliturgie," *Festschrift für R. Bultmann* (Stuttgart, 1949), 133—148; also in *Exegetische Versuche und Besinnungen,* I (Göttingen, 1965), 4th. ed., 34—51.

41. While the references of Manfred Karnetzki ("Der Ort der Taufe im Leben der Gemeinde," *Ev. Th.,* 1957, 52 ff.) to the peculiarity of the New Testament baptismal statements in their generic history are very important, they cannot lead to the conclusion "that the New Testament has no doctrine of Baptism at all, since the New Testament does not teach but proclaim." (53)

42. Cf. Wilhelm Heitmüller, *Im Namen Jesu,* Forschungen zur Religion und Lituratur des Alten und Neuen Testaments (Göttingen: Vandenhoeck & Ruprecht, 1903), 1, Teil 2.

Notes to Chapter Two

1. This applies especially to ἐν.

2. Cf. G. Delling, *Die Zueignung des Heils in der Taufe, eine Untersuchung zum neutestamentlichen "Taufen auf den Namen"* (Berlin, 1961), 89 ff.

3. 1 Cor. 6:11; cf. 1:13-16, Acts 8:16 and 19:5; Matt. 28:19, as well as Gal. 3:27 and Rom. 6:3.

4. Cf. Wilhelm Heitmüller, *Im Namen Jesu,* Forschungen zur Religion und Literatur des Alten und Neuen Testaments (Göttingen, 1903), 1, Teil 2, 328.

5. *Theology of the New Testament,* tr. K. Grobel (New York: Charles Scribner's Sons, 1951—), I, 137.

6. Delling, p. 82.

7. Ibid., p. 80.

8. Ibid., p. 93.

9. The use of this name is found in Acts especially in connection with βαπτίζειν εἰς (8:16; 9:15).

10. Ibid., p. 90.

11. *Theological Dictionary of the New Testament,* I, 539—40; cf. Friedrich Preisigke, *Wörterbuch der griechischen Papyruskunden* (Berlin, 1925—), Vol. 2, 185 f.

12. Cf. W. Heitmüller, "Does faith in the name of Jesus stand in a relationship of

dependence to the Jewish and pagan faith in a name? If in the latter case we must undoubtedly apply the category of superstition and magic, is this true also of the Christian faith in the name? This question, or questions, must be answered with an *unqualified* Yes. . . . The *church* judges the *pagan* faith in a name to be *magic* which she abhors and which can self-evidently not be involved in *her* activity 'in the name of Jesus.' But in reality this is purely a deception which was understandable and excusable for the consciousness of the ancient church but which we cannot share" (252—3).

13. For a magical misunderstanding of Baptism cf. Heitmüller, pp. 138—44.

14. *Die Taufe — ein Sakrament?* (Zollikon-Zürich, 1951), p. 313.

15. Ibid., p. 315.

16. Ibid., p. 524.

17. Oepke, *Theol. Dict.,* I, 540.

18. *Taufe und Sünde im ältesten Christentum bis auf Origenes* (Tübingen, 1908), p. 13. H. Windisch has with considerable clarity worked out the peculiarity of the cleansing from sin through Baptism in distinction from other ideas of forgiveness, but he has oversimplified and underestimated the problematics of sinning by the baptized in the sense of a theory of sinlessness. He apparently did not sufficiently note that in the New Testament we must seek the answer to the familiar question, whether and to what extent the sinful nature of man is put away through Baptism or whether it is retained even after Baptism, not so much in analytical statements about the essence and attributes of the baptized, but rather in the double address to the baptized, on the one hand, of unlimited assurance of forgiveness, justification, renewal, etc., and, on the other hand, the equally unlimited exhortation to righteousness, the new life, etc., as well as the warning against further sinning and the threat of judgment. Withal, assurance and claim belong inseparably together in their seeming contradiction.

19. Op. cit., especially 304 ff.

20. So M. Barth, op. cit., 264 ff., and G. Delling, *Die Taufe im Neuen Testament* (Berlin, 1963), 127 ff. However, this thesis, that in Baptism we did not die with Christ but were only buried, is not maintained by Delling to the extent that he adds, "This dying of the old man on the cross is accomplished in Baptism." (P. 130)

21. In addition to the commentaries cf. especially O. Kuss, "Zu Römer 6, 5a," in *Th. Gl.,* 41 (Paderborn, 1951), 430 ff.

22. The same judgment is made by P. Brunner, *Aus der Kraft des Werkes Christi, Zur Lehre von der Heiligen Taufe und vom Heiligen Abendmahl* (Munich, 1950), p. 23. Even more definite is G. Bornkamm, "Taufe und neues Leben," in: *Das Ende des Gesetzes* (Munich, 1966), 5th ed., 42 f.: "Hence the concept ὁμοίωμα has absolutely nothing to do with the sacrament, however much a being united with Christ self-evidently takes place in Baptism, according to Paul."

23. Op. cit, p. 21. Cf. the analysis of the history of the concept, pp. 20 ff. and 68 ff. In addition see the article by Joh. Schneider on the concept, ὁμοίωμα, in *Theological Dictionary of the New Testament,* V, 191—8.

24. [Bauer] Arndt-Gingrich, *Greek-English Lexicon of the New Testament and Other Early Christian Literature* (Chicago: University of Chicago Press, 1957), translates ὁμοίωμα, "if we have been united . . . in the likeness of his death." Cf. also Ernst Fuchs, "Die Freiheit des Glaubens, Römer 5-8 ausgelegt." *Beiträge zur evang. Theologie (B. Ev. Th.),* 14 (Munich, 1949), p. 30.

25. In this passage the word δικαιοῦσθαι is probably not to be understood in the pregnant sense of Paul's doctrine of justification, but in the sense of being declared and set free (cf. [Bauer] Arndt-Gingrich, p. 197).

26. Such a correspondence (especially between immersion and burial) has indeed often been assumed, but there is nothing in Rom. 6:3 ff. to suggest that this is significant for Paul's understanding of Baptism. What could be the nature of this illustrative correspondence between Christ's crucifixion and Baptism in view of Paul's statement that "our old self was crucified with Him"? Nor do his other baptismal remarks show any interest in presenting and giving a symbolical interpretation to the baptismal process as such.

27. In addition to the reference to the historical man Jesus Christ this, too, marks such a difference between Paul's baptismal theology and the Hellenistic mystery religions that questions have again been raised about a dependence assumed by the history-of-religions school. The most pointed rejection of a relationship is offered by Günter Wagner, *Pauline Baptism and the Pagan Mysteries,* tr. J. P. Smith (Edinburgh and London: Oliver & Boyd, 1967), pp. 30 f.

28. Cf. especially *Das christliche Kultmysterium* (Regensburg, 1960), 4th ed.

29. For a Roman-Catholic critique of the interpretation of Paul see, for example, R. Schnackenburg, *Baptism in the Thought of St. Paul,* tr. G. R. Beasley-Murray (New York: Herder & Herder, 1964), pp. 129 ff. Especially noteworthy in the systematic-theological discussions is Gottlieb Söhngen, *Symbol und Wirklichkeit im Kultmysterium* (Bonn, 1940), 2d ed.

30. Cf. the documentation in Otto Hof, "Taufe und Heilswerk Christi bei Luther," in: *Zur Auferbauung des Leibes Christi,* Festgabe für P. Brunner (Kassel, 1965), 223 ff.

31. "Aus der Kraft des Werkes Christi," 17 ff.; "Die evangelisch-lutherische Lehre von der Taufe," in *Pro Ecclesia, Gesammelte Aufsätze zur dogmatischen Theologie,* I (Berlin-Hamburg, 1962), 138 ff.; see also *Leiturgia,* I, 220 ff. Wilhelm Traugott Hahn, *Das Mitsterben und Mitauferstehen bei Paulus* (Gütersloh, 1937), esp. pp. 40 ff., has discussed the time problem of Roman 6 by means of the concept of contemporaneity.

32. This would also contradict the structure of promise and claim in which Paul makes his assertions about Baptism.

33. The oft-discussed question whether the future tenses in verses 5 and 8 are to be understood in the sense of a temporal sequence or in a logically consistent way may in no case be answered so that the expectation of the future resurrection excludes the present new life, or, vice versa, that the logical following of the already present life excludes its future.

34. Cf. H. Schlier, *Der Brief an die Epheser* (Düsseldorf, 1965), 5th ed., pp. 109 ff.; as well as R. Schnackenburg, pp. 73 ff.

35. For the following cf. the basic studies by R. Bultmann, "Das Problem der Ethik bei Paulus," *Zeitschrift für die neutestamentl. Wissenschaft (ZNW),* 23 (1924), 123 ff., and Hans von Soden, "Sakrament und Ethik bei Paulus," *Ges. Aufsätze,* I, *Urchristentum und Geschichte* (Tübingen, 1951), 239 ff. For the more recent literature see the listings by Niklaus Gäumann, "Taufe und Ethik," 163 ff., *B. Ev. Th.,* 47 (Munich, 1967).

36. See note 35 above; p. 126.

37. Article on "Taufe," 2, *RE,* Vol. 19 (3d ed.), 405.

38. *Summa Theologica,* III, qu. 69; op. cit., Vol. 17, 166 ff.

39. Cf. Ulrich Kühn, *Via Caritatis, Theologie des Gesetzes bei Thomas von Aquin* (Göttingen, 1965).

40. "Taufe und Heilswerk Christi bei Luther," p. 226. See the wealth of documentation at that place.

41. P. 85. Note there the overview of the various exegetical possibilities.

42. Cf. M. Dibelius, "Die Pastoralbriefe," in: *Handbuch zum Neuen Testament*, founded by H. Lietzmann, rev. by H. Conzelmann (Tübingen, 1966), 4th ed., section 13; and Joachim Jeremias, "Die Briefe an Timotheus und Titus," in: *NTD,* 9 (Göttingen, 1968), 9th ed.

43. This is admitted also by R. Bultmann who assumes a later churchly redaction at this place which has inserted the reference to Baptism. "Das Evangelium des Johannes," *Kritisch-Exeget. Kommentar über das NT,* II (Göttingen, 1968), 19th ed., p. 98, note 2. However, the antisacramental stance of the evangelist which is here presupposed is disputed. See opposite view, O. Cullmann, *Baptism in the New Testament,* n., p. 13.

44. Thus a widespread Baptist interpretation. However even Calvin says in his commentary on John that in accordance with the metaphorical usage of the Old Testament prophets this passage (John 3:5) "means nothing else than the inner cleansing of the Holy Spirit."

45. Cf. section 2b below.

46. Article "Geist," IV, *RGG,* 3d ed., II, col. 1274.

47. On the special problems of this text cf. E. Käsemann, "Die Johannesjünger in Ephesus" in *Exegetische Versuche und Besinnungen,* I (Göttingen, 1965), 4th ed., 158 ff.

48. Article "Geist," IV, *RGG,* 3d ed., II, col. 1277.

49. *Die Wirkungen des heiligen Geistes nach den populären Anschauungen der apostolischen Zeit und die Lehre des Apostels Paulus,* 3d ed., (Göttingen, 1909).

50. Cf. E. Schweizer, Article, πνεῦμα, *Theological Dictionary of the New Testament,* VI, 415—37, and the literature indicated there.

51. Cf. J. Behm, *Die Handauflegung im Urchristentum* (Leipzig, 1911); N. Adler, *Taufe und Handauflegung* (Münster, 1951); H. D. Wendland, Article, "Handauflegung" II, *RGG,* III (3d ed.), col. 52—55.

52. Cf. Section 1 c.

53. Cf. Ronald A. Knox, *Enthusiasm, A Chapter in the History of Religion* (New York & Oxford: Oxford University Press, 1950).

54. See the details in P. Brunner, *Worship in the Name of Jesus,* tr. M. H. Bertram (St. Louis: Concordia, 1968), pp. 126 ff., and E. Schlink, "Worship from the Viewpoint of Evangelical Theology," *The Coming Christ and the Coming Church,* pp. 132 ff.

55. Cf. R. Bultmann, *Theology of the New Testament,* I, 311.

56. In current Protestant theology T. F. Torrance especially called attention to this. Cf. "Ein vernachlässigter Gesichtspunkt der Tauflehre," *Ev. Th.,* 16 (1956), 433 ff.

57. *Paulus, der Bote Jesu* (Stuttgart, 1934), p. 197.

58. This does not rule out the thought that the concept of Father, Son, and Spirit as witnesses of Baptism also played a role in the genesis of this understanding. (Cf. G. Kretschmar, "Studien zur frühchristlichen Trinitätstheologie," *Beitr. zur Histor. Theol.,* Vol. 21 [Tübingen, 1956], 62 ff.)

59. Cf. E. Schlink, article "Trinität IV (dogmatisch), *RGG,* 3d ed., VI, col. 1032 ff.

60. Bultmann, *Theology of the New Testament,* I, 140.

61. Bultmann, II (1955), 160.

62. *Das Heilsgeschehen bei der Tau†e nach dem Apostel Paulus* (1950), p. 134. The translator, Beasley-Murray, does not give the text of the German original in full.

63. Albert Schweitzer, *Die Mystik des Apostels Paulus* (Tübingen, 1930), pp. 19 f.

64. Schnackenburg, p. 136.

65. Cf. above, pp.

66. Cf. Adolf von Harnack's collation of the pertinent concepts in his treatise, "Die Terminologie der Wiedergeburt und verwandter Erlebnisse in der ältesten Kirche," *Texte und Untersuchungen zur Geschichte der altchristlichen Literatur,* (Leipzig, 1918), Vol. 42, part 3, 97 ff.

67. Thus Tertullian denied the impartation of the Spirit to Baptism and associated it especially with the laying on of hands (*De haptismo,* chaps. 6 and 8).

68. Ibid., ch. 3—5. But cf. already Justin, *Apology,* I, 61.

69. B. Neunheuser, "Taufe und Firmung," *Handbuch der Dogmengeschichte,* IV, 2 (Freiburg, 1956), p. 33.

70. Jean Danielou, *Origene* (Paris, 1948), p. 71, cited by Neunheuser, p. 33.

71. Article, "Sacrament," *Realencyklopädie* . . . XVII (3d ed.), 353.

72. *Tractate 80,* on John 3.

73. Cf. Werner Jetter, "Die Taufe beim jungen Luther," *Beitr. z. histor. Theol.,* Vol. 18 (Tübingen, 1954).

74. Large Catechism, IV, 8, *The Book of Concord,* ed. Theodore Tappert (Philadelphia: Muhlenberg Press, 1959).

75. Ibid., 10.

76. Ibid., Small Catechism, "The Sacrament of Holy Baptism," 2.

77. Ibid., Large Catechism, IV, 16.

78. Ibid., 22.

79. Ibid., Small Catechism, 6.

80. Ibid., Large Catechism, IV, 27; Small Catechism, IV, 10; Large Catechism, IV, 14.

81. Cf., e. g., C. H. Ratschow, *Magie und Religion* (1947).

82. Article, *"Magie,* religionsgeschichtlich," *RGG* (3d ed.), IV, col. 596.

83. The New Testament understanding of Baptism has often been labeled magical by the history-of-religions school. But the New Testament material does not have in mind an automatic reception of salvation that is given with the baptismal act. Rather, these statements are made by faith in God's saving activity and they summon to this faith. Their presupposition is the recognition of God's freedom. Out of unmotivated love God sent His Son and poured out the Holy Spirit and desires through Baptism to make a reality for the believers what He accomplished in Jesus' Baptism, death, and resurrection. Paul's statement about the so-called vicarious Baptism (1 Cor. 15:29) seems to support a magical understanding of Baptism. But Paul is probably not thinking of a vicarious Baptism for deceased Christians but rather a submission to Baptism on the part of non-Christians who hoped to achieve fellowship with deceased Christians in this way. Cf. M. Raeder, "Vikariatstaufe in 1 Kor. 15:29?" *ZNW,* 46 (1955), 258 ff.

84. *Institutes of the Christian Religion,* Book IV, chap. 15, 5. The Library of Christian Classics, XXI (Philadelphia: Westminster Press, 1960).

85. Ibid., chap. 15, 14.

86. Ibid., chap. 15, 15.

87. Ibid., 15, 5.

88. "Zwinglis Sakramentsauffassung," *Theologische Blätter,* 1931, col. 285.

89. Especially in his *Expositio fidei christianae* (1531).

90. *Theologische Studien und Kritiken* (1882), 205—284, esp. 268 ff.

91. Blanke, col. 289.

92. Cf. the analysis given by Torsten Bergsten, *Balthasar Hubmaier* (Kassel: 1961), 368 ff.

93. Cf. the collection of sources in H. Fast, *Der linke Flügel der Reformation* (Bremen, 1962), p. 20.

94. Thus, for example, Marbeck emphasized the unity of water Baptism and the inner experience over against spiritualism (cf. H. Fast, *Bemerkungen zur Taufanschauung der Täufer,* Archiv für Reformationsgeschichte, Vol. 57 (1966), 141 ff.; Rollin Stely Armour, *Anabaptist Baptism,* Studies in Anabaptist and Mennonite History, 11 [Scottdale, Pa., 1966], 113 ff.).

95. *Glaubens-Bekenntnis der Baptisten-Gemeine in Berlin* (1843).

96. E. g., Joh. Schneider, *Die Taufe im Neuen Testament* (Stuttgart, 1952); George Beasley-Murray, *Baptism in the New Testament* (London, 1962); G. Wagner, *Pauline Baptism and the Pagan Mysteries* (Edinburgh and London: Oliver & Boyd, 1967).

97. *Gesichtspunkt zum Taufgespräch heute* (Kassel, 1965), 8 ff.

98. On this point cf. G. Mecenseffy, "Das Verständnis der Taufe bei den süddeutschen Täufern," in *Antwort, K. Barth zum 70. Geburstag* (Zollikon-Zürich, 1956), 642 ff.

99. *Church Dogmatics,* IV, 4 (Zurich, 1967), p. 45.

100. Ibid., p. 112.

101. Morris A. Creasey, *Das Verständnis der Taufe bei den Quakern,* Studiendokument des Ausschusses für Glauben und Kirchenverfassung (Geneva, 1957), p. 5.

102. R. Bultmann, *Theology of the New Testament,* I, 133.

103. *Institutes* (1559), 3d ed., IV, chap. 15, 20.

104. *Summa Theologica,* Part III, question 68, art. 1, corp., tr. Fathers of the English Dominican Province (London: Burns, Oates & Washbourne, Ltd., 1923), Vol. 17, 141.

105. Ibid., art. 2, corp., Vol. 17, 143.

106. Large Catechism, IV, 31.

Notes to Chapter Three

1. Hymn 401, stanza 7, tr. Richard Massie, *Evangelical Lutheran Hymnbook* (St. Louis: Concordia Publishing House, 1928).

2. In this sense, in the decree on justification of the Council of Trent the Gospel recedes completely behind Baptism as *causa instrumentalis.* Cf. H. J. Schroeder, tr. *Canons and Decrees of the Council of Trent* (St. Louis: B. Herder Book Co., 1955), 3d printing, pp. 29 ff., esp. 33.

3. In this sense the answer of the Heidelberg Catechism to Question 65, concerning the origin of faith, makes the distinction: "The Holy Spirit creates it in our hearts by the preaching of the holy Gospel, and confirms it by the use of the holy Sacraments."

4. This was, in part, the position of Lutheran revival theology in the 19th century. Cf. Eugene Moritz Skibbe, "The Proprium of the Lord's Supper in the German Lutheran Theology of the 19th Century," Heidelberg diss., 1962.

5. In the reports concerning occasional self-administered Baptisms during times of persecution in the ancient church, especially in situations where no baptizer was available, the presupposition was not to question but rather to expect God's saving activity through Baptism, an activity which the believer did not want to do without.

218

6. *De baptismo,* 17, *Tertullian's Homily on Baptism,* tr. Ernest Evans (London: SPCK, 1964), p. 35.

7. *De baptismo,* 17.

8. *Summa Theologica,* Part III, qu. 67, art. 4, corp., tr. Fathers of the English Dominican Province (London: Burns, Oates & Washbourne, Ltd., 1923), Vol. 17, p. 132.

9. *Institutes* (3d ed., 1559), IV, 15, 20.

10. Cf. above, pp. 000.

11. *Summa Theologica,* III, qu. 67, art. 5, ad 1, op. cit., Vol. 17, p. 133.

12. Cf. Luther's translation and, e. g., E. Lohmeyer, "Die Briefe an die Philipper, an die Kolosser und an Philemon," *Kritisch-exegetischer Kommentar über das NT, IX* (Göttingen, 1964), 13th ed., p. 112. The two genitives "do not speak of the object to which faith is directed but of the source from which it comes and which it is itself. For 'power' in an excellent sense expresses the activity of God."

13. There is debate about whether βαπτίζεσθαι is used here and elsewhere in the passive or the middle form. Both are possible linguistically, but in most cases the passive is the more probable (cf. Oepke, *Theological Dictionary of the New Testament,* I, 540).

14. *Die Taufe* (Kassel, 1922), 2d ed., p. 13.

15. Migne, *PG,* XXXVI, 360 ff.

16. *Summa Theologica,* III, qu. 63, art. 4; op. cit., Vol. 17, 52.

17. Ibid., art. 2; op. cit., Vol. 17: 47.

18. Large Catechism, Baptism, 73.

19. Ibid., 40.

20. Ibid., 16.

21. Ibid., 26.

22. Ibid., 43.

23. "Dogmatic Constitution on the Church," 15, *Documents of Vatican II* (New York: Guild Press, 1966), p. 34; cf. also E. Schlink, *After the Council,* tr. Herbert J. A. Bouman (Philadelphia: Fortress Press, 1968), pp. 86—91, 100—125, 245.

24. *Zur Frage nach dem Ursprung der Kindertaufe, Festschrift für Ludwig Ihmels* (Leipzig, 1928), pp. 84 ff.

25. *Die urchristliche Taufe im Lichte der Religionsgeschichte* (Leipzig, 1928).

26. *Hat die älteste Christenheit die Kindertaufe geübt?* (Göttingen, 1938, 1949), 2d ed., *Infant Baptism in the First Four Centuries,* tr. David Cairns (Philadelphia: Westminster Press, 1960).

27. *Baptism in the New Testament,* tr. J. K. S. Reid (London: SCM Press, 1950).

28. *Did the Early Church Baptize Infants?* tr. G. R. Beasley-Murray (Philadelphia: Westminster Press, 1963).

29. *Adversus Haereses,* II, 22, 4.

30. Aland, p. 58 f., comes to a different conclusion.

31. *Church Order,* XVI, 4 f., as cited in Aland, p. 49.

32. Cf. Aland's views, p. 49 f.

33. *De baptismo,* 18, as cited in Aland, p. 61.

34. Ibid.

35. *De anima,* 39.

36. Cf. Aland, *Did the Early Church Baptize Infants?* pp. 65 f.

37. *De baptismo,* 18; Evans, op. cit., p. 39.

38. Ibid.

39. Ibid.

40. Epistle 64, 2—6.

41. On this see J. Jeremias, *Infant Baptism in the First Four Centuries,* pp. 65 f., and K. Aland, *Did the Early Church Baptize Infants?* pp. 47 f.

42. *Commentary on Romans,* V, 9.

43. The 16th Synod of Carthage, 418, explicitly pronounced the anathema upon every one who refused to baptize newborn children.

44. Cf. Jeremias, *Infant Baptism,* pp. 87 ff., and Aland, *Did the Early Church Baptize Infants?* pp. 100 ff.

45. Aristides, *Apology,* 15, 11.

46. Cf. Aland, *Did the Early Church Baptize Infants?* pp. 87 ff., and Peter Weigandt, "Zur sogenannten Oikosformal," *Novum Testamentum,* VI (Leiden, 1963), 49—74.

47. Cf. Ethelbert Stauffer, "Zur Kindertaufe in der Urkirche, *"Deutsches Pfarrerblatt,* Essen, Vol. 49 (1949), 152 ff.

48. Cf. J. Jeremias, *Infant Baptism in the First Four Centuries,* pp. 48 ff.

49. Ibid., p. 40.

50. O. Cullmann, *Baptism in the New Testament,* Appendix: "Traces of an Ancient Baptismal Formula in the New Testament," pp. 71—80.

51. For example, Konrad Grebel supported his rejection of infant Baptism with the argument that "for many years after the days of the apostles, beyond Cyprian and Augustine, for six hundred years, Christians and non-Christians were baptized together 'upon the confession of their faith' " (letter to Thomas Muentzer, 1524, in the collection of texts by H. Fast, op. cit., 21).

52. *WA,* XXVI, p. 167, 1. 23 ff.

53. Ibid. p. 168; cf. Large Catechism, Baptism, 49—51.

54. *Summa Theologica,* III, qu. 68, 9; op. cit., Vol. 17, 157 f.

55. Ibid., qu. 69, 6; op. cit., Vol. 17, 177.

56. *WA,* XXVI, 144—74; "Concerning Rebaptism . . ." LW, 40, 229—62.

57. 1559, IV, 16.

58. Cf., for example, Calvin, *Institutes,* 3d ed., IV, 16, 3—6 and 10—16. "The promise (in which we have shown the power of the signs to consist) is the same in both, namely, that of God's fatherly favor, of forgiveness of sins, and of eternal life. Then the thing represented is the same, namely, regeneration. In both there is one foundation upon which the fulfillment of these things rests [Christ]. Therefore there is no difference in the inner mystery. . . . What dissimilarity remains lies in the outward ceremony, which is a very slight factor. . . . We therefore conclude that, apart from the difference in the visible ceremony, whatever belongs to circumcision pertains likewise to Baptism." (4)

59. *Summa Theologica,* III, qu. 70; op. cit., Vol. 17, 186 ff.

60. *Institutes,* II, 10.

61. Ibid., IV, 16, 5.

62. Ibid., IV, 16, 6.

63. *De baptismo,* 18, 5; Evans, op. cit., p. 39.

64. *Did the Early Church Baptize Infants?* p. 103.

65. On this cf. K. Aland, op. cit., pp. 103 ff.; J. Jeremias, *The Origins of Infant Baptism*, pp. 76 ff.; and Aland, *Die Stellung der Kinder in den frühen christlichen Gemeinden — und ihre Taufe*, 1967.

66. Cf. Torsten Bergsten, *Balthasar Hubmaier, Seine Stellung zu Reformation und Taufertum, 1521—28* (Greenwood, S. C.: Attic Press, 1961), p. 441, cf. 436 ff.

67. In the sources collected by H. Fast, op. cit., pp. 105 ff.

68. Hans Luckey, *Johann Gerhard Oncken* (1958), 3d ed., pp. 232 ff.

69. *Summa Theologica,* III, qu. 69, 6; op. cit., Vol. 17, p. 177.

70. *Die Lehre Luthers von der* fides infantium *bei der Kindertaufe* (Berlin, 1958), p. 81.

71. Ibid. p. 76.

72. Cf. Luther's "The Order of Baptism," *Luther's Works,* American Edition, Vol. 53, pp. 95—103.

73. *Institutes,* 3d ed., IV, 16, 18; cf. 17.

74. John H. Leith, ed., *Creeds of the Churches* (Garden City, New York: Anchor Books, 1963), p. 284.

75. Cf. Usteri, op. cit., pp. 211 f., and August Baur, *Zwinglis Theologie,* (Halle, 1889), Vol. II, pp. 56 f.

76. *Institutes,* 3d ed., IV, 15, 13.

77. *The Teaching of the Church Concerning Baptism* (London: SCM Press, 1948), tr. Ernest A. Payne, p. 54.

78. *Kirchliche Dogmatik* (1967), Vol. IV, 4, 208.

79. *Gesichtspunkte zum Taufgespräch heute* (Kassel, 1965), pp. 86 ff.

80. Cf. the sources collected by H. Fast, op. cit., pp. 57 ff.

81. Leith, op. cit., p. 284 f.

82. *Der Kirchenbegriff der Schwärmer* (Leipzig, 1939), p. 5.

83. See also the discussions concerning the union and the organs of a common administration in the German Baptist movement in the 19th century (H. Luckey, *Gottfried Wilhelm Lehmann und die Entstehung einer deutschen Freikirche* [Kassel, 1939], pp. 125 ff.).

84. F. Heyer has shown "that Anabaptism receives its real weight not from the doctrine of the sacraments, but at another place, from the concept of the church." It performed an important service "for the building of the separated community of salvation" (op. cit., p. 36 and passim).

85. On the changes in Zwingli's understanding of the church see John H. Yoder, *Täufertum und Reformation im Gespräch* (Zurich, 1968), Basler Studien zur historischen und systematischen Theologie, 13, pp. 96—154.

86. Cf. also Bullinger's arguments in his discussion with the Anabaptists (Heinold Fast, "Heinrich Bullinger und die Täufer," *Schriftenreihe des Mennonitischen Geschichtsvereins* 7, [Weierhof, 1959], pp. 132 ff.).

87. *Institutes,* 3d ed., IV, 16, 24.

88. Ibid. IV, 16, 17 ff.

89. *The Teaching of the Church Concerning Baptism,* Thesis V, p. 55.

90. Cf. Otto Hermann Pesch, *Theologie der Rechtfertigung bei Martin Luther und Thomas von Aquin,* Walberberger Studien, IV (Mainz, 1967), chs. V and XII.

Notes to Chapter Four

1. Cf. O. Cullmann, *Baptism in the New Testament,* pp. 71 ff.

2. Cf. O. Cullmann, *The Earliest Christian Confessions,* trans. J. K. S. Reid (London: Lutterworth Press, 1949); J. N. D. Kelly, *Early Christian Creeds* (London, 1950); A. Stenzel, *Die Taufe, Eine genetische Erklärung der Taufliturgien* (Innsbruck, 1958), pp. 29 ff.

3. In addition to being true of Roman Catholic exegetes, this is true especially of High Church Anglican exegetes who look here for the New Testament origin of confirmation, e. g., G. Dix, *The Theology of Confirmation in Relation to Baptism* (London, 1946).

4. Cf. the details by P. Brunner, *Worship in the Name of Jesus,* pp. 217 ff.

5. *Leiturgia,* Vol. V, 1 ff. and 350 ff.

6. *The Teaching of the Church Concerning Baptism* (London: SCM Press, 1948), tr. Ernest A. Payne, p. 10.

7. "Die Geschichte des Taufgottesdienstes in der alten Kirche," *Leiturgia,* Vol. V, 1 ff.

8. Cf. G. Kretschmar, 21 ff.; 24 ff.; 51, 102 ff. et al.

9. Cf. ibid., pp. 24 f.; 27 ff.; 31, 101 ff.; 109 f. et al.

10. Ibid., p. 22; 36 ff.; 71 f. et al.

11. 2 Cor. 1:21; Eph. 1:13; 4:30.

12. Cf. G. Kretschmar, p. 109.

13. Ibid., pp. 77 ff. et al.

14. Ibid., pp. 73 f.

15. Ibid., pp. 111 ff.

16. Ibid., pp. 93 ff. et al.

17. Ibid., pp. 95 ff. et al.

18. *De baptismo,* 6 and 8.

19. Cf. Bruno Jordahn, "Der Taufgottesdienst im Mittelalter bis zur Gegenwart," *Leiturgia,* Vol. V, 355—400; for an English translation of these orders see *Luther's Works,* American Ed., 53, pp. 96—103.

20. Jordahn, pp. 440—48.

21. Ibid., pp. 473—78.

22. Ibid., pp. 511—17.

Notes to Conclusion

1. Cf. G. N. Bonwetsch article "Ketzertaufe," *RE* (3d ed., 1898), Vol. 5, 270.

2. G. Kretschmar, *Studien zur frühchristlichen Trinitätstheologie* (Tübingen, 1956), p. 126.

3. Cf. Bonwetsch, p. 275.

4. Cf. *Ökumenisches Direktorium,* Part 1, with an introd. by Jan Willebrands and commentary by Edward Stakemeier (Paderborn, 1967), pp. 37—49.

5. Cf. Ludolf Müller, *Die Kritik des Protestantismus in der russischen Theologie des 16. bis zum 18. Jahrhunderts* (Wiesbaden, 1951), pp. 41—46.

6. Leonard Hodgson, ed., *The Second World Conference on Faith and Order* (New York: Macmillan, 1938), p. 243.

7. Cf. supra, pp. 133—   and 186—

8. Cf. supra, p. 189—90.

9. See especially the report of the Commission on Faith and Order in *One Lord, One Baptism* (Liverpool and London, 1960), pp. 45 ff., and the report, *Montreal, 1963,* eds. P. C. Rodger and Lukas Vischer (New York: Association Press, 1964), pp. 72 f.

Bibliography

Baptism in the New Testament

Oepke, Albrecht. βάπτω, βαπτίζω. In *Theological Dictionary of the New Testament* (TDNT). Tr. Geoffrey W. Bromiley. Vol. I. Grand Rapids: Eerdmans, 1964.

Bornkamm, Guenther. "Die Neutestamentliche Lehre von der Taufe." *Theologische Blätter* 17, 1938, col. 42—52.

Marsh, Herbert G. *The Origin and Significance of the New Testament Baptism.* Manchester, 1941.

Leenhardt, Franz J. *Le baptême chrétien, son origine, sa signification.* Neuchâtel — Paris, 1946.

Cullmann, Oscar. *Baptism in the New Testament.* London: SCM Press, 1950.

Flemington, F. W. *The New Testament Doctrine of Baptism.* London: SPCK, 1957.

Schnackenburg, Rudolf. *Baptism in the Thought of St. Paul.* Tr. George R. Beasley-Murray. New York: Herder & Herder, 1964.

———. "Taufe." *Lexikon für Theologie und Kirche.* Vol. IX. Freiburg, 1964.

Crehan, Joseph. *Early Christian Baptism and the Creed.* London: Burns, Oates and Washbourne, 1950.

Kuss, Otto. "Zur vorpaulinischen Tauflehre im Neuen Testament," *Theologie und Glaube,* 1951, No. 4, 289 ff.

———. "Zur Frage der vorpaulinischen Todestaufe," *Münchener Theologische Zeitschrift,* 1953, 1 ff.

Barth, Markus. *Die Taufe ein Sakrament?* Zollikon-Zürich, 1951.

Schneider, Johannes. *Die Taufe im Neuen Testament.* Stuttgart, 1952.

Warnach, Victor, OSB. "Taufe und Christusgeschehen nach Römer 6," *Archiv für Liturgiewissenschaft,* 1954, Vol. III, 2.

———. "Die Tauflehre des Römerbriefes in der neueren theologischen Diskussion," Ibid., V, 2.

Lampe, Geoffrey W. H. *The Seal of the Spirit, A Study in the Doctrine of Baptism and Confirmation in the New Testament and the Fathers.* 2d. ed. London, New York, Toronto, 1956.

Torrance, Thomas F. "The Origins of Baptism," *Scottish Journal of Theology,* XI, 158 ff.

Dinkler, Erich. "Taufe, II, Im Urchristentum." *Die Religion in Geschichte und Gegenwart (RGG),* VI (3d ed., Tübingen: 1962), 627 ff.

Beasley-Murray, George R. *Baptism in the New Testament.* London: Macmillan, 1962.

Braumann, George. "Vorpaulinische christliche Taufverkündigung bei Paulus,"

Beiträge zur Wissenschaft vom Alten und Neuen Testament, V, 1962, 1 ff.

Delling, Gerhard. *Die Taufe im Neuen Testament.* Berlin, 1963.

Hahn, Ferdinand. "Taufe im Urchristentum" (Bibliographie). *Jahrbuch für Liturgik und Hymnologie,* 8 (1963), 219 ff.

Marxsen, Willi. "Erwägungen zur neutestamentlichen Begründung der Taufe." *Apophoreta, Festschrift für Ernst Hänchen, Beihefte zur Zeitschrift für die neutestamentliche Wissenschaft,* 30 (1964), 169—77.

Lohse, Edward. "Taufe und Rechtfertigung bei Paulus," *Kerygma und Dogma,* XI, 4 (1965), 308 ff.

Bieder, Werner. *Die Verheissung der Taufe im Neuen Testament.* Zürich, 1966.

See also the theologies of the New Testament (Bultmann, Conzelmann, Meinertz).

Infant Baptism

Jeremias, Joachim. *Infant Baptism in the First Four Centuries.* Tr. David Cairns. Philadelphia: Westminster Press, 1960.

———. *The Origins of Infant Baptism.* Tr. Dorothea M. Barton. Naperville: Alec. R. Allenson, Inc., 1963.

Preiss, Théo., "Die Kindertaufe und das Neue Testament," *Theologische Literaturzeitung,* 73 (1948), 651 ff.

Menoud, Philippe-H. "Le baptême des enfants dans l'église ancienne," *Verbum Caro,* 2 (1948), 15 ff.

Lovsky, F. "Notes d'histoire pour contribuer à l'étude du problème baptismal. I. L'église ancienne baptisait-elle les enfants? II. Notes sur l'inquiétude antipédobaptiste depuis la Réforme," *Foi et Vie.* 48 (1950), 109 ff.

Aland, Kurt. *Did the Early Church Baptize Infants?* Tr. G. R. Beasley-Murray. Philadelphia: Westminster Press, 1963.

De Ru, Gerrit, "Jet Kinderdoop en het NT." Diss., Leiden. Wageningen, 1964.

On the History of Baptismal Theology

Kattenbusch, Ferdinand (Steitz). "Taufe, II, Kirchenlehre." *Realencyklopädie für protestantische Theologie und Kirche.* 3d ed., Leipzig: XIX, (1907), 403 ff.

Landgraf, Artur M. *Dogmengeschichte der Frühscholastik.* III, 1-2. Regensburg: 1954—55.

Lundberg, Per. *La typologie baptismale dans l'Ancienne Eglise.* Leipzig-Uppsala, 1942.

Kraft, Heinz. "Texte zur Geschichte der Taufe, besonders der Kindertaufe in der Alten Kirche." *Kleine Texte für Vorlesungen und Übungen,* founded by Hans Lietzmann, ed. Kurt Aland, No. 174. Berlin, 2d ed., 1968.

Benoit, André. "Le baptême chrétien au second siècle." *La theologie des peres.* Paris, 1953.

Heggelsbacher, Othmar. "Die christliche Taufe als Rechtsakt nach dem Zeugnis der frühen Christenheit." *Paradosis VIII.* Freiburg (Switzerland), 1953.

Neunheuser, Burkhard. "Taufe und Firmung." *Handbuch der Dogmengeschichte,*

IV, 2. Freiburg, 1956.

Stenzel, Alois. "Die Taufe. Eine genetische Erklärung der Taufliturgie. Forschungen zur Geschichte der Theologie und des innerkirchlichen Lebens. Eds. H. Rahner and J. A. Jungmann, VII/VIII, Innsbruck, 1958.

Andersen, Wilh. "Taufe, IV, Dogmengeschichtlich, und V, Dogmatisch." *Evangelisches Kirchenlexikon*, III. Göttingen, 2d ed., 1962, 1295 ff.

Kettler, Franz-Heinrich. "Taufe, III, Dogmengeschichtlich." *RGG*, 3d ed., VI, 631—46.

See also the texts on history of dogma (Harnack, Loofs, Seeberg, Adam), as well as the literature cited by Geo. Kretschmar and Bruno Jordahn in *Leiturgia*, V (Kassel, 1969), 3 ff. and 350 ff.

Orthodox Teaching on Baptism

Kattenbusch, Ferd. "Mystagogische Theologie." *RE*, XIII (1903), 612 ff.

Dyobuniotis, Konstantinos, *Ta Mysteria tes Anatolikes Orthodoxou Ekklesias*. Athens, 1913.

Spačil, Theophilus. *Theologia Orientis separati de sacramento Baptismi*. Rome, 1926.

Jugie, Martino. *Theologia dogmatica christianorum orientalium*, III (Paris, 1930), 62—125; V (1935), 286 ff. and 644 ff.

Heiler, Frierich. *Urkirche und Ostkirche* (Munich, 1937), 243—47, 439—44, 465—68, 498—500, 519—23.

Trempelas, Panagiotis N. *Dogmatike tes orthodoxou ekklesias*. Athens, 1961, 67—116.

Isebaert, Henricus. "Greek Baptismal Terminology." *Graecitas Christianorum Primaeva, Studia ad sermonem Graecum pertinentia* 1, 1962, Noviomagi.

Roman Catholic Teaching on Baptism

Hoerger, P. Concilii Tridentini de necessitate baptismi doctrina in decreto de justificatione. *Antonianum*, 17 (1942), 193—222, 269—302.

Diekamp, Franz. *Katholische Dogmatik nach den Grundsätzen des hl. Thomas*. Münster III (1954, 12th ed., Klaudius Jüssen, ed.), 71—92.

Schmaus, Michael. *Katholische Dogmatik*, IV, 1. Munich, 6th ed. (1964), 136 ff.

Premm, *Matthias. Katholische Glaubenskunde*, III, 1. Vienna (1954), 113—52.

Betz, Johannes. "Taufe." *Handbuch theologischer Grundbegriffe*. Heinrich Fries, ed. II (Munich, 1963), 619—30.

Schlier, Heinrich. "Die kirchliche Lehre von der Taufe." *Die Zeit der Kirche*. Freiburg, 1956, 107 ff.

Holtz, Gottfried. "Die katholische Lehre von der Taufe." *Quellen zur Konfessionskunde*, A, 7. Lüneburg, 1962.

Lutheran Teaching on Baptism

Hoefling, John Friedr. W. *Das Sakrament der Taufe*, 2 vols., Erlangen, 1846 to 1848.

Cremer, Herman. *Taufe, Wiedergeburt und Kindertaufe.* Gütersloh, 2d ed., 1901.

Josefson, Ruben. *Luthers Lära om Dopet.* Stockholm: Svenska Kyrkans Diakonistyrelses Bokförlag, 1944.

Schlink, Edmund. *Theology of the Lutheran Confessions.* Tr. P. F. Koehneke and Herb. J. A. Bouman. Philadelphia: Muhlenberg Press, 1961, 141 ff.

Beckmann, Joachim. "Die Heilsnotwendigkeit der Taufe." *Schriftenreihe der Bekennenden Kirche,* 8. Stuttgart, 1951. (*Im Kampfe für die Kirche des Evangeliums,* Gütersloh, 1961, 75 ff.)

Brunner, Peter. *Aus der Kraft des Werkes Christi, Zur Lehre von der hl. Taufe und vom hl. Abendmahl.* Munich, 1950.

————. "Die evangelisch-lutherische Lehre von der Taufe." *Pro Ecclesia, Gesammelte Aufsätze zur dogmatischen Theologie,* I. Berlin-Hamburg, 2d ed., 1962, 138—64.

Roth, Erich. "Aporien in Luthers Tauflehre," *Zeitschrift für systematische Theologie* 22 (1953), 99—124.

Elert, Werner. "Der Christliche Glaube." *Grundlienien der lutherischen Dogmatik.* Hamburg, 3d ed., 1956, 439—47.

Prenter, Regin. *Creation and Redemption.* Tr. Theo. I. Jensen. Philadelphia: Fortress Press, 1967.

Lohrmann, Walter. *Glaube und Taufe in den Bekenntnisschriften der evangelisch-lutherischen Kirche.* Stuttgart, 1962.

Schott, Erdmann. *Taufe und Rechtfertigung in kontroverstheologischer Sicht.* Stuttgart, 1967.

Grönvik, Lorenz. "Die Taufe in der Theologie Martin Luthers." In: *Acta academiae Aboensis,* Ser. A., XXXVI, 1 Abo. Also Göttingen-Zürich, 1968.

Reformed Teaching on Baptism

Beckmann, Joachim. *Vom Sakrament bei Calvin.* Tübingen, 1926.

Barth, Karl. *The Teaching of the Church Concerning Baptism.* Tr. Ernest A. Payne. London: SCM Press, 1948.

Kreck, Walter. "Die Lehre von der Taufe bei Calvin," *Evangelische Theologie,* Vol. 8 (1948/49), 237 ff.

The Church of Scotland. *Interim Report of the Special Commission on Baptism.* 1955, 1956, 1957, 1958; *Final Report: Baptism in the Church of Scotland. The Doctrine of Baptism Together with Practical Suggestions.* Edinburgh, 1961.

Marcel, Pierre C. *The Biblical Doctrine of Infant Baptism.* Tr. Philip E. Hughes. London: James Clarke & Co., 2d ed. 1959.

Torrance, Thomas F. *Conflict and Agreement in the Church. II, The Ministry and the Sacraments of the Gospel.* London, 1960, 93 ff.

Weber, Otto. *Grundlagen der Dogmatik,* II. Neukirchen, 1962, 656 ff.

Alting von Geusau, Leo George M. *Die Lehre von der Kindertaufe bei Calvin.* Mit einem Anhang über die Kindertaufe auf dem Tridentinischen Konzil. Mainz, 1963.

Neuser, Wilhelm H. "Die Tauflehre des Heidelberger Katechismus," *Theologische Existenz,* new series, No. 139, 1967.

Barth, Karl. *Die Kirchliche Dogmatik,* IV, 4, "Das christliche Leben" (fragment), "Die Taufe als Begründung des christlichen Lebens." Zürich, 1967.

Anglican Teaching on Baptism

Richards, Charles G. *Baptism and Confirmation.* London, 1942.

Dix, Dom Gregory. *The Theology of Confirmation in Relation to Baptism.* Westminster, 1946.

Rawlinson, Alfred Eduard J. *Christian Initiation.* London, 1947.

The Theology of Christian Initiation, Being the Report of a Theological Commission . . . on the Relation between Baptism, Confirmation and Holy Communion. London, 1948.

Davies, John Gordon. *Holy Spirit, Church and Sacrament.* London, 1954.

Baptism and Confirmation. A Report submitted by the Church of England Liturgical Commission. London, 1959.

Baptist Teaching on Bapitsm

Warns, Johannes. *Baptism.* London, 1957.

Robinson, Henry Wheeler/James Henry Rushbrooke. *Baptists in Britain.* London, 1937.

Sondheimer, Friedrich. *Die wahre Taufe. Ein Bekenntnis zur Taufe der Gläubigen.* Kassel, 1951.

Payne, Ernest A. *The Doctrine of Baptism.* London, 1951.

Robinson, Henry Wheeler. *Baptist Principles.* 4th ed. London, 1955.

Hughey, John David Jr. *Die Baptisten. Einführung in Lehre, Praxis und Geschichte.* Kassel, 1959.

———— ed. "Die Baptisten." In *Die Kirchen der Welt,* II. Stuttgart, 1964.

Hershberger, Guy F. ed. *The Recovery of the Anabaptist Vision: A Sixteeenth Anniversary Tribute to H. S. Bender.* Scottdale: Herald Press, 1957.

Beasley-Murray, George R. *Gesichtspunkte zum Taufgespräch heute.* Kassel, 1965.

————. *Baptism Today and Tomorrow.* London, 1966.

Littell, Franklin H. *The Anabaptist View of the Church.* 2d ed. Boston: Starr King Press, 1958.

Current Discussion on Infant Baptism

Freericks, Herman. "Die Taufe im heutigen Protestantismus Deutschlands." *Münsterische Beiträge zur Theologie,* Vol. 6. Münster, 1925.

Berkouwer, G. C. *Karl Barth en de Kinderdoop.* Kampen, 1947.

Althaus, Paul. "Was ist die Taufe? Zur Antwort an Karl Barth," *Th. L. Z.* 74 (1949), 705 ff.

Leenhardt, Franz J. "Pédobaptisme catholique et pédobaptisme réformé." *Etudes Théologiques et Religieuses,* 25, 1950.

Gruenagel, Friedrich, ed., Carl-Heinz Ratschow, Günther Bornkamm, Otto Dilschneider, *Was ist die Taufe? Eine Auseinandersetzung mit Karl Barth.* Stuttgart, 1951.

Mezger, Manfred. *Die Amtshandlungen der Kirche.* I. 2d ed., Munich, 1963.

Mentz, Herman. *Taufe und Kirche in ihrem ursprünglichen Zusammenhang.* Munich, 1960.

Metzger, Wolfgang. "Die Taufe in missionarischen Anfang und in der Gemeindesituation." *Calwer Hefte,* 46. Stuttgart, 1961.

Brunner, Peter. "Taufe und Glaube — Kindertaufe und Kinderglaube," *Pro Ecclesia,* I. 2d ed. Berlin-Hamburg, 1962, 165—82.

Diem, Herman. "Taufverkündigung und Taufordnung," *Th. Ex.* 98. Munich, 1962.

Bijlsma, Roelof. "Die Taufe in Familie und Gemeinde," *Th. Ex.* 103. Munich, 1962.

Perels, Otto, ed., Guenter Harder, Rudolf Herrmann, August Strobel. *Begründung und Geltung der Heiligen Taufe.* Berlin-Hamburg, 1963.

Luescher, Albert. *Grosstaufe oder Kindertaufe?* Langenthal, 1964.

Bromiley, Geoffrey W. and G. R. Beasley-Murray. "The Case for/Against Infant Baptism, *Christianity Today,* 9 (Oct. 9, No. 1, 1964), 7—14.

Hurley, Michael. "Was können die katholischen Christen aus der Kontroverse um die Kleinkindertaufe lernen?" *Concilium,* 1967, 274—78.

Taufverkündigung und Taufpraxis, in *Pastoraltheologie,* Vol. 57, No. 9. Göttingen, 1968.

The Practice of Baptism on Mission Fields

Gensichen, Hans Werner. "Das Taufproblem in der Mission." *Beiträge zur Missionswissenschaft und evangelischen Missionskunde,* I. Gütersloh, 1951.

————. "Taufe, VIII, In der Mission." *RGG,* 3d ed. VI, 657—60.

Vicedom, Geo. F., *Die Taufe unter den Heiden.* Munich, 1960.